THE HUSSITE REVOLUTION
1424-1437

F. M. BARTOŠ

English Edition

prepared by John M. Klasssen

EAST EUROPEAN MONOGRAPHS, BOULDER
DISTRIBUTED BY COLUMBIA UNIVERSITY PRESS, NEW YORK

1986

EAST EUROPEAN MONOGRAPHS, NO. CCIII

DB208
B3713
1986x

František Michálek Bartoš (1889-1972) was Professor of Church History at the Hus and Comenius Theological Faculties in Prague. The Czech original of this work appeared under the title *Husitská revoluce* (2 vols., Praha: Academia, 1965-1966) in the series *České dějiny* (16 vols., Praha, 1912-1966).

John M. Klassen is Professor of History at Trinity Western University in Langley, British Columbia, Canada.

TABLE OF CONTENTS

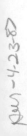

INTRODUCTION

Most of the work in English on the Hussite movement deals with its early years. F. Heymann's, *John Žižka and the Hussite Revolution,* ended with the death of the Hussite military hero in the fall of 1424. H. Kaminsky's, *A History of the Hussite Revolution,* also ended in 1424. The reformation and revolution strains in the movement ceased creating novelty through their interaction, and the evolution of Taboritism had become fulfilled. Žižka's death was coincidental to those developments in Kaminsky's treatment.

A general study in English of the period from 1424 to King Sigismund's death in 1437 is lacking. These later years saw the Hussites make considerable gains. Whereas the early years brought remarkable innovations in the economic, social, religious and political spheres, in the later years the Hussites converted their military triumphs into diplomatic and political fruits.

Professor Bartoš, with his comprehensive grasp of the Hussite material, provides us with the details of the Hussite achievements, with their frustrations and with what he calls the deceitfulness of the Council of Basel, and of King Sigismund. He takes us step by step along the way as the Hussites and the Catholic church in fifteenth-century Europe took that unique step and agreed with reluctance to live together.

We begin this translation of *Husitská revoluce* with the last chapter of volume one which takes up the narrative just after the death of Žižka. He died, most likely of the plague, while the Hussites were on their way to Moravia to help free that land from the domination of Duke Albert of

of Austria. By the time of Žižka's death, the Hussites were divided into
three main parties.

The moderates diverged from the medieval church in their claim that
lay people should receive both bread and wine at communion. Although
with varying degrees of fervour, they also accepted the other three points
of the common Hussite program, the so-called *Four Articles:* freedom to
preach the Word of God, prohibition against the clergy owning property,
and an end to "public mortal sins." In general this group was made up of
the people of Prague, especially Old Town, and of some noble families.

The radical parties were separated primarily by geography and somewhat by politics. The Orebites, centered near Hradec Králové in eastern
Bohemia, were somewhat less extreme as indicated by their earlier accommodation with moderate Prague. More radical groups existed in New
Town, Prague, and in Tábor, in southern Bohemia. To them the true
church was one patterned on that of the New Testament, which meant
that the power of the clergy was greatly diminished. They disagreed with
the Praguers on the importance of the seven sacraments, wishing to dispose
of those which were not observed by the primitive church. In addition
they insisted that Christ was not corporeally present in the eucharistic
bread. They stood for a greatly simplified life, objecting to any signs of
luxury such as the ornate vestments worn by the moderate Hussite priests,
or the rich fineries of the Prague burghers. They destroyed church build-
ings which they felt were not used for proper worship, and stole valuables
found there in order to help the poor. All Hussite parties agreed that the
Scriptures were the one authority that should be binding on all Christians.

It was the task of leaders, such as Jakoubek of Stříbro and John Žižka,
to keep the tensions which existed just below the surface in the Hussite
movement, from breaking into destructive internecine quarrels. The latest
such agreement before Žižka's death occurred in New Town, Prague at
Špital (Hospital) field where Žižka and Prague agreed that whoever in-
fringed upon the compact would be buried beneath the stones piled on
Hospital field to commemorate the pact. Immediately preceding the
campaign in Moravia, during which Žižka died, the Bohemians, both
Catholics and Hussites, extended the area of agreement by taking a major
step to try and solve the religious dispute within their own land.

This was the *Zdice Accord,* so-called because the meeting or diet which
drew it up met at Zdice, a town just west of Prague. Its significance rests

on the fact that the Czechs decided to solve their problems on a national or land level. It planned an assembly for the next year to meet at Kouřím in eastern Bohemia, dominated by the radicals. Here the religious issues summed up in the *Four Articles,* were to be submitted to a hearing before a jury of one hundred laymen, both Catholic and Hussite.

The Accord also called for an armistice which applied only to the Bohemian parties. Thus the Hussites were free to continue their struggle against King Sigismund and his foreign allies, but the king was deprived of his royalist Czech allies. Both Czech parties put up armed forces to enforce this agreement. For the duration of the armistice, some six months, and until the verdict on the religious dispute had been issued, everyone was to be free to worship as he or she pleased.

The following translation is an abridgment of the Czech original. The original draft was the work of Mrs. J. Weir and the general decisions as to what to include and what to leave out are hers. I have revised her draft only to rid it of what seemed to me the most glaring idiomatic expressions and have added material when I felt the meaning would thereby be enhanced. Mrs. Weir had omitted all footnotes. I have decided that this was regrettable and that they should be included. In translating and editing them I have followed Bartoš' advice, given in his preface to the English edition, that his polemics with Czech researchers be eliminated. Furthermore, information that referred to material omitted in this abridged edition was naturally left out unless I felt it might clarify an issue. Bartoš was quite nonchalant about consistency in style in his footnote references. In a few of his references I have been unable to locate the dates of publication. Information which I added is contained in square brackets.

The Czech version includes a long "Exkurs" (vol. 2, 237-248) on sources and historiography for the Hussite period.

Lastly I take pleasure in thanking Professor Jarold K. Zeman, of Acadia Divinity College, for his many helpful suggestions. It is certain that without his encouragement this project would never have been completed.

August 1985

John M. Klassen
Professor of History
Trinity Western University
Langley, British Columbia

PREFACE TO THE ENGLISH EDITION

My book, *The Hussite Revolution* appeared in 1965-6 as part of the "History of Bohemia" series which Jan Laichter, the publisher, had introduced in 1912. Professor Václav Novotný, its first editor, died in 1932, leaving his contribution unfinished. Professor Kamil Krofta, the new editor, entrusted to me the writing of the Hussite history (1378-1437) as I had been working in this field since 1909 as a pupil of Novotný, our leading specialist on that period. At that time I received a professorship at the Protestant Faculty which then bore the name of Hus, and was thus granted the great privilege of devoting myself entirely to the study of what Palacký, our greatest historian, had called the culminating epoch of our history. I was thus able to present an essentially new picture of the foremost Central European state in the period when it made a bold attempt at a radical solution of the crisis of contemporary Christian culture.

The very foundations of this culture were then imperilled by the rival Roman and Avignon papal factions which for forty years made war against each other, involving several states of Europe in it. To put an end to this outrage it was necessary to convene the Council of the Church which met at Constance in 1414, deposed the two popes and restored unity to the Church and Europe. However, the Pope whom the Council elected in 1417, turned all the strength of the Church against the Hussites in whom he sensed the greatest danger to papal imperialism. With the consent of the Council which had put Hus to death at the stake, the Pope, in 1420, launched the first crusade against the followers of Hus, and refused to consider any negotiations with them, maintaining till his death (1431) that only the horrors of war would bring them to their senses. The Czechs, however, repulsed all five invasions into their country and fought out peace negotiations at the new Council of Basel which resulted in an honorable peace settlement as well as penetrating changes in the body of the Church. Some years later, when the Popes repealed the reform decrees of Basel as well as the peace treaty with the Hussites, and even sent another crusade to Bohemia, King George of Poděbrady successfully maintained the independence of the Hussite Church and in 1485 his statesmen set the seal on his effort by working out an agreement between the Hussites and Catholics based on mutual toleration. The Czech State was thus the first in Europe to secure for its citizens freedom of worship. Within half a century, Luther called on the German nobles to follow the path of the Hussites, and before the end of the 16th century, other countries, England among them, severed their ties with the papacy.

This is, in broad outline, the historical importance of the supreme epoch of our history, as presented in my book.

The Hussite state, being born of twenty-two years of continual struggle, could not succeed in maintaining self-defence in the face of the overwhelming enemy, when the Habsburgs became its kings and marshalled the German and Spanish imperialist forces of their house against it during the Thirty Years' War. Nevertheless, they failed to make the triumph of the world's counter-revolution permanent. The memory of the glorious achievements of the Hussite revolution and the admiration they excited abroad brought new strength to the inextinguishable tradition at home and supplied the moving force in the rebirth of the Czech nation in the 19th century especially after Palacký revealed its glorious past. And when Thomas G. Masaryk, the great champion of the Hussite tradition, launched his struggle for spiritual and political independence of his nation, he was guided by the ideals of the Hussite revolution and by its motto "Truth prevails" under which free Czechoslovakia was born in 1918.

The Hussite Revolution is the sequel to my Bohemia at the Time of Hus (published in 1947), a history of the Czech religious movement from 1378 to the death of Hus in 1415. The English reader will find a substitute in the first three chapters of the book by Howard Kaminsky which deals exhaustively with events up to 1415. However, the title of the work of the eminent American hussitologist, A History of the Hussite Revolution

(University of California Press, 1967) is somewhat inaccurate as the book does not go beyond 1424. As a matter of fact, the struggle of the revolution went on for at least another thirteen years terminating in the peace agreements of Basel and the final victory over Sigismund.

My two books, *Bohemia at the Time of Hus* and *The Hussite Revolution,* sum up the results of many years of intensive research in libraries and archives at home and abroad. These findings appeared as articles in numerous periodicals, as essays, monographs and contributions to various collective works. I joined the ranks of hussitologists at the propitious time when accurate and systematic catalogues of the two largest collections of Hussitica became available to scholars and opened to them a world of discovery. I am referring to the catalogue of the Prague University Library completed by Joseph Truhlář in 1906, and that of the Prague Cathedral Chapter Library compiled by Antonin Podlaha in 1910-22. To these I was able to add in 1927 the catalogue of the National Museum Library which is the third largest in the country. These catalogues revealed to hussitologists hitherto unsuspected sources the importance of which is comparable to the opening of the Vatican Archives. This work was due to the efforts of Professor Jaroslav Goll, the founder of a large school of historians of which I was one of the last pupils, and whose work painstakingly continued all through the period of the First Republic. It supplied copious material to generations of researchers, enabling them to tackle problems which hitherto had seemed insoluble.

I hope the reader may find evidence thereof. My chief concern was to stress the great effort of the revolution towards the fundamental reconstruction of the Czech state. At the outbreak of the revolution, the state was under the almost boundless control of several families of lords. In the course of sixteen years, the government of the country was widened by the inclusion of the strata of society which had previously been denied a share of power, the yeomen and the Knights, and the population of the Royal towns which became considerably more populous by having acquired larges estates from confiscated Church property. Henceforth, the lords had to share power with the two new estates and meet their representatives as equal partners in regular diet sessions. The democratization of the constitution which gave political power to incomparably more numerous classes was certainly the most radical change the Hussite revolution had brought about.

To trace this particular change in the inadequate sources is perhaps the most difficult challenge a hussitologist is faced with. The struggle for democratization was fought not only on the many battlefields but, above all, in diet sessions and assemblies whose minutes were seldom handed down. More than anywhere else we realize the sad truth of Palacký's sorrowful words: "In vain may a historian send thousands and thousands of questions into the dark and deaf night of the past ages; even if he may catch a gleam it is doubtful whether it is light or will-o-the-wisp." This applies above all, to the effort to ascertain the lives and characters of the warriors and statesmen of the revolution who had shaped its history. Yet these questions are so urgent that no historian can afford to evade them even at the risk of making mistakes and coming up against until now insurmountable obstacles. I drew strength from the heartening words with which Palacký had prefaced his last publication on Hussitism, *Urkundliche Beiträge zur Geschichte des Hussitenkrieges* (1872) as if to remind the Czech historians of their indebtedness to the heroes of the Hussite revolution who were frequently reviled as coarse and uneducated fanatics: "On the contrary, they were the first men in Europe to take up arms only because they were forced to do so, not for worldly possessions or power, but in defense of the highest values of man: the right to self-determination and freedom of conscience; they not only undertook the terrible and long struggle against the rest of the world which strove to exterminate them, but wonderfully brought it to victory. Hus went along the same path as many men before him. But his followers had no predecessors, no example in history to guide them. They were the first people on earth to rise in defence of their spiritual freedom and stake their whole existence on it."

To make progress in this direction, to ascertain the fluctuating programmes and compositions of parties and factions, and to discover the lives of revolutionary leaders, I suppressed a good many details offered by our sources which tend to be long-winded on irrelevances and stop short when it comes to essentials. Instead of dwelling on battle scenes and campaigns, I endeavoured to probe the deeper forces determining the course of the revolution and find out something about its unfathomed history and the persons who had made it.

Only this laborious process will, in my opinion, result in a worthy picture of the revolution as part of the struggle for justice. To men, history in its highest and deepest sense is the quintessence of that struggle.

This work which has extended over more than sixty years, has had the support of several generations of Jaroslav Goll's school and has matured through lively discussions with workers at home and abroad. The Czech public helped by its interest which was stimulated by the 500th anniversaries of the great Hussite events, beginning with the commemoration of the death of Hus in 1915 and continued by official remembrances under the First Czechoslavak Republic, of the great Hussite victory in 1919, the death of Žižka in 1924 and the tragedy of Lipany in 1934. The 550th anniversary of Hus in 1965 helped this book to go to the press. I could thus realize the dream which had been on my mind since the early days of my university studies, and fulfill the expectations of my readers, friends and pupils. In my *Reminiscences of a Hussitologist* (1970) I expressed my indebtedness to most of those who had assisted me with advice, encouragement and criticism. This little book of gratitude is dedicated to the memory of my wife who did not live to see the day of issue.

The Czechoslovak Academy of Sciences which had, after nationalization of private enterprise, taken over the *History of Bohemia* series, accepted this book for publication. For the English version I have introduced various modifications originally made for the 2nd Czech edition which was sent to the press in 1969 and later withdrawn.

Various details of little interest to the foreign student, such as polemics with Czech researchers, details of battle descriptions, etc., have been omitted.

F. M. Bartoš

ABBREVIATIONS

AČ	F. Palacký, et al., eds., *Archiv Český,* 37 vols. (Prague, 1840-1944)
ADB	*Allgemeine Deutsche Biographie.*
Altmann	W. Altmann, *Regesta Imperii XI, Die Urkunden Kaiser Sigmunds* 2 vols. (Innsbruck, 1896/1900).
Andreas	G. Leidinger, ed., *Andreas von Regensburg. Sämtliche Werke* (Münich, 1903).
Anděl	R. Anděl, *Husitství v severních Čechách* (Liberec, 1960).
Antoch	F. Bartoš, ed., "Zápisky Antochovy" in *Časopis archivní školy,* 12 (1943).
AOeG	*Archiv für österreichische Geschichte.*
Bartoš	The following are abbreviations of his most frequently cited works.
Do čtyř	*Do čtyř pražských artikulů* (2nd ed., Prague, 1940).
Čechy	*Čechy v době Husově* (Prague, 1947).
Dvě studie	"Dvě studie o husitských postilách," *Rozpravy Československé akademie věd* 4 (1955).
Husitika a Bohemika	"Husitika a Bohemika v několika knihovnách jihoněmeckých a švýcarských." *VKČSN,* 1931.
Husitství a cizina	*Husitství a cizina* (Prague, 1931).
Korybut	"Kníže Zikmund Korybutovič v Čechách," *SH,* 6, 1959).

xv

Bartoš
LČ Jak　　　　*Literární činnost M. Jakoubka ze Stříbra* (Prague, 1925).
LČ Rok　　　　*Literární činnost M. Rokycany, J. Příbrama a P. Payna*
　　　　　　　(Prague, 1928).
Manifesty　　 "Manifesty města Prahy z doby husitské," *Sborník pří-
　　　　　　　spěvků k dějinám hlavního města Prahy* 7, (1932).
Prokop Vel.　 "Několik záhad v životě Prokopa Velikého," *SH* 8
　　　　　　　(1960).
Z politické　 "Z politické literatury doby husitské," *SH* 5 (1958).
Z Žižkových　 "Z Žižkových mladých let," *ČSPS* 30 (1922).
Žižka　　　　 "Žižka a Korybut," *JSH* 20 (1951).
Bartošek　　 *Bartošek z Drahonic,* J. Goll, ed., in *FRB* 5 (1893).
Bezold　　　 F. Bezold, *König Sigmund und die Reichskriege gegen
　　　　　　　die Hussiten* 1-3, (Munich, 1872-1877).
Biskupec　　 *Chronicon Taboritarum,* K. Höfler ed., *Die Geschichts-
　　　　　　　schreiber der hussitischen Bewegung* 2 (Vienna, 1865).
Bretholz　　 B. Bretholz, "Uebergabe Mährens an H. Albrecht V. von
　　　　　　　Oesterreich im J. 1423," *AOeG* 80 (1894).
Caro　　　　 J. Caro, *Geschichte Polens,* 3-4 (1869/1871).
CB　　　　　 J. Haller et al., eds., *Concilium Basiliense,* 8 vols. (Basel,
　　　　　　　1896-1936).
CDLS　　　　 R. Jecht, ed., *Codex diplomaticus Lusatiae superioris*
　　　　　　　(Görlitz, 1903).
CDS, CDSR　 H. Ermisch, ed., *Codex diplomaticus Saxoniae regiae.*
CE　　　　　 J. Szujski and A. Lewicki, eds., *Codex epistolaris saec.
　　　　　　　XV* in *Monumenta medii aevi Poloniae* 2, 12, 14
　　　　　　　(1876-94).
CIM　　　　 J. Čelakovský et al., eds., *Codex juris municipalis regni
　　　　　　　Bohemiae* 1-4 (Prague, 1886-1954).
Chronicon Treb. K. Höfler, ed., *Chronicon Trebonense* in *Fontes rerum
　　　　　　　Austriacarum* I/2 (Vienna, 1856).
Cochlaeus　　 J. Cochlaeus, *Historiae Hussitarum libri* XII (Mainz,
　　　　　　　1549).
CW　　　　　 A. Prochaska, ed., *Codex Witoldi in Monumenta medii
　　　　　　　aevi Poloniae* 6 (1882).
ČČH　　　　 *Český časopis historický* 1-50 (1895-1949).
ČČM (ČNM)　 *Časopis českého musea.*

ČsČH   Československý časopis historický (1953ff.).
Chronicon vet. Höfler 1, 78ff and *JSH* 19 (1950) 37ff.
  colleg.
ČKD   Časopis katolického duchovenstva.
ČMM   Časopis Matice Moravské.
ČSPS   Časopis Společnosti přátel starožitností českých v Praze.
Dlugoš   J. Dlugosz, *Historica Polonica* 4 (1887).
Dobiáš   J. Dobiáš, *Dějiny královského města Pelhřimova a jeho okolí*, 1-3 (Prague, 1927-1954).
Doc   F. Palacký, ed., *Documenta M. J. Hus vitam, doctrinam, causam in constantiensi Concilio actam . . . motas illustrantia* (Prague, 1869).
DPŽ   F. Heřmanský, trans. *Deník Petra Žateckého* (Prague, 1953).
Durdík   J. Durdík, *Husitské vojenství* (2nd. ed., Prague, 1954).
Finke   H. Finke, *Acta Concilii Constantiensis*, 4 vols. (Münster-Regensburg, 1896-1928).
Frankenberger O. Frankenberger, *Naše velká armáda* (Prague, 1921).
FRB   *Fontes rerum Bohemicarum.*
Goll   J. Goll, *Čechy a Prusy ve středověku* (Prague, 1895-97).
Grünhagen   C. Grünhagen, *Die Hussitenkämpfe der Schlesier 1420-1435* (Breslau, 1872).
Hardt   H. Hardt, ed., *Magnum Oecumenicum Constantiense Concilium*, 1-6 (Frankfurt-Leipzig, 1697-1700).
Hlaváček   I. Hlaváček, "Husitské sněmy," *SH* 4 (1956).
Höfler   C. Höfler, *Geschichtsschreiber der hussitischen Bewegung* in *Fontes rerum Austriacarum*, I, 2 and 6 (Vienna, 1856/1865).
Hrady   A. Sedláček, *Hrady, zámky a tvrze království českého* 1-15 (Prague, 1883-1927).
Jecht   R. Jecht, *Der oberlausitzer Hussitenkrieg*, 2 vols. (Görlitz, 1911-1916).
JSH   *Jihočeský sborník historický* 1 (1928ff.).
Kalivoda   R. Kalivoda, *Husitská ideologie* (Prague, 1961).
Kejř   J. Kejř, *Právní život v husitské Kutné Hoře* (Prague, 1958).
KJ   *Kostnické jiskry.*

KR	*Křestanská revue.*
Laurence	Laurence of Březová's chronicle in *FRB* 5 (1893).
Lůžek	B. Lůžek, *Po stopách husitství v ústeckém kraji* (1959).
Macek	J. Macek, *Ktož jsú Boží bojovníci* (Prague, 1951).
Macek 1, 2	J. Macek, *Tábor v husitském revolučním hnutí,* 2 vols. (Prague, 1952-1955).
MC	*Monumenta conciliorum generalium,* XV, 1-2 (Vienna, 1857-1873).
Michl	K. Michl, *Husitství na Hradecku* (Prague, 1957).
MUP	*Monumenta universitatis Pragensis,* I-III (Prague, 1830-1834).
MVGDB	*Mitteilungen des Vereins für Geschichte der Deutschen in Böhmen.*
NA, NASG	*Neues Archiv für sächsische Geschichte.*
Nejedlý	Z. Nejedlý, *Dějiny husitského zpěvu za válek husitských* (Prague, 1913).
Neumann	A. Neumann, *K dějinám husitství na Moravě* (Olomouc, 1939).
Neumann, Prameny	A. Neumann, *Nové prameny k dějinám husitství na Moravě* (Olomouc, 1930).
Novotný	V. Novotný, *M. J. Hus,* 2 vols. (Prague, 1919-1921).
Orig. Tab.	*De origine Taboritarum* in *SH* 2 (1954), 83ff.
OSN	*Ottův slovník naučný.*
Palacký	F. Palacký, *Dějiny národa českého,* final rev. ed., 5 vols. in 11 parts (Prague, 1876-78).
Pekař	J. Pekař, *Žižka a jeho doba,* 4 vols. (Prague, 1927-1933).
Pelcl	F. Pelzel. *Lebensgeschichte des römischen und böhmischen K. Wenzeslaus, Urkundenbuch* 1-2 (Prague-Leipzig, 1788-1790).
Prokeš	J. Prokeš, *M. Prokop z Plzně* (Prague, 1927).
PŽ	F. Palacký, ed., *Deník Petra Žateckého* in *MD* 1.
PŽP	F. Palacký, ed., *Deník Petra Zateckého* in *MC* 1.
Reg	A. Sedláček, *Zbytky register králův římských a českých z let 1361-1480* (Prague, 1914).
RTA, RA	*Deutsche Reichstagsakten* 1-6 (Gotha, 1867-1888).
Richental	M. R. Buck, ed., *Ulrich von Richental, Chronik des Constanzer Concils* (1882).

Rynešová   B. Rynešová, *Listář a listinář Oldřicha z Rožmberka* 1
               (Prague, 1929).

Segovia   *Joh. de Segovia. Historia gestorum synodi Basiliensis* in
               MC 2, (1873).

Silvio Eneáš   *Aenaes Sylvius, Historia Bohemica* (Prague, 1766).

SH   *Sborník historický.*

SL   F. Palacký, ed., *Staří letopisové čeští* (Prague, 1829).

SLK   F. Šimek, ed., with introduction by M. Kaňák, *Staré
               letopisy české z rukopisu Křížovnického* (Prague,
               1959).

SLŠ   F. Šimek, ed., *Staré letopisy české* (Prague, 1937).

SSRPruss   *Scriptores rerum Prussicarum.*

SSRS, SSRSiL   C. Grünhagen, ed., *Scriptores rerum Silesiacarum* 6
               (1871).

St Chr   *Chroniken der deutschen Städte vom 14. bis ins 16.
               Jahrhundert* (Leipzig-Stuttgart, 1862-1931).

Stöller   F. Stöller, "Oesterreich im Kriege gegen die Hussiten
               1420-36," *Jahrbuch f. Landeskunde von Nieder-
               österreich* NF 22 (1929).

Svejkovský   F. Svejkovský, *Staročeské vojenské řády* (Prague, 1952).

Theobald   Z. Theobald, *Hussitenkrieg* (2nd ed., Nurnberg, 1621).

ThPř   *Theologická příloha Křest'anské revue.*

Toman   H. Toman, *Husitské válečnictví* (Prague, 1898).

Tomek   V. V. Tomek, *Dějepis města Prahy,* vols. 3-4 (Prague,
               1893/1899).

Tomek, Základy V. V. Tomek, *Základy starého místopisu pražského* 1-3
               (Prague, 1866-1875).

UB   F. Palacký, *Urkundliche Beiträge zur Geschichte des
               Hussitenkrieges* 1-2 (Prague, 1873).

ÚČL   *Ústav pro českou literaturu, Ceskoslovenská akademie
               věd.*

Urbánek,   R. Urbánek, "K historii husitské Moravy," *ČMM* 63
Morava   (1940)

Varsik   B. Varsik, *Husitské revolučné hnutie a Slovensko* (Brati-
               slava, 1965).

Varsik 1, 2   B. Varsik, "Husitské posádky na Slovensku a ich vplyv
               na svoje okolie," *Sborník Fil. fakulty univ. Komen-
               ského, Historica* 11 (1960) and 12 (1961).

VČA   *Věstník České akademie.*
VKČSN   *Věstník královské české společnosti nauk.*
Wackernagel   R. Wackernagel, *Geschichte der Stadt Basel* 1 (Basel,
               1907).
Windecke   E. Windecke, *Denkwürdigkeiten zur Geschichte des Zeit-
               alters Kaiser Sigmunds,* ed. V. Altmann (Berlin, 1893).
ZVGMS   *Zeitschrift des Vereins f. Geschichte Mährens u. Schle-
               siens.*

NOTE: For more complete bibliographic information on these and other works, see Jarold K. Zeman, *The Hussite Movement and the Reformation in Bohemia, Moravia and Slovakia (1350-1650): A Bibliographical Study Guide* (Ann Arbor: Michigan Slavic Publications, The University of Michigan, 1977).

CHAPTER ONE

THE STRUGGLE FOR ŽIŽKA'S LEGACY*

John Žižka's unexpected death did not at first seem to affect his army's progress. The priests, Ambrose and Prokůpek, later a distinguished Orphan (Orebite) leader, took Žižka's body to Hradec Králové and buried it in front of the main altar of the largest church.[1] Meanwhile, the Hussite armies had taken Přibyslav and marched on to Moravia where their help had long been urgently needed.

The Prague alliance's previous expedition to Moravia in 1423 had achieved moderate but short-lived success. Led by Diviš Bořek of Miletínek, Hašek of Valdštejn and the Kunštát brothers, Victorin and Hynek, it reached Brno, taking Slavkov, Vyškov and Kvasice but suffering heavy losses at the hands of John Železný near Kroměříž. Nevertheless, the Prague forces had taken the town and having entered Přerov, probably without fighting, hastily returned home.[2]

The autumn expedition in 1424 aimed at stopping the advance of Albrecht of Austria who had invaded Moravia for the second time that year in order to secure his previous conquest. Under the leadership of Korybut and Nicholas Sokol, son of John Sokol, a participant in the "Great War" in Poland, the Hussites seized Přibyslav with the help of the Taborites under John Hvězda's command.[3] Strengthened by Diviš Bořek's unit, the combined Hussite army was able to conquer Třebíč, a strongly fortified monastery, as well as Ivančice, Boskovice, Letovice and Mohelnice. After these successes they returned home in November.

1

Pressing problems of maintaining the peace of Špital Field and implementing the Zdice Accord brought the campaign to a premature end. Before marching off to Moravia, Žižka had suggested that the Taborite and Prague priests should meet on 16 October to settle their differences of opinion and thus implement the peace of Hospital field. After Žižka's death the old dissensions broke out again not only between Prague and the brotherhoods but also within the brotherhoods themselves. One such attempt at reconciliation had already been made at Konopiště in June 1423, but it had failed; hence Žižka's prophetic remark that the peace of Hospital field would be equally short-lived.

The topics of the Konopiště talks had been clerical vestments and liturgy and the Prague theologian, John Příbram, passionately attacked Nicholas Biskupec, the Taborite bishop for his views of the Lord's Supper.[4] The two sides had soon reached agreement on the first point declaring the differences of liturgy as immaterial, and Prokop Holý, a new member of the Taborite brotherhood, clinched the matter by wearing canonicals during the service. The other subject had proved intractable. Although it is true that the priests of both parties had signed Příbram's formula on the Lord's Supper, Nicholas continued to resent Příbram's attack on him, for which he had not received satisfaction. Nicholas had given his tract to two elected arbiters, Gall (Havel) of Sušice, a Taborite, and to Příbram, but the latter's tract, which had been entrusted to a priest, Wenceslas, and to Jakoubek of Stříbro for corrections, had been left unchanged because Jakoubek had supposedly not taken any action.

This is understandable if we accept the probability that the other arbiter was Wenceslas Koranda, who of course could never find any common ground with Jakoubek, or any other Prague master. Koranda was likely behind the whole conflict. He may not have been at Konopiště at all. If he was, he refused to sign the Prague formula unlike the other eight Taborite priests, and had also openly condemned Žižka for the executions of Martin Húska, Peter Kániš and their adherents. He kept fomenting ill-will towards Prague with Biskupec's connivance, just as Jakoubek had been pressured by Příbram who continually fanned the flame against Tabor. The belligerent pamphlet, which Příbram wrote earlier in 1424, had created the situation which the theologians of both cities had to face at their meeting on 16 October 1424 in the castle of Prague.

The Prague masters submitted a fairly comprehensive confession of faith consisting of twenty-four not very controversial articles, most of which followed up the resolutions of the Prague synod of 1422.[5] Nevertheless a turbulent debate followed and the Taborite priests promised to give a detailed answer a few weeks later. This was probably worked out by Nicholas Biskupec and adopted by the Taborite synod at Klatovy on 11 November.[6] On the whole, it was reserved in expression but resolute in substance, defining Tabor's fundamental stand against Rome in the essential matter of faith. It reflected the Taborites' irreconcilable opposition to Roman rites which the synod of Klatovy condemned as a disfigurement of Christ's teaching. It also reflected their ardent desire to renew Christianity and the Church solely on biblical foundations by rejecting later innovations.

With these resolutions the Taborite priests came back to resume the debate with the masters in the Prague castle on 23 November.[7] The presidium then transferred the meeting to the Carolinum at the university. The Klatovy resolutions were read out after which Příbram picked out the introductory articles on the Eucharist for special attack and quoted from several Taborite tracts to show that there were still Pikarts in their midst. The only preserved record quotes Prokop Holý as declaring that the Taborite priests condemned Pikartism and that he himself had burnt three or four such tracts. Seeing that even some Prague masters protested against his views, Příbram shifted his ground and accused the Taborite priest Markolt of denying bad priests the right to administer the Eucharist, an accusation which Markolt refuted. Thus the meeting ended with each side, as Biskupec put it, going its own way. As far as we know, nobody suggested that the debate should be continued or that Žižka's prophetic warning be heeded. The politicians who might have been expected to take the initiative, were too preoccupied with other disputes between the brotherhoods requiring immediate action.

Žižka's consistent adherence to the alliance with Prague had frequently caused dissatisfaction at Tabor and ill-will among her priests especially since he had refused to adopt the reduced liturgy of 1420, preferring Jakoubek's simplified and partly Czech mass.[8] Since his breach with Tabor, Žižka had drawn closer to the Orebites who had joined the Německý Brod alliance which he had founded in 1423. Žižka struck up a close friendship with the Orebite priest, Ambrose,[9] and found in Hradec Králové a substitute for Tabor. He nevertheless remained in military alliance with Tabor and acted as mediator in disagreements between the Orebites and Taborites. After his death, the brotherhoods became alienated from one another and began to quarrel about the possession of certain towns, especially those Žižka had seized after the battle of Malešov.[10]

In the end, good sense and discipline prevailed and a line of demarcation was drawn up between Taborite and Orphan (Orebite) possessions. Hradiště, on Tabor Hill remained the capital of the Taborites who also held Pelhřimov, Řečice and the newly acquired Nymburk; to these Slaný was later added. Písek, the second Taborite center, had Klatovy, Sušice, Domažlice and Horažd'ovice in its territory. Hradec Králové, the Orphan capital, held Jaroměř, Dvůr Králové, Trutnov, Přibyslav, Kouřim, Český Brod and Mladá Boleslav. In 1425, it was to acquire Mýto and Litomyšl from the Prague association to which Kolín was to be added in 1427. Čáslav became important as the second center of the Orphan domain. Kutná Hora, still badly damaged, passed into the joint ownership of both brotherhoods.

The Royalist Party and the Prague conservatives hastened to take full advantage of the differences in the Hussite camp. Žižka's death, the dispute between the brotherhoods and the failure of the Prague and Tabor theologians to find common ground encouraged Ulrich of Rožmberk and Čeněk of Vartemberk to seek the abrogation of the Zdice Agreement whose terms they had accepted under duress. The opportunity presented itself when Prague and the brotherhoods went on a joint expedition to Ústí on the Elbe, a formidable fortress, belonging to Frederick, the Margrave of Meissen, whom Sigismund had raised to the status of the Elector of Saxony as compensation for his losses resulting from the battle of Vítkov. Fearful lest his numerous enemies should snatch the electorship from him, and in obedience to the king, Frederick had not signed the Zdice Accord although he had taken part in the truce talks with the Hussites. Soon he renewed his attacks on the Hussites living in the foothills of the Ore Mountains. At the beginning of December, a large and well equipped Hussite army struck at Ústí in retaliation, and then suddenly raised the siege for reasons unknown. Bad weather or, more likely, disagreement among the commanders stopped the operation and only a small part of the Hussite army was left on patrol duty between Hazmburk and Třebenice.[11]

This was a serious setback. It led to recriminations and the renewal of old disputes just when it was necessary to prepare for the diet of Kouřím. Now the royalists went into action. As a substitute for the diet, they proposed a meeting between the Hussite and the Catholic party including a disputation on the Four Articles for which, they claimed they had King Sigismund's support. The proposal split the arbiters of the Zdice Agreement. The representatives of the brotherhoods voted against, those of Prague, in favor. The royalist party succeeded in swaying the majority of Korybut's council including the prince himself who had been disillusioned by the outcome of the peace of Hospital Field. In June the previous year he had arrived in the country styling himself "Prince of Lithuania by the Grace of God and the desired and elected King of Bohemia and Moravia," and thus he signed the treaty of Špital Field, after which he reverted to the simple title of "Prince of Lithuania." He must soon have concluded that Prague had promised more than it was in a position to grant when it had declared him the desired king.

He also soon realized that two important reasons which had prompted Prague to contemplate his election no longer existed. Wladyslaw II, king of Poland, and Witold, grand duke of Lithuania, had publicly and almost demonstratively disowned him as soon as he returned to Bohemia in defiance of their probibition. He then lost any claim to the crown of Poland when a son and heir was born to the aged King Wladyslaw on 18 October 1424.[12] Furthermore, a general diet of the lands of the Bohemian crown was the only authority that could have bestowed the crown on Korybut. But a diet could not be contemplated at the time of the Špital Field peace when anything likely to disturb the cohesion of the Hussite armies before the Moravian campaign had to be avoided. The death of Žižka, the father figure and the only reliable guide in the intricate Bohemian situation, shattered Korybut's hopes more than anything else. Žižka's successors did not possess his authority nor was anyone so well-disposed towards the prince. He therefore attached himself more closely to those men who had called him to the throne, men such as William Kostka, Heník of Kolštejn and John Smiřický who stood closer to the royalists than to the brotherhoods. All this alienated Korybut from the country in general and frustrated the hopes of those who wished him to feel at home in Bohemia. Sometime in February 1426[13] the confused prince decided to accept the proposal of the royalist party. In reprisal the brotherhoods apparently threatened to sieze the towns which they had conquered for Prague as her allies in the spring of 1421. When the threat was ignored, they took up arms.

The Taborites came to blows with Menhart of (Jindřichův) Hradec in a skirmish which ended at the beginning of February by their seizure of Kamenice (on the river Labe).[14] War began in earnest in the middle of March when the brotherhoods exploited Korybut's difficulties and concluded a lightening fast operation in east Bohemia, snatching Litomyšl and Mýto from Prague, justifying their claim to these towns by pointing out that they had been captured with their participation in Žižka's spring campaign of 1421.[15] As a result, Korybut and Prague veered further to the right and made a clean break with the brotherhoods by arranging with the royalist lords to send delegates to Brno to negotiate with the representatives of the Catholic Church. It was no secret that the idea had emanated from Hašek of Valdštejn, the bloody-minded instigator of John Želivský's execution and of the fraticidal Malešov battle. He had shortly before defected to King Sigismund and thereby earned the highest office in Moravia.[16] Expecting that public opinion in Prague—where the very name of Hašek was detested—would be specially indignant, the brotherhoods changed their plans.

Instead of invading Moravia as everybody expected, they turned in the opposite direction and on 31 March 1425 appeared outside the walls of Prague.[17] At the head of the Taborites were John Hvězda and Bohuslav Švamberk, the leaders of a similar attack in 1422; with them came the Orphans under the command of John Roháč and a detachment from Hradec Králové, led by Hertvík of Rúšinov. Prague had been forewarned and the attackers were beaten off nursing their wounds. In reprisal for their defeat, the brotherhoods struck at Slaný, the town to which they laid claim because in 1421 they had helped Prague to conquer it. They took Slaný after twelve days' seige and inflicted much suffering on the lay and clerical defenders.[18] After that, they burnt down the town of Roudnice although the archbishop's castle withstood their attack. The next target was the royalist party, especially the Podbrský association, which they accused of violating the Zdice Agreement, and the *Landfríd* of Plzeň, an inveterate enemy of the Hussites. At the beginning of May, the brotherhoods unsuccessfully attacked Žebrák and Točnik, royal castles, after which they burnt the towns of Žebrák and Hořovice, and later

Obořiště. They also took Švihov castle in the Plzeň area. Meanwhile the Taborites made a futile attempt at Třeboň on the Rožmberk estate and burnt down Nové Hrady. Fragmentary sources record the fall to the brotherhoods of Chlumec on the Cidlina and of Rychmburk near Skuteč, the property of Lord Ernest Flaška of Pardubice. In August, the brotherhoods took hold of Liberk near Rychnov, Opočno and perhaps also Lanšperk. On 2 September 1425, the forces of Žatec conquered the large Duchov fortress from the possession of Meissen. Apart from a minor victory, the Praguers' only other gain was that Hynek of Poděbrady transferred his loyalty from the brotherhoods to Korybut. By then the war of the brotherhoods against Prague and Korybut had come to an end.[19] This was partly due to the lack of progress at the Brno meeting between Prague and the royalist party.

The Brno negotiations took place under the auspices of Albrecht of Austria, the new lord of Moravia. King Sigismund sent as his delegation, his council of state, headed by Günter, the archbishop of Magdeburg, Ulrich of Rožmberk and John Krk Švihovský. Günter, an expert in Bohemian affairs, had already encountered the Hussites in May 1420 at Kutná Hora and had lost none of his intransigence.[20] The delegates from Prague were escorted by a few more loyalist lords including Čeněk of Vartemberk. The talks proved that the principles of the two opposing sides were absolutely irreconcilable, and achieved nothing. The failure of the negotiations, which had originally embroiled the Hussite camp in internecine war now gradually brought the brotherhoods and Prague together so that they prepared for another military campaign to Moravia. At the beginning of September, their joint forces again fought the fortified city of Jihlava, but without success.[21] At the time, the Hussites in another part of Moravia were threatened by a fresh royalist attack increasing the need for reconciliation between the various wings of the movement.

There was no time to lose. The fortified monastery of Třebíč, the major Hussite conquest in Moravia in 1424, was under fire and ready to capitulate. Before going to its rescue, however, the Bohemian Hussites had to gain time by concluding a truce with the royalists as in 1424. To achieve this, it was necessary to improve the relationship between the brotherhoods and Korybut. In the past, Žižka's personality would have been a sufficient guarantee of their cooperation; now it was resolved to seek a permanent solution, that would guard against any breach of the alliance. The beginning was difficult. Švamberk's abortive attack on Prague was still fresh in people's memory; this time, however, he brought his army to Prague and stayed to take an active part in the peace negotiations. John Hvězda, his erstwhile partner, died just before Vožice was captured from the royalists on 18 October 1425. The situation which had led to the outbreak of war in the spring of 1425 had changed and the memory of the Špital Field peace and of the solemn oath sworn to Žižka revived the spirit of reconciliation. On 17 October 1425, close to the first anniversary of Žižka's death, peace was concluded and promulgated at Vršovice near Prague.[22]

The treaty of Vršovice was a unique document giving a good insight into the internal life of Hussite democracy. It made ample use of the experience gained since the previous peace and took every possible precaution to prevent another failure. Both contracting parties unreservedly pledged to submit to the verdict of a panel of twelve elected representatives, six for the Prague association and six for the Tabor and Žatec group. Prague delegated William Kostka of Postupice and John Smiřický, both of the rank of captain, and four burghers, of whom Simon of the White Lion was the most prominent. Their opposite numbers were four Tabor captains, Bohuslav of Švamberk, Zbyněk of Buchov, Matthew Louda and Nicholas of Padařov, and one burgher each of Žatec and Louny.[23] Strangely enough, the Orphans were not represented on the panel. To guarantee the inviolability of the pledge, each party gave the other, twenty-two men as hostages; in the event of a broken pledge, the guilty party was to pay 300,000 groschen, failing that, submit to custody of their own accord.[24]

The verdict exhorted both parties to live in sincere and truly Christian peace, and announced that the arbiters intended to call a diet where they would make every effort to lead the priests of both parties to harmony, unity and love. They also ordered the release of prisoners and the cancellation of any obligations the release might cause. The burghers of Prague and of any other town who had been exiled from or left their cities were to be allowed to return. A measure of special importance concerned the restitution of property which either side had acquired from the other by conquest. To shorten the procedure and save time, the arbiters reserved the right to select a team of four who were empowered to take instant action. These immediately returned three estates which the brotherhoods had occupied, to Heník of Kolštejn. A number of similar cases were referred to the future diet, and if it should fail to reach an agreement, the team of four would be empowered to decide. Lastly, the peace treaty made new provisions concerning fines for breaking the peace, and appealed to those who wished to avail themselves of the benefits of the peace to declare their acceptance of it; but the peace was binding even on those who would not do so.

Judging by the letters of acceptance from the brotherhoods as well as from Korybut and the Prague association, the peace of Vršovice was received with gratitude and joy. The presence of the Moravian Hussites had made a noticeable contribution, and like the peace of the Špital Field, it cleared the way for a campaign to Moravia. The treaty was signed by the spokesmen of both Hussite parties and by some royalist groups, such as the leading towns of the Podbrský association. The head of the garrison in the royal Karlštejn castle, which had been included in a truce agreement with Prague since 1422, and a few nobles from the Plzeň region, although not the *Landfríd,* also signed. The treaty was to last for a year but, unlike the Zdice Accord, it did not attempt to provide a final solution to the conflict between the Hussites and the royalists. This was a major victory for the royalist party[25] because lasting peace (which they now relinquished) had been a goal of the brotherhoods in 1424.

The united Hussite armies led by Prince Korybut first struck at Jihlava but, lacking the resources, had to give up after a few days. Then they moved towards Třebíč from which Duke Albrecht beat a hasty retreat. Next they marched on Moravské Budějovice and Znojmo; unable to tackle the latter they burnt out the nearby monastery at Louka instead. Thereupon they invaded Austria and on 24 November took Retz after a week's siege. With a large booty and numerous prisoners, including John Hardegg, the lord of Retz, they returned home to deal with a more difficult problem.

In accordance with the terms of the Peace of Vršovice, the select committee of four[26] called a general assembly of all Hussite parties to meet in Bethlehem chapel in January 1426. As already contemplated in October, the theologians met first to smooth out their differences. On 11 January, Jakoubek opened the synod with a moving address recalling the early days of the great struggle for Hus' legacy, the famous rallies of 1419 which produced the famous Four Articles and the unanimous resolutions of the spiritual leaders of both Prague and Tabor to take up arms in defence of God's law.[27] Here the record of the synod ends; it is known for certain that Jakoubek's endeavor to reconcile the divergent opinions was of no avail. The same applies to the deliberations of the secular participants, the record of which has not survived. Nevertheless, it can be gathered that the problem of Korybut's kingship was at the root of the trouble.[28] The Peace of Vršovice had deferred its solution to the assembly in Prague specifying that order and constitutional power be jointly emphasized. By this was meant that Korybut's position should be defined at least on the basis of Žižka's bond of the alliance with Korybut and Prague, as recorded by Žižka and his Taborite fellow captains in 1422.

It is understandable that under existing conditions and after the shifts and changes of the previous three years, the brotherhoods were reluctant to enter into a similar alliance and indeed, rightly, felt threatened by it. However, they felt the need to justify their case to the public and did so at their regional assemblies to avoid an open refusal. We know only the resolution of the regional assembly of Písek of 6 February 1426 which declared that the Taborites ". . . were ready to obey, if it were not in disagreement with God's Law, a properly constituted secular power which they could accept of their own free will."[29] This was a clear "no" even though the memorandum which was sent to Prague with the assembly's resolution stressed that "even though for the present things pleasing to God and good cannot prosper, it would not be proper to cease working permanently for the common good." On the Orphan side no such manifestation is recorded. Their attitude to Korybut hardly differed from that of Tabor. The Orphans could not forget his coup at Hradec Králové, his overtures to King Sigismund or his alliance with the barons. Moreover, they were especially vulnerable since they had acquired more territories from the Prague association and the pro-Korybut lords than Tabor had. To ally themselves again with the Prague association would have meant surrendering their independence. The net result was that neither brotherhood could second Prague's proposal to elect Korybut king.

On the other hand, the Orphans did not turn down the appeal for cooperation in renewing the regional constitution, although it came from their enemies and was meant to harm the brotherhoods. The Orphans' positive response testified both to their strength and their understanding for the needs of the state.

In pre-revolutionary times, regional administration[30] had been the prerogative of the lords who had the exclusive right to the office of the regional captain with the police and military forces of the region at his command. The brotherhoods generally regarded the system with distrust because Sigismund and the lords, and later perhaps even Korybut, used it against them. However, the regional constitution had always been an integral part of the structure of the Czech state and the brotherhoods had to admit that opposing it in principle branded them as enemies of the state and its institutions. Now the Orphans changed their attitude and began to turn the regional constitution to their advantage.[31]

They seem to have taken the first step when Korybut reintroduced regional administration in the territories where they were in the majority. This probably happened about 20 December 1425 during their assembly at Kouřim shortly before the January diet opened. While Korybut appointed regional captains at Kouřim and Čáslav, the Orphans went further and appointed a joint captain for Hradec Králové and Chrudim. He was a member of the gentry, John Královec of Hrádek, a young and competent soldier. In these regions, more than anywhere else in the kingdom, knights, squires and freeholders predominated, and most of them had joined the revolution. During the famous spring campaign of 1421, Prague and Tabor had acquired a number of fortified towns and reduced the importance of the lords most of whom had accepted the chalice under compulsion. The gentry and the towns therefore gained control of these East-Bohemian regions and secured the rule of the chalice more securely than the Taborites had done in south Bohemia. It was a worthy continuation of the work of Žižka who had built in East Bohemia, on Orebite soil, an alliance whose effectiveness equalled that of Tabor. It seems that the new name, the Orphans,[32] officially dated from the Kouřim assembly, probably at the suggestion of Victorin of Kunštát and Kuneš of Bělovice who had been at Žižka's death-bed.

Compared with the Orphans, the Taborites were at a disadvantage. Their widely spaced town fortresses prevented them from taking control of more than two regions, those of Písek and Bechyně (Tabor). By February 1426, the organization of the Písek region was completed. Tabor had little chance of extending its control westward beyond Domažlice because in every direction the territory was dominated by the power of the Plzeň *Landfríd.* Tabor could spread its influence eastward in a narrow strip across Moravia and even into Slovakia where, however, the chance of maintaining control was nil.

Consequently, the Taborites lagged behind the Orphans in their concern about the importance of regional constitution, or the interests of the state. The political center of both brotherhoods was steadily moving towards east Bohemia following the tendency of the last two years of Žižka's life. In 1427, Kutná Hora became the joint possession of both, and from the time Prokop Holý made it his residence, it overshadowed Tabor as well as Hradec Králové.[33]

A year and a half after the loss of Žižka, the Hussite movement was no less strong than at the moment of his death. It had passed through the dangerous storms of the immediate past from which it emerged steeled and strengthened. The brotherhoods retained the initiative and led the revolution and remained faithful to Žižka's undying spirit. The adherence of his policy resulted in the idea which probably issued from the mind of Prokop Holý, that the internal tension of the movement be reduced by turning its combined forces against the enemy abroad who was just about to strike another blow, and against whom attack was the most effective defence.

CHAPTER TWO

THE HUSSITE CAMPAIGN TO ÚSTÍ AND THE FALL OF KORYBUT

In March 1425, Cardinal Branda, the organizer of the two unsuccessful crusades against the Hussites, returned to Italy, and the pope had to find a new nuncio. Branda was then seventy-five. After a good deal of trouble, Martin V chose a considerably younger man with the necessary status and of the same Roman lineage as the pope himself, Giordano Orsini.[1] A hard canonist, as was the pope, Orsini had already shown his prowess in persecuting those within the Franciscan order who opposed the pope. In 1421 he had had two towns in Italy razed to the ground and had the population massacred. Prior to leaving Rome in March he had done his homework so thoroughly that before he reached Florence his propaganda machine was already working in Vienna, the residence of King Sigismund's son-in-law, Albrecht, Duke of Austria, a man directly threatened by the Hussites. A former Augustinian preacher from Prague, Osvald Reinlein, who had known John Hus and was now based in Nürnberg, officially launched the anti-Hussite campaign with a solemn mass in Vienna to which John, the king of Portugal, made a special contribution. He wrote a devotional pamphlet "for the salvation of all the fighters against the faithless Hussite heretics" and sent it to Vienna along with his son who had been exiled from Portugal for murder and was now touring Europe with a resplendent retinue.[2] After three months' of ceaseless preaching, Reinlein

13

suddenly gave up. At the same time Orsini's mission ended in failure as the Hussites had smashed the greatest army assembled against them that year.[3]

The Hussites' idea to send an army against the crusaders was probably born at the January diet in Prague, but could not be carried out before spring. The enemy helped the Hussites to decide where to send their forces. Frederick, the elector of Saxony and, next to Albrecht, the most dangerous neighbor of Bohemia, had already launched a series of preventive attacks from Most and Ústí on the Elbe. While his attacks relaxed in February, both Hussite parties were busy planning a concentrated and effective blow. The elector left his wife in charge of his cantry and went to Nürnberg to seek the help of King Sigismund and the imperial diet while Orsini was heading in the same direction.

The Orebite vanguard, led by John Roháč of Dubá, set out in the direction of a strong royalist bastion, Česká Lípa, destroyed Benešov on the Ploučnice and caused panic in Upper Lusatia, where forces were quickly mobilized against the unexpected attack. Roháč, however, turned back, burned down Bělá near Bezděz and arrived at Mladá Boleslav just in time to put out the fire which the enemy had set to the town and to the nearby Michalovice castle. On 5 May, the Hussite commanders held rallies at Mladá Boleslav and Starý Bydžov. The elite of the Orphan gentry joined Roháč in laying seige to Česká Lípa, which capitulated on 19 May with favorable terms probably owing to the efforts of the Orphan gentry.[4] The edge of the Hussite occupied territory thus advanced deeper into the north-westerly direction, and closer towards Lusatia. But instead of advancing against Žitava, the Orphans turned west and encamped outside Ústí, probably according to the plans laid down at Mladá Boleslav. They were soon joined by the Praguers and the Taborites.

The Prague army was led by Korybut himself with his Polish retinue, followed by the town captains and the Moravian allies under John Tovačovský and Wenceslas of Strážnice. The Taborite campaigning force was led by Bleh of Těšnice and Jaroslav of Buchovice, but Prokop Holý, the spiritual leader of the troops, had the main responsibility. The troops from Žatec, Louny and Slaný were headed by Jacob of Vřesovice, the captain of Bilina, whose territory lay in the first line of attack from Saxony. The four armies occupied positions around Ústí which was well protected by the Labe (Elbe) river and the nearby Střekov castle. The

Hussites launched the first attack on 6 June but were repulsed by the stiff resistance of the defenders who were hoping to get relief soon. After sustaining considerable losses, the Hussite high command refrained from further attacks and withdrew to a gently rising hill west of Ústí, called Běhaní, with a commanding position over a broad valley and overlooking the probable path of the hostile attack from the Ore mountains. This vantage position made it possible to lure the enemy into a dangerous spot and was reminiscent of the strategy of the Vítkov battle in 1420.

Catherine, the elector's wife, rallied and inspected the combined Saxon and Lusatian forces at Freiberg in Saxony on 11 June 1425, and gave them a moving send-off. The well-equipped army was so large that it had to split before crossing the Ore Mountains through three passes, heading for Most, Osek and Duchov, and Krupka respectively, to join near Chabařovice in the broad valley above which the Hussite army was waiting inside a formation of wagons. After slow progress, caused by a difficult search for food, the German army reached its destination on the night of 15 June, and the following morning, Sunday, revealed its immense size to the Czechs.[5] The Czech command, in its customary way, sent messengers to the enemy camp to negotiate details of combat, including observance of fair play and the special demand that those who wished to capitulate should not be killed,[6] and that the battle should be put off by a day to prevent desecrating the Sunday. These demands were arrogantly turned down and the Saxon army launched an attack on the wagons.

The Hussites allowed the enemy to ascend the easy slope and form quite close to the front row of the wagons. Then they fired fiercely with guns and howitzers and started making inroads among the attackers. The wind blew dense clouds of smoke into the eyes of the Saxons and, in the confused hand to hand fighting that followed, caused complete havoc among them. The depleted front lines turned back and carried the rest with them. The firing stopped and the Hussite cavalry rushed in pursuit with the infantry in the rear. The Hussites paid the Saxons in their own coin and spared few captives even though some stuck their swords into the ground to show that they wished to surrender. The page-boys who had been brought over for the first taste of blood were spared. The dead lay like sheaves on the field. Those who sought refuge in the nearby villages were encircled and burnt. Very few got away. One of them was the Saxon supreme commander, Boso of Fictum, who was denounced in his country as a traitor.[7]

The defeat decided the fate of the formidable fortress of Ústí. The Saxon garrison and a large number of citizens evacuated the town at night and the conquerors entered it almost without a fight. Knowing that the fortress was difficult to hold, the Hussites demolished and burned it. Three years later Ústí was rebuilt[8] and colonized by the Hussites after their further conquests in the area. After Ústí, the Hussites took Střekov and Blansko castles,[9] and thus opened the way for the greatest Hussite campaign of all in 1429.

The defeat of one of the largest armies the Church had ever sent against the Hussites was a triumph and a testimony to the political and strategic ingenuity of their party's statesmen and commanders. Unfortunately, it was followed by a lamentable anti-climax at home which might have deprived the Hussites of the fruits of their victory. The failure of the January diet of Prague had convinced the right wing of the Hussite revolution that neither the Taborites nor the Orphans would ever accept Korybut or become reconciled with the Church by seeking a fair hearing with King Sigismund's assistance. Of course neither Korybut nor Prague could refuse to help with the expedition to Ústí, which was a matter of extreme urgency for the state. But once back from the battle, Korybut offended the Hussite susceptibilities by keeping in touch with King Sigismund in order to arrange a hearing, knowing full well that the previous effort had sparked off the war between Prague and the brotherhoods. In any case, it might have been thought that those negotiations were over when the Prague messengers had returned from the Brno meeting. But some delegates had apparently gone from Brno to Hungary and had been deliberately detained by Sigismund in a remote part of the country. Later they were released, and having encountered many dangers on route, returned safely to Prague.[10] Their delayed return caused consternation among the brotherhoods as well as speculation as to why they were so late, and about what they may have been talking about with the hostile king. The suspicion became stronger when Korybut accepted an invitation from Sigismund to join him in negotiations in Vienna.[11] The royalist aristocracy tried to seize this new opportunity to get the upper hand. Žižka had thwarted their previous attempts in 1423-1424, and this time they had to cope with the vigorous growth and rising political power of the Hussite lesser nobles who were turning the renewed regional administration to their own advantage. The royalist aristocracy sought out Korybut, who was their only hope in this difficult situation.

The way was prepared for them by a member of a powerful noble family, Hynek of Poděbrady. In 1424, he was still a loyal supporter of Žižka, whom he and his brother Viktorin had rescued from a trap near Poděbrady. For this help both brothers were then taken hostage and released only when their political friends guaranteed that the hostages would pay a high ransom. Whereas Viktorin paid the fine, Hynek refused.[12] During the 1425 war Hynek had defected to Korybut and by the end of the same year treacherously captured his uncle, Puška of Kunštát and starved him to death. When he joined the east Bohemian royalists, the worst enemies of the Orphans, a clash became inevitable. As soon as the battle of Ústí was over, his adversaries rushed at him and would have beaten him to death, if the captains had not intervened in the name of military discipline. This violent incident unleashed hostility between Korybut and the brotherhoods, and it was only through the statesmanship of the leaders of the two sides that war was averted. Meanwhile, the Hussite troops disbanded, leaving Most castle in the hands of the elector of Saxony for the duration of the Hussite wars. In the end, fighting did break out between Hynek and the brotherhoods, and in spite of its local character, deepened the conflict between the brotherhoods on the one side and Korybut and the Prague alliance on the other.

The rules of war which prohibited personal feuds between all participants of the battle of Ústí, allowed Hynek to return safely from the battlefield to Poděbrady. But at the moment of his return he lost this immunity and very soon both the Taborites and the Orphans besieged Poděbrady, wishing to make a public example of Hynek. Their main concern was, however, to save the achievements of the pacts of Špital Field and of Vršovice, and yet their involvement in this local dispute was to affect both their own and the fate of Prince Korybut.

The large forces of the brotherhoods were commanded by Prokop Holý and Kuneš of Bělovice; and the regional troops were led by Captain John Kralovice.[13] The fortress of Poděbrady was well protected and Hynek resisted very effectively. One day a single shot from his canon killed eleven men in a crowd of people who had gathered for worship. The success of the garrison raised the hopes of the royalists and their sympathizers in the Hussite ranks. It seemed that events were creating the kind of situation in which, after eight years, the brotherhood armies were to suffer the terrible final defeat at Lipany. Even traitors came out of hiding. Sometime before, a Hussite defector had helped the Swabian cavalry to cross from Bavaria and advance toward Klatovy, and even capture a formation of Hussite wagons.[14] Prokop Holý became aware of the danger and withdrew from Poděbrady at the beginning of October, after a three week seige. The proud magnate hastened to snatch Nymburk, a Taborite town, but was crushed to death by a gate that closed behind him. The Poděbrady estate was inherited by his brother Viktorin, the lord of Pardubice, and became again part of the Orphan territory. Viktorin, however, died on 1 January 1427, leaving a son aged seven; the future King George of Poděbrady. His guardians and managers of the estate remained loyal Hussites.

Hynek's sudden death stopped the war but did not bring lasting peace. The dangerous tensions between the brotherhoods and Korybut remained, and the latter's position was becoming increasingly unstable.

It is possible that at King Sigismund's invitation Korybut at this time sent messengers to Vienna; in any case the king made a fresh attempt to bring the Catholic and Hussite theologians together at the request of both the Catholic and Hussite nobility. The new nuncio, Orsini, had no idea of the Hussite strength and of the reluctance of Germany to make another war on the Czechs. Three days after Orsini's flat refusal[15] to consider a hearing for the Hussite nobles, his attemped crusade collapsed near Ústí. The diet of Nürnberg, which he had launched with his militant speech was soon dissolved and the nuncio himself eventually left for Italy. All he could do from that time on, was to promise indulgences to contributors towards the so-called daily war. Since Sigismund was involved in the Turkish wars, he had not even attended the diet of Nürnberg. The direction of the daily war was given to four German princes in the immediate vicinity of Bohemia,[16] but Albrecht of Austria was the only one who could undertake any major action. Frederick of Saxony took extensive measures for the defence of the Ore mountains, but was glad for a temporary lull in the fighting.

Albrecht's position was more difficult. At the beginning of March 1426,[17] the Hussites not only invaded south Moravia, where they took Podivín and set fire to Valtice and Mikulov, but also penetrated into Austria. As soon as the harvest was over, the duke struck at Břeclav, fulfilling resolutions made by the Nürnberg diet. By the end of August the town was completely surrounded by a large army reinforced by troops from Sigismund and Peter, the prince of Portugal. After an eight week seige, when Albrecht was preparing for the final attack and felt sure of victory, Prokop Holý suddenly appeared on the scene with a large force from Tabor and Ivančice and saved Břeclav at the last minute. Albrecht retreated hastily on 29 October 1426, after which the Taborites could restock Břeclav and again carry out raids deep into Austria. A month before these events, the brotherhoods had acquired Stříbro, a powerful fortress in west Bohemia. Přibík of Klenovy, with the troops of Peter Zmrzlík, took it by surprise without losing a single warrior, and thus moved the frontier of the Hussite territory close to Plzeň.

This double defeat of the anti-Hussite forces on the battlefield was almost offset by a simultaneous victory of papal diplomacy in Prague which brought Korybut a spectacular, if short-lived success.

Because Orsini had refused King Sigismund's request that he should grant a hearing to the Hussite theologians of the Prague party, Korybut made a fresh attempt, and this time turned to his native country. Already in March he had sent a letter to his uncle Witold, in which he had given an account of all his unsparing but futile efforts to bring about a fair hearing for the Hussites. He had stressed that he was ready to accept any findings based on the Scriptures in order to put an end to the wars and bloodshed, and begged his uncle to intercede with the pope. Witold never replied to his nephew's plea and protestations of loyalty, although the letter had repeated almost literally what Witold had written to the pope four years earlier before sending Korybut to Bohemia. Having achieved all his aims through the alliance with Sigismund, the grand duke had washed his hands of Hussite affairs and left Korybut to his fate.[18]

In Cracow, Korybut's prospects were brighter. The victory of Ústí which he could partly claim as his own, raised his prestige and impressed the court. Wladislaw gave ear to his nephew's request and promised to send messengers to Rome with the important concessions Korybut was prepared to make to Sigismund. He found an obliging helper in Archbishop Conrad whom Martin V had punished for his defection to the Hussites in 1421, by placing the diocese and the chapter of Prague, which had been exiled in Žitava in 1420, in charge of John, the bishop of Litomyšl. Anxious to obtain the pope's pardon and in order to prove his determination to abandon the Hussites and return to the Church with his officials and bring along the Hussites, the archbishop issued orders which he passed off as resolutions of the synod.[19] He instructed that the old rites be reintroduced and all deviations be extirpated in the spirit of the university circular of 1417, which had been directed at Jakoubek.[20] Those who would not submit within a fortnight were to be removed from church office. This highly reactionary document, together with Korybut's supplication, was taken to Rome by the messengers of the King of Poland and presented to Martin V at the end of September. Strangely enough, the pope was affable and responded by requesting Wladislaw and Witold to use any appropriate means to help this commendable effort. Of course he added that the Hussite delegates must be unconditionally empowered to accept the decision of the holy see.[21] He must have concluded from Conrad's document that the capitulation of the truculent heretics was a *fait accompli.* The pope's answer reached Prague early in November and got a stormy reception.

The content of the pope's letter to Korybut is not known but it is possible to imagine that Martin V couched his demand of unconditional surrender in suave language calculated to captivate the young prince's heart. And indeed Korybut took on the task all the more readily because he had remained estranged from the spiritual essence of the Hussite revolution and now received unreserved support from the right-wing university masters who had long been waiting for their chance.

These masters had been driven into the reactionary camp by the steady decline of the university, resulting partly from the ravages of war, and partly from the loss of its property, the only source of their regular income. Moreover, in 1421, the city council had abolished the so-called perpetual payments or rents, the most popular securities of the time, on which their salaries depended.[22] As a result, lectures and examinations were discontinued, the university was reduced to the philosophical faculty and functioned irregularly, only when an election or a rector or a dean was due.[23] The disgruntled masters found powerful allies among the well-to-do citizens of Prague and the associated towns, and welcomed Korybut's efforts because they promised their rehabilitation and the repeal of the odious law on perpetual rents.

The masters appreciated these allies, since their most talented colleagues had left the university to earn their living in the Prague parish churches, where they could influence public opinion by preaching. Křišt'an of Prachatice, Peter Mladoňovice and John Příbram were outstanding examples.[24] Christian was a senior master with influential connections among the nobility and a reputation, at home and abroad, as a famous astronomer and physician. His disciple Mladoňovice, the chronicler of John Hus' trial, had met many Hussite and Polish nobles at the Council of Constance and later promoted contacts between Hussites and Poles. He had reasons to fear King Sigismund's vengeance because, in his chroncile, he had unmasked the king's hateful treatment of Hus. John Příbram surpassed all in vehemence and fanaticism. He called himself proudly ". . . the solicitous persecutor of all heresies and especially of the Wycliffite and Pikard heresies." He was now in his element. He was convinced that the best way to an agreement with Rome was an attack on Wyclif whose teachings had been condemned as heresy by the Council of Constance in 1415. Příbram's invective met resolute resistance as the Evangelical Doctor had been widely respected in Prague from the time of John Hus. Master English-Payne spoke in defence of his famous compatriot at the university. In reply, Příbram plunged into other vehement controversies, old and new, and challenged Payne and Jakoubek, whom he had branded as Wycliffites, to state their views on the Lord's Supper. The two masters did so without touching on the scholastic formulae which had led Wyclif into questionable speculations.[25] The speakers of both parties engaged in heated public disputes and swayed their audiences to the point that they also got involved. Korybut attended on several occasions and declared his agreement with Příbram.

The struggle was not confined to the university which had now come to life, and to theological topics which only academicians could follow. There is a fragmentary record of the sermon delivered by Jakoubek at Bethlehem chapel on 22 December 1426, which bore witness to the lively activity of the preachers.[26] Jakoubek, who had earned as much respect as Hus by his lifelong struggle for the chalice defended himself against the unceasing attacks from the reactionary elements at the university. His colleagues hated him, he said, believing him to be the source of the evil that was spreading in the kingdom and the author of the law which had impoverished them, and even more as an advocate of talks with the Taborites whom they wanted to destroy.

The nobles, including even those who temporarily accepted the chalice under duress, had narrowly missed their chance to destroy the campaigning armies of the brotherhoods in 1423, when they succeeded in ousting the towns from their leading position in the realm. Žižka's victory at Malešov and the peace of Špital Field had restored the superiority of the brother-hoods. Then the treachery of Hynek of Poděbrady and Korybut's success in Rome gave the royalists fresh impetus to concerted action.[27] The Prague alliance had been coexisting peacefully with the royalist Podbrský group by annually extending the truce of 1422. At the same time a few prominent captains had maintained connections with the royalist east Bohemian nobles who in turn had kept in touch with the powerful league of Silesian princes. The royalist loss of Ústí led, at the beginning of July 1426 to the formation of a military alliance between the Six Towns of Lusatia and the duchies of Swidnice and Jawor in Upper Silesia. Almost simultaneously, Conrad, the Bishop of Breslau and commander of the Silesian duchy opened negotiations with the foremost royalist nobles in Bohemia, John Městecký of Opočno, Púta of Častolovice and Krušina of Lichtenburg, the captain of Klodzko, as well as with three noblemen of Korybut's party. In September the Silesians met with all noblemen from Bohemia, of which only two were said to have remained true to the Hus-site faith.[28] It was a situation which foreshadowed the crushing defeat of the brotherhoods at Lipany in 1434. It had become clear that the first prerequisite for success was to seize Prague and make it fight against the brotherhoods. This was impossible as long as Jakoubek kept preaching in Prague.

In his pre-Christmas sermon, in 1426, Jakoubek analysed in detail his relationship with the Taborites and denied their assertion that their litur-gical and dogmatic deviations were nothing but conclusions drawn from his own teachings. He rejected equally firmly any attempt to make a pact with Rome, and the demands of the reactionaries that he should break off relations with Tabor. He would not abandon them although he failed to bring about an agreement with them in January 1426. As his disciples, they were infinitely nearer to him than the university colleagues who hated him. This decision by the most powerful Prague preacher had a far-reaching effect. A vast majority of the population of Prague and of its alliance voted against sacrificing the fundamental Hussite principles to a reconciliation with the pope, and against Korybut's policy to eliminate Tabor.

Korybut, however, did not give up. The barons, whom he had been brought up to regard as the embodiment of the state, went on with their preparations which apparently coincided with the decisions of the pope and King Sigismund to launch another crusade against the Hussites. The military league of Silesian princes was finally set up at Strzelin and it concluded a pact in mid-February 1427 with the royalist nobles from Bohemia. It contained a clause allowing the inclusion of the Hussite nobles of Korybut's party. Late in March, the brotherhoods and Korybut were on the brink of war. It was however prevented by the intervention of the leaders of the Taborites, of the Orphans and of Žatec whose arrival in Prague on 24 March 1427 had however dangerously intensified the tension in the capital.[29] A passionate battle of pulpits had split the city into two hostile camps, ready to strike at each other at any moment. It was Korybut who in the end turned the tables.[30]

Intelligence from Silesia convinced him that the right moment had arrived.[31] After consultations with his Polish confidants on 16 April, he invited his foremost officials, the vice-chamberlain, Svojše of Zahrádka and John Rozvoda of Stakory,[32] to dinner and sent them to the Prague commanders, Heník of Kolštejn and John Smiřický with detailed instructions. Both guests, however, understood the situation better and decided to act according to their conscience. At dawn on Maundy Thursday, as soon as the city gates were opened, they handed the damning documents containing the instructions to influential members of the city council and to Rokycana. At the sound of the city bells, the military forces of Prague rallied and Korybut was taken prisoner at his home in Old Town Square and taken to the castle. Priests of Příbram's party were arrested and chose to leave the city rather than accept Rokycana's authority. Later, Korybut was secretly deported to the Valdštejn castle near Turnov and after his release in the autumn of 1428, was escorted to the Odry castle by Dobeslav Puchala, never to return to the kingdom which had offered him its crown three years earlier.[33] The revolution may have judged leniently a politically immature man but it could not put up with a convicted plotter.[34]

This bloodless overthrow of one man had fateful consequences for the revolution. It buried the hopes that the country would have a Hussite king in the person of the young Lithuanian prince. The Hussites would not be spared the accusation that they did not want a renewed order but were bent on anarchy, so that they could fish in troubled waters. waters.

King Sigismund, the man who gained the most from these events, ominously reappeared on the scene, ready to make a profit from his fallen rival's misfortune and to enjoy the swing of public opinion. The revolution which had deposed him did not have many alternatives. He was still the only heir to the throne. To set up a republic was even less feasible than to impose the Four Articles on the whole population of the country. Since the Hussites had failed to find a king of their own faith, it would now be much more difficult to challenge Sigismund's accession. The Polish party disintegrated and men like William Kostka, who had called Korybut to the throne, now turned to Sigismund. In the end Sigismund was to find adherents even at Tabor. Later, two prominent Tabor captains were to betray the brotherhood and help Sigismund to win the battle of Lipany, and the crown.

CHAPTER THREE

THE FOURTH CRUSADE AND THE BEGINNINGS OF
THE HUSSITE OFFENSIVE

It dawned on most people only gradually what significance the fall of Korybut in April 1427 had for the revolution. At that time, the attention of the whole nation was directed towards events abroad where preparations for another crusade were in full swing. Its organizer, the most powerful elector in Germany, had a personal interest in it.

Frederick Hohenzollern,[1] the Margrave of Brandenburg, had been the head of the electors who had formed an opposition group against Sigismund in 1424. The king, however, succeeded in breaking up the group and Frederick eventually resigned the margraviate in 1426, in favor of his son, John. Frederick withdrew to the original estate of his family in Franconia, and thereafter devoted his spare energy to high-level politics. The Hussite problem was an eminently suitable subject to deal with and he had acquired first-hand knowledge thereof at the Council of Constance, as well as during the siege of Karlštejn castle, and had many contacts with the Bohemian royalist and Hussite aristocracy as well as with the papal court. Moreover, his other son, Frederick, had become engaged in 1421 to Wladyslaw's daughter, Jadwiga, and had been promised the crown of Poland. Elector Frederick was not well disposed towards Korybut because he was a potential rival of his son. Even before Korybut's fall, Frederick Sr. set in motion preparations for a new crusade against

25

the Hussites and made the Franconian knights, of which he was the first,
take the initiative. On 15 January 1427, they issued a manifesto in which
they bitterly deplored the corruption of Christianity in Bohemia and the
general apathy to this evil. They declared themselves ready to give up, in
the current year, jousting and other entertainments, and to dedicate themselves to wage war against Bohemia under the banner of the Virgin Mary
and of St. George, their patron saint.[2] They invited all knights to rally
at Cheb on 15 June for a six week's war against the Hussites. The manifesto was issued at Bamberg and distributed all over Germany. Frederick
and his bishops sent an urgent request to the pope that he should declare
a crusade against the Hussites and send a nuncio or appoint a German
bishop in that capacity. The imperial diet was announced to take place
at Mainz on 9 February, but did not meet until the end of April in Frankfurt, with however, a large attendance. Its prepared resolutions bore the
stamp of Frederick's forceful authorship.[3]

The six electors who attended the diet (the seventh, King Sigismund,
was absent) issued orders on 27 April, that the attack should be launched
on 29 June 1427 by four armies: one from the Rhineland, Swabia, Franconia and Bavaria which was to rally at Nürnberg; one from central and
north Germany under Frederick, the elector of Saxony, to gather at
Freiberg; and another two from Silesia and Austria. Frederick issued the
first detailed military regulations stressing strict discipline. By that time
the fall of Korybut had become known and Elector Frederick tried to
enlist the services of two prominent Czech nobles, John Smiřický and
most likely, Heník of Kolštejn, expecting them to help him win the Bohemian crown and to instruct the crusaders how to break the formation
of wagons, used by the Hussites.[4] Before tackling this risk-laden task,
the two Czech noblemen stipulated that if the crusade failed they would
receive compensation in Germany for their lost possessions in Bohemia.
They advised the elector that the main Hussite attack was aimed at Sigismund and that, if adequate crusading forces were available and if Slaný
fell first, Prague would become demoralized and capitulate. They advised
him to proclaim that Bohemia had nothing to fear from him, who was
bringing reconciliation and peace, as long as the Czechs pursued decency
and fairness. The appropriate letters of intent were to be sent to Prague,
Žatec and Louny and to eight prominent politicians including Archbishop
Conrad, Diviš Bořek, Černín of Vysoká and to the Hussites, Přibík of

Klenová and Peter Zmrzlík, who had taken the royalist city of Stříbro in a joint attack. This treacherous plan failed because it was based more on wishful thinking than on knowledge of Hussite affairs.

The overthrow of Korybut eventually strengthened the middle-of-the-road elements, who tried to win over the defeated party instead of crushing it. This was no doubt due to the efforts of the Hussite clergy, especially Jakoubek, who issued guidelines for a new order.[5] These decreed observance of the Four Articles of Prague and obedience to the newly elected administrator of spiritual affairs, John Rokycana, the preacher at the Týn church. The guidelines also prohibited: the reintroduction of the liturgy which Prague had abolished at Jakoubek's insistence; propaganda favoring the return to Rome; obstruction of authorities attempting to punish public sins; attacks on confiscations of church property, and attacks on individuals accused of heresy. All these matters were to be submitted to the administrator and his council. Příbram's new interpretation of the Lord's Supper was rejected, and Jakoubek's confession of simple faith adopted instead. The Catholic doctrine of transubstantiation was foreign to Jakoubek's way of thinking. He felt closer to the Taborites in spite of the old differences of opinion. Sanctions were imposed on those who defied the new order and Příbram and others left Prague, hoping that it would be a temporary exile. After a time all of them submitted and returned except Příbram and Mladoňovice. The election of a new city council concluded the stabilization of conditions in Prague and in its allies.[6] The exodus of the right-wing masters also strengthened the relationship between Prague and the brotherhoods. The common danger made both more interdependent.

The Taborite field army was already in combat.[7] On 12 March 1427 it attacked Zwettl near Weitra in Austria but was repulsed by a strong Austrian force which even pierced the line of wagons. As soon as the Austrians started looting the Taborites struck back strongly and dispersed them but they could not resume the siege, and so turned back.

The fear of a possible coup by Korybut's adherents slowed down the drive of the brotherhoods for the time being although preparations continued. At the beginning of May, a joint Taborite and Orphan expedition led by Prokop Holý (the Great), Prokůpek (the Little) and Velek Koudelník was headed for Upper Lusatia and Silesia where it could expect support from the Slav population oppressed by the Germans.[8] On 10 May, the Hussite army stopped outside Žitava, a superbly equipped fortress brimming with forces from far and wide including a select contingent from the Teutonic Knights. The overconfident defenders rushed upon the be- siegers who lured them a good distance away from the town and then struck so hard that there were no survivors in the field. Some, in panic saved themselves by fleeing back to the city before the gates shut. But the Hussites could not take the fortress. After razing the suburbs they moved north to Görlitz, the largest of the Lusatian Six Towns, but did not attempt to take it because it was too well guarded. Instead they seized and set fire to the town of Luban whose defenders made the same mis- take as those of Žitava. Near Lwowek in Silesia the brotherhoods met and defeated a strong enemy force and also conquered Goldberg after which they speedily returned to Bohemia via Trutnov carrying rich spoils.

After sharing it the army separated. The Orphans turned off towards Červená Hora, belonging to their enemy, Hynek of Dubá, which had for some time been besieged by brotherhood armies from east Bohemia. The castle capitulated on 8 June and was demolished. The Taborites then went to Jaroměř, an Orphan fortress, and garrisoned it with their own men and the Orphan priest there was replaced with one of their own. This was probably the last stage of the demarcation adjustment of 1424 between them and the Orphans. The last conquest of the campaign was the capitulation, on 24 June 1427 of Žleby, a castle which used to belong to Hašek of Valdštejn.

Just at that time, consultations between the statesmen and commanders of both brotherhoods and the Prague alliance on how to defend against the crusaders were in full swing. Fighting had already broken out in some places. It was necessary not only to coordinate forces against the imminent attack but also to deal with treason in the Hussite camp.

On the day after the fall of Žleby, Elector Frederick sent off the letters to the Hussite towns and to prominent individuals such as John Smiřický had advised. According to the records he received only two answers.[9] Prague reacted courteously but stated that it must first consult its allies, the brotherhoods. Žatec avoided making a flat refusal but warned the elector against the corrupt clergy and indicated no willingness to negotiate with him. The Hussite nobles, although more favorably disposed, also took no concrete action. Only Smiřický and Kolštejn found an excuse for not taking part in the defenses of the country against the crusaders. The elector's overtures were too late and had practically no effect on events. Furthermore, he was not chosen as the supreme commander of the crusading forces and the resulting fiasco occurred partly because he strongly resented this.

Since the diet of Frankfurt failed to make arrangements for a unified command, Frederick may have hoped to be proposed as commander by the new nuncio. Hence he worked for the reappointment of Cardinal Branda who had put him in command of the crusade in 1422. But Martin V appoint Cardinal Henry Beaufort, the great uncle of the King of England, as the new legate because he implicitly trusted his ability.[10] Beaufort was a soldier and a diplomat rather than a prelate, with plenty of experience in both fields from the time of the Hundred Years War between England and France. Unfortunately for the royalist cause, he only arrived at Nürnberg on 13 June and stayed only until 28 June. The mysterious delay was explained by a letter[11] he sent to the Praguers five days after his arrival at Nürnberg. He knew about the answer which Frederick had received from Prague and perhaps he felt it was his duty to observe the proper form.

The cardinal used threats in his letter and began with appropriate quotations from the Scriptures adding his own exhortations to the Czechs that they should remember the times when the kingdom was a shining example of virtue and obedience. Would they, now dangerously isolated, renounce the pestiferous errors and return to the flock of Christ under one shepherd? Whether the letter reached Prague or had any effect is not known. The cardinal probably expected a prompt reply and eventually left Nürnberg, after a futile wait, for Bohemia, only to find the crusading army disintegrating.

Frederick Hohenzollern bore part of the responsibility for the disaster. Wishing to impress the Czech nobles as the supreme commander, he ignored the decision of the Frankfurt diet that the army should rally at Nürnberg. Instead he stuck to the manifesto of the Franconian knights and insisted on their meeting at Cheb. The Swabian forces which had gathered at Nürnberg were led by Otto, the archbishop of Trier. They, heading for Tachov, in Bohemia, a large royalist frontier stronghold on the road to Plzeň, had encamped near Planá. Frederick was forced to follow them to Weiden, where they agreed that Frederick would join the Saxons at Mašt'ov and proceed with them towards Slaný and Prague. At Mašt'ov he got a message from the duke of Saxony that he should meet him near Kadaň where Jakoubek of Vřesovice and his west-Bohemian Hussite forces kept the Saxon army dangerously isolated. The promised relief for the Saxons did not arrive; nor did Duke Albrecht, who had stayed behind, and who like his father-in-law, granted the imperial princes all the joy of dealing with the Hussite armies. Frederick tried to persuade the reluctant archbishop Otto to help the Saxons but since Frederick refused an invitation to meet for discussion at Tepla, Otto returned to his army at Planá.

He found its situation grave. The ever-growing German troops were idling away time and grumbling at the irresolution of the command. "It would have been better if we had not come at all. The princes and the council of war think the same . . .", wrote a commander of the Swabian troops on 20 July, adding that the council of war was disunited and everybody was glad to get home.[12]

Without waiting for Frederick, the massive army moved from Planá to Stříbro which the Plzeň *Landfríd* was anxious to get back from Příbík of Klenové who had conquered it for the Taborites. Meanwhile, Frederick was diverted by rumors from the Saxon camp that it was threatened by alleged concentrations of Hussites near Karlštejn. The Saxon commander declared that he would return home if he did not receive help. The war-weary Frederick knew that the plan to seize Prague would come to nothing and like most crusaders longed to be at home. When asked for help with the siege of Stříbro he persuaded the Duke of Saxony to come along with him but when he assessed the hopeless situation near Stříbro he pretended to be ill and withdrew to Tachov to be nearer to his home. This was welcome news to the Hussites. Prague was safe and the enemy had to withdraw from several fronts in order to strengthen the siege of Stříbro, an exhausting task in itself without a guarantee of success or even of an orderly retreat.

The siege began on 22 July with the support of the troops of Frederick and the Duke of Saxony as well as late arrivals from Germany. The town resisted artillery fire, and dissatisfaction and dissensions in the crusading army grew. A rumor that a Hussite army was on the way frustrated the plan for an all-out artillery attack and the council of war decided to raise the siege and move towards Plzeň to meet the enemy. The decision was not clearly understood by the rank and file, but by night guns began to move towards the frontier. When the order to raise the siege and burn the tents was issued, the whole army was seized by panic and wagoners jammed the road to Tachov believing that the Hussites were very close. Only the cavalry put up a semblance of military discipline but in the end it too turned back. Within a day the whole army had returned to Tachov and some had already crossed into Germany. Fortunately for the crusaders, the Hussites just about then reached Stříbro having been delayed by a detour around the hostile Plzeň.

At Tachov, the council of war made a fresh attempt to resume fighting with the small residue of the army. By that time Cardinal Beaufort arrived at last and took command. In the last meeting of the council of war he unrolled the banner which he had brought to Germany and offered to face the enemy without weapons and shield, ready to lead to victory or die trying. This proposal met with a mixed reception after which the cardinal handed his banner to the zealous Elector-Palatine John, challenging him to lead the fight. In the ensuring quarrel the banner was torn down, the cardinal was outvoted and he quickly departed from Bohemia.[13] On the same day, 4 August, the Hussites arrived from Stříbro and besieged Tachov.

The rendezvous of all the Hussite armies between Prague and Slaný probably had been arranged soon after the conquest of Žleby on 24 June 1427. The Hussite command seems to have expected an attack from Saxony and Lusatia, which had formed a military alliance. The Orphans, who were entrusted with a campaign against them carried out a successful attack. On 2 July they seized Česká Dubá whereby they not only moved the frontier of their territory deeper into enemy land but also forced the Six Towns to refrain from sending troops to Freiberg.[14]

When it became clear that the focus of the crusade would be the west, the main Hussite army began to gather near Karlštejn. Their passage through Prague started on 12 July.[15] First to arrive were the Orphans, after them the Tabor field army led by Prokop Holý and lastly the forces of the Moravian nobles, Wenceslas of Strážnice, Hlaváč of Mitrov and Ernest of Leskovec. They brought along Menhart of Hradec, the only Bohemian nobleman it was said who obeyed the summons of the Hussite command.[16] They all set out on 18 July together with a Prague force which was sent out to take independent action against the enemy, and after having won a victory at an unknown place, returned to Prague and set out again on 28 July to join the main army.[17]

Tachov, which had withstood Žižka's attacks in 1421,[18] was now defended not only by its own vassals but also by the residual crusading
forces, especially those left behind by the elector Frederick and the Plzeň
Landfríd. They were well supplied with heavy guns salvaged from Stříbro
including a "Chmelík," a very big cannon which had become popular
at the time of Wenceslas IV. The Hussites had perfected their siege tech-
nique at Žleby and elsewhere. They dug tunnels under the town, lit
fires and occupied it after a bloody hand-to-hand fight on 11 August.
The defenders, about 1500 of them, found refuge in the castle but food
shortages forced them to surrender three days later. The Moravian nobles
requested favorable terms for the captured barons who, however, abused
the magnanimous treatment and twenty-four of them escaped.[19] This of
course led to indignation on the part of the brotherhoods and to tighter
measures. The castle and town were given to the Orphans who had probably made the greatest sacrifice and Buzek of Smolotely became its
captain.

The victorious army next went to Roupov near Přeštice, made its
owner declare his loyalty to the Hussites and then encamped outside
Plzeň. The army did not have sufficient means for besieging the biggest
stronghold of the *Landfríd* and was glad of the services of the Podbrd-
ský association through which a truce between the two parties was established which lasted to the end of April 1428.[20] The terms included a
disputation between the Hussite and Catholic theologians, a standard
phrase which neither side took seriously but which they could not afford
to omit.[21] Prokop Holý was probably more eager for a truce than the
royalists, because he had other more urgent business on his mind. He was
in a hurry to crush the partisans of Elector Frederick who was already
taking advantage of the fact that the brotherhood forces were engaged in
west Bohemia and was preparing an attack on Prague. The conspirators
somehow got hold of Kolín, east of Prague, from which they wanted to
launch their attack on the main city.[22] Their leaders were John Smiřický
and Heník of Kolštejn, who were known as men who did nothing to help
defend the country. They managed to persuade Bořek of Miletínek, a
prominent Hussite, to join them, and were thus a dangerous trio.

Having no time to waste they struck before the Hussite leaders signed
the truce agreement with the *Landfríd*.[23] Early on 6 September, 600
mounted men entered the New Town of Prague through the gate which

John Rak, the reeve, had opened to them and got as far as Old Town square. Shouting the slogan "Holy Peace" they tried to sway the population into joining them but the councillors had been forewarned. One of them, Simon of the White Lion, had received a hint from William Kostka who had remained in the conspirator's confidence as one of the recipients of Elector Frederick's letters. The council had the city center cordoned off and opened fire on the intruders. Some were killed, many were arrested, a few saved themselves by flight and a considerable number were hidden by Korybut's adherents. Smiřický was captured but managed to escape. Heník of Kolštejn was flung from a window of the house where he was hiding and dragged dead to the stocks. It turned out that armed men of John Městecký and Púta of Častolovice were also involved. The population of Prague turned on all the captives whose lives were saved through the intervention of Rokycana and a few other priests. They put on their robes and covered the prisoners' heads to save them from lynching and took them to the town hall. Later some executions, expulsions and confiscations of property took place.

Five days later Prokop Holý returned to Prague with the brotherhood forces, and soon besieged Kolín bringing the Prague forces as well. Diviš Bořek of Miletínek, once an experienced Orebite and later a defector, resisted the siege for three months until he was forced, by heavy fire and the pressure of the population, to surrender Kolín. The garrison was allowed to go and the town was handed over to John Hertvík of Rušinov,[24] an Orphan captain and once a friend of Bořek's.

The Orphans who had conquered Česká Duba and other forts, still bore the brunt of the raids from Silesia. The Silesians had been too late to join the crusade but continued harrying their Bohemian neighbors. They invaded the region using as their base Hostinné, the town of John Krušina of Kumberk, a former Orebite commander who had defected to Sigismund but later apparently maintained a truce with the Hussites. Now, however, he sold Žacléř, an important frontier stronghold to the Silesians who tried in vain to conquer Dvůr Králové and then struck heavily at the nearby castle Náchod which withstood the onslaught with heavy losses to the garrison, civilian population and property.[25] This was the first known engagement of the Orphan captain, Čapek of Sány, who fell into a trap set by the enemy and only saved himself through desperate flight. The Silesians very nearly got inside the town and inflicted much suffering on the defenders and old people in the suburbs.

The long siege of Kolín had halted the Hussite military operations a-
broad. This gave their leaders time to plan new campaigns to replenish
urgently needed provisions. This was also the first time the idea was
broached that the Hussites ought to explain the cause for which they
were fighting to the peoples abroad. They proclaimed it to be a fight for
the liberation of the Law of God; they were fighting in God's name. The
first of several Hussite manifestos, signed by the captains and commanders
of both brotherhoods was issued in 1428.[26] It can be inferred from the
tone of the manifestos that one of the spiritual leaders Prokop Holý or
the priest Prokůpek, may have initiated these moves. Both were equally
concerned that this should not be a mere adornment of the Hussite conquests nor only a propaganda slogan.

The next Hussite campaign headed for Silesia because some support
could be expected from the large Slav population of the rural areas oppressed by the German towns. Silesia was still a dangerous neighbor, all the
more as the princes and towns had strengthened (after the fall of Tachov
to the Hussites) the Střelin association, by imposing specific military obligations on its members.[27] As the direct route was blocked by Žacléř and
Broumov, both of which were held by the Silesians, the Hussites made a
broad detour via Moravia and south Slovakia,[28] where they were sure of
reinforcements. John Tovačovský of Cimburk joined the Orphans in Moravia and helped them take Uherský Brod without fighting. Both brotherhoods went on to Skalice, crossed the Little Carpathians in Slovakia and
approached Bratislava. As King Sigismund was on the Turkish front,
Queen Barbara had concentrated a large force in the city which the Hussites could not hope to take by force.[29] After burning the suburbs and
looting the surrounding countryside, they turned towards Trnava and
Nové Město on the Váh river and crossed back into Moravia along the
Hrozenkov pass.

On their way northward through Moravia, their forces steadily increased. They were joined by Moravian Hussites, Dobeslav Puchala of Polish-
Slovak descent and by Frederick of Ostroh, who had probably arrived with
Korybut and later joined the Orphans. They all entered Silesia early in
March and gained two more allies, Wenceslas of Hradec, son of the Prince
of Opava, and Bolek Jr. of Opolé. After having put to rout a large force
assembled near Nysa, by Bishop Conrad of Breslau and Půta of Častolovice, they spread like a flood over the wide country and forced John of

Münsterberg and Bernard of Opolé to capitulate. They got as far as Břeh, the largest fortress of Upper Silesia whose ruler, Ludwig, surrendered the town on 25 March. This was followed by the capitulation of Ludwig Jr. of Olawa. A month of continuous fighting weakened the victorious sides as well, and both brotherhoods called for reinforcements from Bohemia. Thanks to the success of the campaign, the relief forces could come unimpeded along the Náchod and Mittelwalde passes, and take Lewin and Homole castles on the way to the town of Klodzko (Glatz). Avoiding the heavily fortified Klodzko, they took Frankenstein and reached the main Hussite army at Dzierźoniów (Reichenbach).

The following month was largely spent in transporting the rich spoils to Bohemia, through the hostile territory of the enemy. In April the Střelín association had to some extent recovered from the blow. Ludwig of Břeh, who had been accused of treason and was, moreover, the son-in-law of Frederick of Brandenberg, met the princes of the Silesian association at his Legnica residence and agreed to join in. Bishop Conrad also renewed his efforts and secured the cooperation of his brother Conrad of Olesnice, of Přemek of Opava, Bolek of Těšín, Kazimir of Oswiecim (Auschwitz) and the forces of Princess Helena of Ratibor, the widowed sister of Korybut. A Lusatian official, Hanuš of Polensko, and the captain of Klodzko, Půta of Častolovice, promised their help. This combined army of Upper and Lower Silesia was now ready for an attack. The Hussites, however, first drove away the Lusatians and they in turn spread panic in the army of Lower Silesia which withdrew to Legnica and to other bases. Afterwards, the field army demolished Chojnow, but failed to conquer Lubin and on 1 May appeared outside Breslau. Although they could not challenge the impregnable and heavily garrisoned stronghold, the Hussites caused enough damage in the outskirts to cut the communications between Conrad and his Upper Silesian allies. These princes even paid them a ransom in return for immunity from attack. Having thus safeguarded themselves, the Hussites set out on a journey home and arrived in Bohemia on 15 May.

The Silesian campaign did not fulfill all that they had hoped for. Nevertheless, the rich booty especially the cattle they brought, very much relieved the relentless economic blockade which the pope consistently decreed, and in addition Bohemia was for a time less vulnerable to attacks from Silesia. Soon the Orphans went on a minor expedition to the Upper

Palatinate using Tachov, which was now in their hands, as their base. They followed the route taken by King Wenceslas's forces twenty-two years earlier, at that time led by two prominent prelates. Some participants of the journey of 1406 certainly went along with the Orphans.[30] First they took Bärenau on the road to Nürnberg, then set fire to Mosbach, pulled down the dam of the landgrave's large fishpond at Nittenau, reduced to ashes the monastery at Walderbach and returned to Domažlice via Kaube and Waldmünchen which they also burnt. The Taborites, in their turn, carried out a lightning invasion of Austria, in order to inflict losses on the enemy and gather booty. Starting from Břeclau, they penetrated through the Morava Field (Marchfeld) as far as Vienna but could not get beyond the Danube.[31]

When the expedition returned home, the leaders of all three Hussite associations met on 25 June, the date set down for the opening of a new crusading war. In the crusaders' camp, Cardinal Beaufort had, immediately after the Tachov disaster, called a diet which was to derive conclusions from the mistakes of the past and draw up effective plans for another expedition in which he intended to take part.[32] The diet of Frankfurt did not meet until November 1427. Beaufort and Frederick Hohenzollern elected the supreme commander and put to a vote a well-thought out and detailed law on a war tax and how it was to be levied. A special office was set up at Nürnberg consisting of the supreme commander and nine assessors, six German princes and three town representatives. Frederick controlled this important office from Nürnberg but even its considerable funds were not likely to cover the cost of a new invasion of Bohemia. Cardinal Beaufort's recall to the French theater of war in March 1428[33] put an end to war preparations, but the measures introduced by the Frankfurt diet remained in force. Although these facts likely were known in Bohemia, the Hussites had to be prepared. Nevertheless, their assembly was relieved to hear that the crusade, to all appearances, would not come off. There were still many urgent matters to take care of. The idea of an elected head of state survived Korybut's regency[34] but could not be realized because of disagreement in the Hussite camp as to who would get which towns and territories. An immense effort was needed to settle the disputes. Kutná Hora was an outstanding example.[35] For four years it had been jointly administered by the brotherhoods but some citizens of Prague had in vain been claiming the restitution of their property in the town to which they were entitled in accordance with the peace of Špital Field. At last on 25 June 1428, a compromise was reached and justice done to the Prague landowners. There were undoubtedly other similar agreements between Prague and the brotherhoods. The next step towards inter-party peace was the decision that the field armies should attempt to conquer royalist property in Bohemia because it was inadvisable to send them abroad now. Accordingly, the Taborites laid siege to Bechyně which belonged to Hynek of Lažany and battered it with artillery from July until October, when the garrison surrendered on its word of honor. The Orphans, under John Královec, laid siege of Lichnice, the property of John Městecký of Opočno, but they did not have adequate ammunition for a sustained operation. Since the castle was solidly surrounded by Orphan territory they hoped to starve it out.[36]

Jakoubek, an indefatigable conciliator who was painfully aware of the deep rift between Prague and Tabor, made a fresh attempt to bring over his disciples to the formula which he expounded in his last known writing. His was a voice of one crying in the wilderness, since Prague tried to misuse even this tract against Tabor.[37] This failure led him to turn to the Prague city council to get it to settle the dangerous political and ecclesiastical issues in the capital.

Since its foundation, the New Town of Prague had felt itself the inferior partner of the Old Town except for the brief period of independence between 1424 and the return of Korybut. The conflict between the two towns revolved partly around the joint administration of the large property expropriated from the Church, departed citizens and from those declared unreliable. The New Town wished to assert its independence against the managing board in which the Old Town had the greater influence. Apart from that, the New Town was opposed to Rokycana, who had been elected, with Jakoubek's assistance, as head of the clergy of Prague and its association. The New Town favored the priest Jacob Vlk, John Želivský's successor, and refused to obey Rokycana. Ever since Rokycana's election there had been tensions and frequent clashes, outward signs of a deeper crisis which the royalist party did not fail to exploit.

Peace between the two towns was eventually concluded,[38] granting the New Town freedom to worship, the appointment of Jacob Vlk as its spiritual administrator and half of the joint property. The two sides were admonished to consult each other on important matters. As an interim

measure, a committee of an equal number of councillors from each town
was set up to deal with various exigencies. One of the committee, Milota
of Bohdaneč, scored a quick success by bringing to an end the war between Prague and John Smiřický, a skilled warrior with powerful royalist
backing on the northern borderland and in Lusatia, who granted asylum
at his Roudnice fortress to runaway adherents of Korybut. Now Smiřický
arranged for them to return to Prague and at the same time secured, in
the autumn of 1428, the release of Korybut from internment. Korybut
took up residence at Odry castle in Silesia, the property of Dobeslav
Puchala.

During Korybut's difficulties, Sigismund had believed it more important to fight the Turks than exploit the fall of his rival. The safest
crown he had ever worn depended on his defence of Hungary. He was
not sorry when the Elector Frederick and Cardinal Beaufort between
them had relieved him of the cares of the empire and the campaign against
the Hussites. However, the crusade which had been planned for the summer of 1428 came to nothing because the cardinal had to leave Germany.
Frederick, as the supreme commander designate and the manager of the
funds from the war tax, could combat the Hussites with a different weapon. He used the money, to be sure, against the Hussites, but also to further his own and Sigismund's political ends. He got in touch with his old
acquaintences, the nobles of the Bohemian royalist party who quickly
found allies among the lords from the disintegrated Korybut party, and
even in the Old Town and other towns of the Prague alliance. This success
for the royalists sprang partly from the general longing for peace and
partly from an aversion to an alliance with the brotherhoods. Sigismund's
negative attitude to the Hussite religious program was of course an obstacle, but the royalists spread the hope that negotiations might dispose
of the difficulty, and tried to convince the king that he would achieve
his aims without further bloodshed.[39] This was the main propaganda
weapon which was used, for the time being, only by those privy to the
royalists' plans.

Their plan was quite reasonable. Cardinal Beaufort, the legate who was
to preach the crusade in England, was a sincere advocate of the conciliar
principle. In 1424, he had obtained a request from the English government to the Holy See to speed up the convocation of a general council
of the Church which Martin V had promised to call for Basel. The cardinal,

while at Constance, had for four years employed the Italian humanist, Poggio, the author of the record of the trial and death of Jerome of Prague, and had gained considerable insight into the Bohemian situation. As he had hinted in his letter to Prague in 1427, his idea was to use the council of the Church as a forum where the Bohemian heretics should be invited because they were adverse to direct negotiations with the pope. But the cardinal had left Germany before he could complete his plan. The Elector Frederick took over and set his propaganda machine in motion. After the experiences of 1422 and 1427, another crusade was ruled out. The leaders of the Bohemian royalists were at one with Frederick and paid calls at Nürnberg to get money for the common cause. Even the zealous Plzeň *Landfríd* did not hesitate to extend the September truce with the brotherhoods. The elector thus gained access to those of the aristocracy who professed to be Hussites only under duress, and to the Prague recipients of his letters of July 1427. All these became Frederick's invaluable intermediaries, informants and eventually willing tools.

Sigismund's Turkish war dragged on until the end of 1428 without tangible results but his party had prepared the ground and was only waiting for the news that the king was ready to return to Buda. Menhart of Hradec, a leading Hussite lord who had an understanding with the royalists, asked Prokop Holý to call a diet which would decide on direct negotiations with the king who, as Menhart said, wished him to arrange a meeting with the Hussite spokesmen.[40] Considering the wide political implications, Prokop could not refuse, and called the diet which was to meet on New Year's day 1429 at Český Brod.

The expectations of Sigismund's party were truly fantastic. They spread the word that the Hussite towns were fed up with the dictatorship of the field armies, and if the "rabble" would not play they could be sent to Lusatia for the winter, and the agreement with the king could be made without them.[41] Český Brod was an Orphan town and the diet was one of the stormiest in the history of the revolution. The proposal that the king's demands should be accepted met with stiff opposition from the host party, the hatred of the treacherous king being part of Žižka's legacy. In the end the Orphans agreed that the royalist messengers should notify the king of their terms, which were made entirely unacceptable to him. Peter English, whom the Orphans could regard as their man was chosen as the chief spokesman. The diet asked that the king with all his subjects should

accept the Four Articles of Prague, but if he found the terms too hard the
Hussites would be willing to sign a truce with him and his son-in-law,
Albrecht of Austria, on condition that the inhabitants of the castles in
the joint ownership in Bohemia and Moravia would accept the Four
Articles and join the Hussites. These harsh terms were very probably
the work of the Orphan statesmen, and their acceptance by the diet
pacified the brotherhood. The king was requested to attend a meeting
on 6 March, at Moravský Krumlov which was on Hussite territory.[42] The
resolutions caused dissatisfaction in other quarters, and Prokop Holý and
Velek Koudelník had to intervene to prevent a direct conflict between
the New and Old Towns of Prague. They were able to conclude a truce
which was to last until the end of July.[43]

On the appointed day, the Hussite messengers arrived at Moravský
Krumlov and awaited the king's arrival. But he had been at Lutsk in Lithuania trying to sow discord between Witold and King Wladyslaw and to
prevent them from allying themselves with the Hussites. On 6 March he
passed through Jager in Hungary on the way back.[44] The idea of meeting
the Hussite messengers on their native soil held no attraction for him, all
the more so as he had certainly heard of and been provoked by the resolutions of the Český Brod diet. He intended to receive the Hussite delegates
at his court at Budin where they were however reluctant to go.[45] Hence
they passed the time at Moravský Krumlov preparing for their encounter
with the Catholic theologians who, as they knew, were assisting the king
in his attempt to split the Hussite camp. Before dispersing, the Hussite
delegates gave their leaders full powers to carry on with the negotiations.
In the end the two sides arrived at a compromise solution, to meet half-
way at Bratislava.

This historic meeting of King Sigismund and the representatives of the
revolution which had deposed him took place at the beginning of April
1429. It was the first step towards the long and interrupted negotiations
which were to culminate, seven years later, in peace between the revolution on the one side and the king and Church on the other.

CHAPTER FOUR

THE GLORIOUS CAMPAIGN

The momentous meeting began on 3 April 1429, when the Hussite delegation, two hundred strong, reached Bratislava to meet the assembled Catholic dignitaries.[1] Before the Hussites arrived it had been arranged for them to receive Přemek, the Duke of Opava, his son Nicholas and two German noblemen as hostages. The head of the ecclesiastical delegation was John Železný, the bishop of Olomouc and now cardinal, who had taken refuge at Bratislava because he did not feel safe in his see. The others were King Sigismund's chancellor John, the Archbishop of Zagreb, three bishops from Hungary, three from Silesia and Nicodemus, the bishop of Friesingen. The temporal delegates were Albrecht, the duke of Austria, William, the duke of Bavaria, brother of Sophia, King Wenceslas' widow,[2] four princes from Silesia and Nicholas Gara, the county palatine of Hungary. Ulrich of Rožmberk led the magnates of the royalist party of Bohemia. There were a number of doctors of divinity from the various universities who were responsible for anti-Hussite propaganda and for preparing the speedy convocation of the Council of Basel. Four of them came from Paris,[3] four from Vienna and possibly from Hungary, three from Bavaria and at least one from Burgundy. He was Giles Charlier who was to encounter the Hussites at Basel four years later and pay a visit to Prague.

41

King Sigismund addressed the Hussite messengers in a kindly and prudent speech, as recommended by his advisors, and assured them a fair
hearing. After a few words by Prokop Holý, the main speaker, Peter
English (Payne) addressed himself to the assembly on behalf of the diet
of Český Brod. It was an inspiring speech, interspersed with frequent
references to the Bible and ancient history. In the introduction the speaker
presented Jesus Christ as the invincible knight and champion of Prague
and the real giver of Hussite victories. For the theme of the main speech
he chose the Hussite motto "Truth prevails over all." He gave many examples of the invincibility of truth and reminded the king that, while
he was on the side of God, his superior forces fought victorious battles
against the heathens, but were beaten many a time by a handful of peasants, since he had fallen away from truth. "Verily I declare to you," he
said to the assembled celebrities, "that one single spark of truth for which
we fight you, is more powerful than all kings, princes, popes, legates and
masters." He ended with an emotional appeal to Sigismund to adopt the
just cause of the Hussites, for which they would loyally serve him.

After Payne's speech the meeting rose and negotiations were referred
to the confidants of both parties who were expected to reconcile the
widely divergent views. It can be gathered from the fragmentary record
that the Hussites wished to defend the Four Articles before a large assembly of the laity, while the Catholic theologians argued that an ecclesiastical
forum was the only appropriate arbiter. Thereupon Sigismund produced
a ready-made solution which in his opinion was infallible: the Hussites
were to promise to accept *a priori* the findings of the Council of Basel
which was to meet within two years.[4] The Hussites in turn insisted on
Payne's formula that the answer should be sought in the Gospels and
those ecclesiastical doctors who were firmly based on them. They also
requested the king to ensure the acceptance of their terms by the council of the Church. This was rejected.[5] Similarly, all efforts of the royalist diplomats to make the Hussites sign a truce for the whole period before the beginning of the Council of Basel were fruitless. This was a clumsy
attempt to disarm the field armies, based on the wish that the Hussite
forces might disband or be outlawed.

By 6 April the deadlock was complete. The Hussite confidants returned
to their camp and their commanders decided to send the king their final
answer.[6] Addressing him as "Your Grace," they pointed out that he had

failed to appear at Moravský Krumlov, for a meeting requested by him to meet their spokesmen. They restated the demands of the diet of Český Brod; that he was refusing to consider these demands and was only interested in a truce; that only the diet was competent to decide whether a truce or the Hussite participation in the Council was desirable. If the king meant a general truce and, if the Council were exclusively controlled by the Church, and the temporal rulers had no power to put in force what the Hussites would convincingly prove, scarcely anybody from Bohemia would attend. Would "His Grace" consider the matter carefully and answer under his own seal? The notice giving the date of the next diet would be delivered to Karlštejn.[7] The letter was sent off with the transcript of Payne's speech and the defence of the Four Articles as enclosures. The Hussite commanders wished these to be brought to the attention of the foreign doctors and answered in due course.

The letter was a fine example of the clear and straightforward thinking of the Hussite leadership and it is a pity that it was handed down only in the Latin translation. Its dignified and resolute tone and, moreover, the content of Payne's address which may not have been clearly understood when spoken with his English accent, caused an uproar in the king's council. Sigismund burst out and spoke of an instant war against the Czech heretics. On 8 April, Prokop, with a small retinue, called at Bratislava in order to sound the reaction to the letter from the Hussite commanders, pretending interest in the composition of the king's council. Sigismund called his council and promised to reply on the following day. Nothing is known of the results of the session.

The king did not answer in writing. But, the members of his party from Bohemia, Moravia and Silesia were much too anxious to allow negotiations to stop now. It had become evident that the only way for him to regain the crown of Bohemia, which the intransigent pope and his fanatical prelates, such as John Železný,[8] had several times blocked, required the help of the royalist lords and the presence of the Hussites in Basel. Sigismund therefore, could not give the Hussites a direct answer in writing, nor could he break off the negotiations. Instead, he left a verbal message that he would send his delegates to the diet.

Next day, the king's officials began to issue letters describing the failure of the Bratislava talks and the king's decision to lead a new crusade at the end of June.[9] Neither the Elector Frederick nor Martin V took the royal promises very seriously. Frederick knew the king too well and had plenty of inside information. Sigismund's initial zeal was beginning to wane and even when his letters seemed to arouse Germany from its apathy he started to back out, and to make very particular demands, or to stress that without thorough preparations the campaign had better be abandoned. In the end nothing happened and the negotiations seemed, for a time, to hold out better prospects then war.

The diet met at the Carolinum in Prague on 23 May to deal with the king's terms, brought by his noble representatives.[10] He reaffirmed his peaceful intentions and promised the Hussite delegates safe-conduct to Basel and back in the event that no agreement was reached at the Council. He did not wish to be reminded of the safe-conduct he had given John Hus. In return, he asked for a truce until the convocation of the Council, followed by a further six months in the event of the Council's failure. He also promised amnesty and apologized for not sending the doctors' response to the defence of the Hussite program. At the end of a stormy debate at the diet the dissenting Orphans were outvoted. The majority decided not to press the demand that Sigismund convert to their faith and even assented to the truce negotiations.[11] The dissidents could, of course, hope that the terms which the diet presented after consulting the priests from the university, from Tabor and the Orphan brotherhood, would wreck the prospects of the negotiations. These clergy demanded that the Council should be ecumenical and include the representatives of the Greeks[12] with the patriach of Constantinople as well as the Armenians because they all partook of the chalice. Furthermore, decisions should be made, not only by the pope, but by all Christendom according to the Law of God, not according to the Roman canonical law. The terms of the diet also precluded a truce with the royalists who had first enrolled as members of the Hussite party but had not joined it, and with those who had defected. The people of Meissen and the Bavarians were to be similarly excluded and Duke Albrecht was asked to appoint a lord or a prince of Czech or Slav blood as a governor of Moravia. Lastly, the diet elected delegates who were to travel to Bratislava with the returning royal messengers to meet with King Sigismund. They reached their destination as late as the beginning of July, after a month's delay, because the members for the New Town Prague, Žatec, Hradec Králové and Orphans refused to take part.[13]

This refusal weakened the position of the delegation which included Prokop Holý and even a few nobles from Bohemia and Moravia. In any case, their task was most difficult. Sigismund appeared to be in agreement with the diet, on the whole, and treated the delegates with a special courtesy that almost displeased his adherents, but he flatly refused to discuss the composition of the Council and concentrated on secular matters instead.[14] He asked for three concessions: that the Hussites should return all the revenues from their erstwhile Catholic subjects; give up besieging castles, and extend the truce to the defectors. By that time, the preamble of the truce agreement was almost completed which suggests that the two sides had moved considerably closer to each other.[15] This placed Prokop in an awkward position but fortunately the Hussite delegates had no powers to sign binding agreements because they failed to get Sigismund's complete acceptance of the diet's terms. Sigismund's demands had to be deferred to the next session of the diet.

This took place on 15 August. As could be expected, the recent talks with Sigismund were declared invalid and no new approach to him was made.[16] Despite these promising overtures, the two sides were not to meet for more than a year which allowed the revolutionarry forces in Bohemia to patch up their internal conflicts and prepare to deliver what was up to that time their most powerful thrust against the enemy.

There is no doubt that the determined rejection of Sigismund's terms was partly due to the death, on 9 August, of Jakoubek of Stříbro.[17] He had been the master mind behind the proposal of the Hussite clergy that the Council of Basel should be ecumenical. Sigismund's refusal to consider this was felt as a slight upon the revered teacher whose loss made his followers acutely aware of his greatness as a man, preacher, statesman and leader of the revolution. Laurence of Březová appropriately started his chronicle of the Hussite movement with Jakoubek's first defence of the chalice.[18] Jakoubek was remembered as an indomitable fighter who for decades had been stirring the spiritual life of the nation and upholding the legacy of John Milíč and John Hus regardless of opposition from any quarter. The story goes that he had called his friends and disciples to his death bed at the Bethlehem parish and urged them to uphold his formula for reconciliation between Tabor and Prague and to maintain their opposition to the perpetual payments in order to preserve the far-reaching social changes in the Prague associations.

Jakoubek's death deprived the moderates in Prague of their chief spokesman and the restraining force which could curb reactionary elements, mostly at the Old Town. Now these circles hastened to secure the return of the few prominent masters who had left Prague after Korybut's fall in protest against Jakoubek's simplified liturgy and uncompromising anticatholic tendencies. Although it is true that the masters, on their return had to pledge to refrain from attacks on Jakoubek's liturgical reforms and writings, as well as those of John Hus,[19] their presence in the Old Town hardened the feeling against the brotherhoods while the New Town was steadily drawing closer to the Orphans.

The uncertainty surrounding the protracted July negotiations at Bratislava kept both the New Town and the Old Town in suspense. It wrecked the reconciliation of September 1428 as well as the truce which had lapsed on 25 July 1429. All attempts to bring about a peaceful solution to their differences failed and the vehement quarrel, in the August session of the diet, between the Prague association and the brotherhoods brought both the Old and the New Towns to the brink of war.[20] This was however averted through the intervention of friendly arbiters, three Orphan captains, and on 25 September, peace was promulgated in the same place that Žižka had proclaimed a similar peace in 1424, near the pyramid of stones on the boundary between the two cities.

The record of the arbitration consists of only three sentences. The details were left to the two new trustees. One was appointed for each town and they had to divide the city's considerable property, much of it confiscated from the Church, between the New and Old Towns, or to decide on the joint tenure of some of its parts. Their decision was published on 15 October.[21]

As part of the peace agreement, a special panel was set up on 30 September to settle the old controversy regarding Wyclif's doctrine of the Lord's Supper. The rival speakers at the Carolinum were Peter Payne and John Příbram. The latter welcomed this chance to return from exile and brought into play his explosive temperament, so that the disputation drew crowds of spectators who cheered and heckled and had to be kept in order by the panel comprising eight theologians.[22] Of these, Václav of Dráchov (Jakoubek's successor), John Rokycana, Nicholas of Pelhřimov and Peter Němec of Žatec, were on Payne's side. The other four are not known. The findings of the panel were submitted to the well attended synod of the Prague clergy during which Rokycana was appointed archiepiscopal vicar and Václav of Dráchov the consistory official, succeeding John Kardinál.[23] This was done with the permission of Archbishop Conrad, who had made peace with those priests of Prague who had renounced their allegiance to him during the Korybut crisis, and now was confined to his Roudnice residence for reasons of health. Rokycana, the faithful disciple and follower of Hus and Jakoubek, thus became the permanent head of the clergy of Prague and its association for the next forty years, piloting the Hussite church through many storms and making it strong and unified. In the main synod session held on 19 October, Rokycana made a memorable speech on the Lord's Supper, steering a middle course between Payne and Příbram as, in his opinion, befitted his role as an arbiter, thereby encouraging Příbram to assert that both Rokycana and William of Dráchovec had adopted his point of view.[24] However, the verdict of the panel showed that unanimity was not reached and that Payne's group was far from agreeing with Příbram. It suggested a kind of truce which was to last until 4 June 1430. Until then the rivals were told to confine their polemics to written exchanges, submit them to the panel, avoid bandying about the word "heretic" and strive for the glorification of the Lord's Supper instead.

Příbram thought this was unfair and provoked a number of exchanges with the synod of Tabor. He published his own confession of faith and an account of the Carolinum disputation to which he appended a defamatory pamphlet, "The Lives of the Taborite Priests."[25] In answer to this, the synod of Tabor, on 6 January 1430 condemned his action and laid down rules requiring tolerance for its priests. It also stated its views on liturgy, namely: it recognized that the Tabor order of worship was justified by the example of the early church; it promised that its clergy would not restore nor extol the ceremonies rejected earlier, especially serving the mass in vestments. The synod was on the whole in agreement with Jakoubek's teachings, and firmly dissociated itself from Příbram's doctrine on transubstantiation.[26] Příbram parried with a new treatise aiming chiefly at Prokop Holý, and went on fighting from his voluntary exile probably spent in the varous estates of Lord Menhart of Hradec. As the powerful magnate's star was steadily rising, despite occasional declines, and the Hussite fortune appeared, to Příbram, to be at a low ebb, he was hoping to return to Prague before long with his patron's help. He miscalculated badly; his exile was to last for nine years.

His impression may have been justified by the way the siege of Lichnice was going.[27] The Orphans, led by John Královec and the priest Prokop, were encamped around the castle, the property of the royalist lord, John Městecký of Opočno. Wishing to seize the castle intact, the Orphans tried to starve it out but found, within three months, that their own supplies were running out. This induced part of the force to go foraging in Lusatia at the beginning of November.[28] After setting fire to Friedland, they were repulsed at Löbau and had to retreat to north Bohemia where on 16 November, large forces of the Lusatian Six Towns caught up with them, and defeated them. The Orphans lost many lives and a great deal of equipment, even wagons, but succeeded in fighting their way home and saving some of the spoils. Yet this first victory over the invincible enemy caused great rejoicing in Germany.

The next Orphan expedition into Silesia went better.[29] At first, it made incursions into the open country surrounding Klodzke castle and took only Bystryca on the Upper Nysa. After Christmas, the Orphans came under attack from a large Silesian army led by Prince John of Münsterberg, son-in-law of Půta of Častolovice, who came with relief forces from Breslau. The Orphans soon scattered the attack with gunfire and gave chase. Only a few Silesians saved themselves in the Klodzko fortress. Prince John himself perished in a bog. This victory opened the path for the Orphans through Silesia as far as the Oder where they captured Brzeg and Olawa with the help of the Taborites and the Moravian Hussites who had joined them in January. The next conquest was the town and castle of Niemcza which surrendered to them. After setting fire to Münsterberg and the rich monastery at Henrykón, the Hussites turned towards Swidnica which they failed to capture but where they accumulated a rich booty which they took home at the beginning of February 1430.

This success made amends for the defeat at Machnín but it did not help the siege of Lichnice from which John Královec had been called in June 1429 to make a futile attempt at capturing Trosky, the castle of a leading royalist, Otto of Bergov. Despite the severe damage by fire, Trosky remained in its owner's hands.[30]

The Taborites were not doing any better with the siege of Zvíkov castle in south Bohemia, waiting for the capitulation of its captain who was dissatisfied with his pay.[31] At King Sigismund's bidding, Ulrich of

Rožmberk stepped in after three months and concluded a truce whereby he saved the castle for the king. About the same time, detachments from Tabor and Prague under the command of Carda of Petrovice returned from a short raid of Lusatia where they had pillaged the open country near Görlitz and Žitava without tackling the towns themselves.[32] On finding that Lubań was evacuated, they ended up by taking Boleslavec in Silesia after which there was no need for further fighting because John, the Prince of Sagan, who had been deserted by his Silesian allies, signed a year's truce with the Hussites and paid them a large sum of money. The Czechs returned home with a rich booty, leaving their prisoners of war at Jaroměř, from where they were released a year later against ransom money deposited at Žitava. The Taborites who had withdrawn from Zvíkov were now free to further enterprises such as the siege of Lanšperk, another estate of John Městecký, which threatened the Hussite route to Silesia. The castle surrendered on its word of honor after ten weeks' siege and was handed to a Taborite captain, John Šárovec.[33] By then Jacob Kroměšín, the commander of the expedition, had left for Prague to take part in consultations with all Hussite leaders which resulted in the peace of 25 September.

This peace agreement, the work of two friends of the late Žižka, ended in an appeal to all Hussites to unite in the conduct of an expedition abroad. This was reminiscent of Žižka's exhortations five years earlier. The revolutionary forces had to be roused from their languor and petty inter-party squabbles, and to take advantage of the collapse, in Germany, of the plans for a summer crusade. It is possible that the Glorious campaign was already anticipated.

In spite of his reluctance to make war on the Hussites, King Sigismund had to pretend, under pressure from both the pope and from public opinion in Germany, that he seriously considered organizing the crusade with which he had threatened the Hussite messengers at Bratislava. His pretentious letters eventually reached Cardinal Beaufort who took his bragging at its face value and promptly offered his help. He reproached himself for having left Germany in 1428 when there was a chance to make up for the shameful flight from Stříbro and Tachov in which he had been involved. He suddenly informed Sigismund that he would arrive at Cologne on 13 July and take command of the crusade. The king was greatly alarmed and at the beginning of August, sent word to the cardinal with the latter's messenger, Hartank van Clux, whom he had kept at Bratislava as the alleged reporter of the July talks with the second Hussite delegation.[34] But by the time the messenger reached Germany, Cardinal Beaufort, who had stopped in Belgium, had been instructed by the royal council of England to divert his army which had been recruited in England, to France, where Joan of Arc, had brought about a turning point in the Hundred Years war and had had Charles VII of France crowned at Rheims. An outstanding commander and his picked men were thus lost for the Bohemian theater of war.[35]

The tidings of the near-miraculous victory of a country girl over a superior army echoed throughout Bohemia and encouraged those who desired to unify the Hussite movement in order to deal a decisive blow to the enemy. The salutary victory of the revolutionary elements, on 25 September, produced some more clear and definite plans as to the direction of the impending Hussite attack. In view of the exceptionally large scale of the operation it was decided to carry out a preliminary test that would ensure final success. Owing to the suddenness of the decision, only the field armies of both brotherhoods took part in the rehearsal.[36]

The first to set out was the chief captain Jacob Kroměšín whose Taborite army was freed for action after the surrender of Lanšperk. On 28 September 1429, they tried in vain to conquer the Ojvín monastery near Žitava. They were soon joined by Prokop Holý with another Taborite force and by the Orphans under Velek Koudelník and Prokůpek. They made their way to Görlitz and set fire to the suburbs but could not scale the ramparts. A similar attempt on Stolpen, the castle of the bishop of Meissen failed. One flank turned west and occupied Kamenz in Saxony, and got quite close to Dresden, while the main army laid siege, on 14 October, to Bautzen, the third largest town of the Lusatian Six. The garrison resisted valiantly but in the end Bautzen, Kamenz and another two towns agreed to a truce.[37] These events had a tragic sequel in February 1430 when a Bautzen town clerk, Peter of Prišvice, was accused of collaboration with the Hussites, interrogated under torture and brutally executed.[38] The Hussites got as far as Lower Lusatia where they took Gubin, on 27 October, and Boleslawiec in Silesia. On the way back they invited Görlitz to surrender but their negotiator was put into a sack and drowned. The probable aim of this expedition was to neutralize Lusatia in order to prevent it from helping Silesia and central Germany. The campaign was only a partial success but a useful weapon. On 11 November the Hussites returned home with rich spoils.

After a short rest, the Orphans increased the pressure on Lichnice and on 25 November forced it to surrender to their captain, John Hertvík Rušinovský who became its new lord.[39] But the main concern of the brotherhoods and the Prague association was to gather forces for their greatest campaign that ever went into action. On 6 December their leaders met in Prague and spent a week in consultation.[40] About 14 December, all the Hussite armies were marshalled against Saxony, with "retaliation for 1426" as their slogan.

Their force was made up of the field and town armies of the Taborites and Orphans, the troops of the Bohemian and Moravian nobles and the army of Prague and its allies. On 20 and 21 December they crossed the Ore mountains, mainly along the Nakléřov pass, and a few other westerly routes.[41] The Saxon army did not offer serious resistance in spite of its size and the presence of auxiliary forces from local bishops such as John Hofmann of Meissen, former rector of Charles University, and Nicholas Lubich of Merseburg, an alumnus of Charles University. Lubich later became the chancellor of the margrave of Meissen and obtained for him the charter for the University of Leipzig.[42] The Saxons hoped that the Hussites would wear themselves out in sieges of Pirna or Dresden, and prepared themselves for a joint attack from Leipzig and Belgern on the Elbe. But the Czech armies spread out far and wide like a flood and struck terror into the countryside on the left bank of the Elbe as far as Magdeburg, after which they unexpectedly turned southwest, a tactic which may have been part of the original plan.

A serious accident occurred when the Hussite wagons were trying to ford the Mulde (near Grimme) in triple line. Some wagons were torn apart, drowning their drivers, when Hanuš of Polensko, the bailiff of Lower Lusatia, appeared on the opposite bank with the spearhead of the cavalry. However, John Zmrzlík scattered them, and the rest of the wagons crossed safely in single file. After that, Frederick, the elector of Saxony, disbanded his large army because he had fallen out with his allies over the financial responsibility for the war.[43] This enabled the Hussites to proceed unimpeded in five parallel streams a few kilometers apart, capable of closing up in the event of attack. The Prussian victories of 1866 and 1870 were won with similar strategy. Fear of the Hussites thus completely paralyzed the population of the region, which sought refuge in very large fortresses such as Altenburg, Kronach and Wunsiedel, leaving their property as booty for their enemies. At the end of January the Hussites took Plavno, killing some of the locals in revenge for the massacre of their negotiators for which local monks were probably responsible.[44] The Hussites also suspected Henry of Plavno, who earlier, through deception had escaped from their custody and had been their sworn enemy ever since.

The Hussite army soon reached Franconia, the territory of Frederick of Hohenzollern, and stormed Hof, Bayreuth and Kulmback in quick succession on 30 and 31 January 1430.[45] At the time of the Hussite penetration into Saxony, Frederick was attending the Imperial diet at Bratislava and returned to Nürnberg as late as 13 January to take command of his army from his deputy, Ludwig of Oettingen. Frederick promptly freed all the assets of the Nürnberg war fund but was still not prepared for an attack because his royalist informants in Bohemia had told him that the Hussites would return home from Plavno via Cheb. This may have been their original plan but they were either tempted to venture further, or keen to come face to face with Frederick who, after all, had been supreme commander of the armies against them. The Hussite command, therefore, immediately asked Caspar of Waldenfels, with whom they were bargaining over the terms of the preservation of Hof castle, to arrange a meeting with the elector to negotiate an end to war. Waldenfals complied, but the final arrangements were delayed by the fall of Bayreuth and the Hussite advance into the diocese of Bamberg. Bishop Frederick of Aufsess, a major enemy of the Hussites, had already fled from his open town, with the clergy and most of the burghers, leaving the property at the mercy of the poor who plundered the deserted houses. To avert the ruin of the town, the representatives of Bamberg and two other towns offered to pay the Hussites ransom which Prokop, and his military command, fixed at 50,000 florins.[46] The Hussites were ready to waive the sum if the towns accepted the Hussite faith. As the two minor towns had since been taken by the Hussites, the fee for Bamberg was reduced to 12,000 florins.[47] The elector Frederick arrived from Nürnberg for the final settlement, escorted by ten representatives of the five Hussite armies and with letters of safe conduct from the Orphan captain, Jíra of Řečice, and three noblemen, Smil of Šternberk, William Kostka and Beneš

Mokrovousky. The agreement with the elector was signed after some delay because some of his allies were not ready until the rapid advance of the Hussites forced them to do so. On 7 February the Hussite armies moved across Pottestein and Beheimstein, the old feudal territories which Charles IV had added to the Czech crown lands, and then through Pegnitz to the Upper Palatinate where they occupied the deserted Auerbach, near the evacuated Sulzbach, the residence of the Count Palatine John. Another detachment took Gratenberg on the Nürnberg territory. Now at last the proud republic was ready to sign a treaty to save its land from desolation. This was done about 10 February 1430 at the Beheimstein castle with John and his father Ludwig, the elector palatine, as the contracting parties.[48]

The treaty guaranteed the victorious party a moderate sum which amounted to 12,000 florins from the city of Nürnberg of which it paid a half on the spot, realizing that it was the cheaper solution. Elector Frederick pledged to pay 9000 florins, the count palatine, 8000. Apart from that, the two princes made a commitment which the Hussites valued above money: a written guarantee of safety for a Hussite delegation to come from their fortresses to Nürnberg and return. On 23 April, they were to have the opportunity to explain publicly in Nürnberg, "truly, without obstacles or humiliation" the cause for which they fought, the Four Articles of Prague, and to show that they were truly and inexorably founded on the Bible. The Hussites stipulated that the guarantee must not be declared invalid if opposed by Sigismund or any spiritual or temporal princes, who were at war with them. They also reserved the right to worship at Nürnberg according to their own faith, with the interdict lifted.

After the signing of the Beheimstein treaty, Prokop Holý called on Frederick at Nürnberg to discuss how to carry out this unprecedented proposition.[49] Prokop agreed that the elector could not act without the pope's or Sigismund's authorization nor could he provide, within two months, the theologians for the disputation. They worked out a plan according to which the elector was to appeal to the pope and to the king for permission, and to request the six archbishops of the German empire to delegate the theologians. Frederick was as good as his word and even accompanied the Hussites part way on their homeward journey[50] and helped them to transport their enormous booty. When the armies reached west Bohemia they laid waste to Kynžvart, the estate of Henry of Plavno and to the surroundings of Cheb. The town paid a ransom in order to be included in the Nürnberg truce until 25 July. On 21 February the Hussites returned to Prague and were joyfully received in the customary manner.

A Bohemian diet, called to choose the delegates to the Nürnberg disputation, met at the Carolinum on 8 March.[51] Apart from representatives of the Hussite towns, twenty-nine leading priests, commanders, Hussite lords and knights from Bohemia and Moravia were elected.[52] The diet also received, and rejected, the message from King Sigismund, presented by the burgrave of Karlštejn, Zdislav Tluksa of Buřenice, in which the king pressed again for the acceptance of his Bratislava proposals of 1429. The diet broke up early in April without receiving an answer from Nürnberg. Just prior to 13 April Elector Frederick wrote that he could not secure the transit through so many German territories within the short time allotted, and that the Church authorities regarded the Hussite terms of safe conduct as impossible. Frederick had sent his confidant, Dr. George Fischel, to Rome and beyond doubt approached the king. But before the negative answers arrived he put before the Nürnberg diet, at the end of April, the memorandum of certain unnamed theologians which had most certainly been influenced by Dr. Henry Toke, a former professor at the university of Rostock, who was now teaching at the cathedral school at Magdeburg. The memorandum advocated what the Hussites had long been asking for; a Church reform as the only means of eradicating heresy and abuses among the clergy. It suggested, instead of war against the Hussites, a peaceful discussion with them, preferably somewhere on the border of Bohemia, by carefully selected persons representing the German archbishoprics and universities, which would be in preparation for the intended meeting of imperial electors and archbishops, as well as for the future Council of the Church.

For the time being, the memorandum was the voice of one crying in the wilderness. Nevertheless, Frederick invited the Hussite messengers to meet him at Cheb and set out, on 16 May, with John, the bishop of Zagreb, who was the steward of the Archbishop of Mainz as well as King Sigismund's chancellor and with Peter Volkmar, a prominent Nürnberg diplomat. Their journey's end is wrapped in mystery. They never arrived at Cheb and on 25 May the Hussites turned back after a futile wait. It appeared that the ecclesiastical opposition was stronger than the elector's good will.[53] Another two years and another disastrous crusade were to bring together Prokop Holý and the elector Frederick in the famous talks of Cheb in May 1432.

The stillborn Nürnberg disputation deprived the Hussites of the principal gain of what an old chronicler had called the Glorious Campaign.[54] It was a personal defeat for Prokop Holý and to some extent a blow for his prestige. But in spite of the growing number of his adversaries he was still recognized as the undisputed head of the revolution, its ablest statesman and chief spokesman. For the time being, he could ride out the storm.

Without waiting for the utter collapse of the negotiations with Frederick, the Hussites had shaped their new weapon. They resorted to making their program public in the customary contemporary form, the manifesto. On 25 May, while still at Cheb, they issued a detailed interpretation of the Four Articles which was probably written in German and handed down in print and thus became available, in 1524, to the young German Reformation. The second manifesto was addressed to all Christendom and stated that the Lord had revealed to the Czechs the irrefutable truths (the Four Articles) and that they had been forced to meet violence with violence; there was an account of the "Glorious Campaign" and of the broken promises, and a declaration of the Hussites' readiness to submit their cause to all peoples and to abide by any instruction that would lead to peace and truth.[55]

Perhaps simultaneously, the Taborites issued an extensive German manifesto signed by Prokop Holý and four other priests.[56] It expounded the Four Articles and some innovations of their own, such as the condemnation of splendour in churches and the wealth of the clergy, using popular, even extreme language and some of Wyclif's imagery. The manifesto dealt with various accusations against them and with the need for a public hearing. "If the pope and your priests are right why are they afraid of us? They resist us out of fear. We urge you to meet us as friends and bring your bishops and doctors and we will bring ours, and let them fight it out with the Word of God, not with craftiness and violence. If we are proved wrong we will do penance according to the Gospels. But if your doctors are defeated come to us. If they resist we will help you to make them mend their ways or to expel them from Christendom. Do not be afraid you will be left without sacraments, God will provide better priests. If they prevail upon you that you should not listen to us, leave them alone with their false indulgences and stay at home with your families. Let the pope and his cardinals, his bishops and priests come to fight us and thus to deserve in person all the indulgences and mercies they give to you. We will fight with the help of the almighty God and give them a chock-full of indulgences."

This down-to-earth language did not fail to impress the masses in Germany, or even in France, England and Spain. The manifestos were also effective in the countries which were not covered by the Beheimstein treaty, and still open to Hussite attack. Silesia was one of them. The Taborites took advantage of the consultations between Sigismund and the Silesian princes at Bratislava and invaded Upper Silesia in the second half of March.[57] In Moravia they were joined by Dobeslav Puchala, and here they laid waste to the surroundings of Kozlé. After crossing the Oder they were met by Korybut and then launched a joint attack on Oleśnica, the land of Conrad the White, brother of the bishop of Breslau. This conquest was relatively easy because Silesia was divided into many small principalities, some of them jointly owned by various branches of the ruling families. On 17 April Gliwica fell and was handed to Korybut. With Bolek Jr. of Opole, an ally of two years' standing, the Taborites reoccupied Brzeg which they turned into a Taborite supporting base. Niemcza, the prominent and well-supplied fortress, was entrusted to the priest Frederick of Strážnice who could not stand his ground in South Moravia. In mid-May the Taborites returned to Prague with extensive booty.

The Orphans were less fortunate. They had planned an expedition to Slovakia because King Sigismund had announced that he would attend the diet of Nürnberg, feeling that he had been neglecting the stricken empire for too long. When warned of the Orphan plans, and fearing that he might lose the Hungarian crown as well as his political position in Europe, he yielded to the pressure from the Hungarian magnates and put off his journey in order to gather a large army. Sigismund's friends held up the Hussite expeditionary army consisting of the Orphans, a force from the New Town and a detachment from Tabor, led by Velek Koudelník, the priest of Prokůpek, John Zmrzlík of Orlík and Philip of Padařov, the Taborite captain of Ostromeč. After a late start in the middle of April, they were soon intercepted at Podivín near the Austro-Moravian border but reached, in spite of very heavy casualties, Trnava, the key post on the so-called Czech highway from Hodonín to Parkáň, one of the most important Hungarian trade routes.[58] At Trnava, their progress was checked by a heavy onslaught[59] led by Stibor Jr. of Stíbořic, who owned large estates in the Váh valley and the adjacent Moravian districts, and by Frederick of Ostrog (in Volynia) who had arrived with Korybut, joined the Orphans and then crossed over to King Sigismund's side and tried to seize Uherský Brod in 1429. The enemy troops managed to penetrate the lines of the Hussite wagons and became trapped inside but Stibor and Frederick escaped after a fierce battle, leaving their men to their fate. The Hussites lost many men including the valiant Velek Koudelník. Their army had to retreat and fight its way through marshes for nine days before reaching safety beyond the Moravian border.[60]

After a month's rest, there was a need for immediate action. The Silesians who resented having the Hussites dangerously close to Breslau and Swidnica, began about 20 May, to bombard Niemcza with heavy artillery almost as soon as they had pulled out of Silesia. Frederick of Strážnice effectively returned the fire until, after three weeks, the Silesians hastily retreated when a two-pronged Hussite army from east Bohemia approached to join somewhere between Strzegom, Jawor and Bolkenhain. Seeing that Niemcza was safe, the Hussites moved on until they met resistance near Vedrov on 14 June. After four local gentry had accidentally set their own forts on fire and then been overwhelmed, there was a general demand for peace. Herman Cettric, and old Silesian knight, appealed to a few Hussite nobles whom he knew personally and accepted their truce terms on behalf of the nobles and towns of the Swidnica principality, whereby this Hussite expedition ended.[61]

At the beginning of June, Prokop Holý and the Taborites set out to relieve their allies in Moravia. After some fighting near Brno, they besieged Moravský Šternberk. Perchta, the chatelaine of Šternberk, was the widow of the staunch enemy of the Hussites, Peter, who had been killed in the battle of Vyšehrad. For ten years since his death, Perchta had allowed her subjects in Bohemia to profess the Hussite faith. In the middle of August, the siege of the castle ended when she capitulated. The Orphans were also on the move. Having elected Čert, a man from the New Town, as a successor to the late Velek Koudelník, they took preventive measures against the Plzeň Landfríd, and against a possible invasion from Bavaria, by occupying Hořovice and demolishing the outer fortifications of the royalist castle, Libštejn.[62]

The ravages of the Glorious Campaign in Saxony, Thuringia nad Franconia aroused horror all over Germany and caused a wave of indignation which also spread to France. Joan of Arc sent a letter to Bohemia in which she heaped reproaches and threats on the Hussites challenging them to send their messengers to France to be told how to mend their ways, or else she would set out for Bohemia herself and pay them out with supreme power, human and divine. The letter was sent off on 23 March, was widely circulated by the enemies of the revolution even after her death on 30 May 1431.[63] Nürnberg had to defend itself against widespread indignation by pleading desperate necessity and claiming that it had gained a truce without committing itself, or weakening its stand against the heretics. In spite of a general clamour for war, fear of the Hussites was stronger than enthusiasm. Moreover, the king was absent from Germany and had twice failed to attend the diet which he had convoked. At last he appeared in the new session at Straubing to find only a few princes waiting for him. Now he had to reap what he had sown and try to keep on the right side, both of public opinion in Germany and of the pope, who was becoming increasingly important for his aspirations to the crown of the Holy Roman Empire. The only party who had to take his threats seriously was the Hussite headquarters, especially Prokop Holý. The Hussites ordered a general mobilization and a rally to take place near Plzeň, pillaging the estates of the wealthy city and of the whole *Landfrid* to provision their army.

Later in August, the allied armies began to gather.[64] The Taborites returned from Šternberk and the Orphans from Libštejn leaving behind an adequate force to which the castle later surrendered. Some lords from Moravia and Bohemia joined in, including even John of Opočno, who was hoping to regain Lichnice by this gesture. On 30 August Sigismund indeed made an urgent appeal to German towns to send their forces to a rally at Kaube for a two-month war on behalf of Plzeň. He simultaneously announced an allout attack on Bohemia from Saxony, Silesia, Hungary and Austria.[65] However, he soon reverted to the old game; postponed the date, transferred the rally to Cheb, and on 27 September, cancelled the rendezvous replacing it by a "daily war." A new diet was called to meet at Nürnberg at the end of November to plan a crusade for the next year and to take defensive measures against a Hussite invasion but on 31 October the king left Nürnberg for a tour of south Germany. A Hussite reconnaissance party checked at Kaube and found that no invasion was on the way. Prokop Holý therefore decided to lead a campaign to Silesia.[66] The war scare had cost the Hussites a lot of money and not a few lives outside Plzeň; but it was a rewarding preparation for the next, and last crusade.

The main objective of the Taborite campaign[67] was to save Niemcza, threatened by the Silesians, who in September had destroyed a fairly large Hussite convoy of supplies and then seized Münsterberg which was later demolished. Early in October, they launched a series of attacks on Strzelin and Niemcza. As soon as the Taborites entered Silesia in mid-November, they resupplied Niemcza and seized Otmuchów with a daring operation although it was thought impregnable, and for that reason housed the treasures of many Silesian ecclesiastical institutions. Nicholas Zedlitz, the commander of Otmuchów, who yielded to the Hussites in order to save the castle from destruction was later executed at Breslau for his action. The nearby Vrbno Castle also fell to the Hussites, after which the Silesians rallied for counter-attacks. When the Taborites summoned the well fortified Namslaw to negotiate a settlement, they received no answer and so spent eight days in a futile siege.[68] Then they moved towards Bolkenhain pillaging the countryside. On 26 December they eventually entered Lusatia where they made arrangements for the Orphans to join them. The Orphans came by a direct route from Bohemia and attacked Bernstadt whose defenders took shelter in the church but capitulated on 25 December. They were spared their lives on condition that they would never again fight against the holy truth of the gospels, or the Hussites, and that they would pay them taxes. A similar thing happened at Reichenbach, between Bautzen and Görlitz, where the population desperately resisted for two weeks. When the Taborites were making incursions into the Bautzen area, the town received reinforcements from Saxony led by Elector Frederick himself in the company of John Hoffmann, the Bishop of Meissen. As on the previous occasion in Saxony, neither risked an attack on Prokop Holý. Prokop was hardly displeased at the enemy's retreat which enabled him to take his troops home without hindrance. His mind was fully occupied with the next diet which he had called after Christmas, while still in the field. By about 13 January both armies were back on their native soil.

CHAPTER FIVE

THE BATTLE OF DOMAŽLICE AND THE INVITATION OF THE HUSSITES TO BASEL

In 1431, although the Church and the German Empire marshalled their forces for the greatest blow they had ever aimed at the Hussite revolution, the defeat they suffered was so terrible that they decided to seek peace through negotiations. This time, however, a notable change occurred. The pope was kept out and the Council of Basel, as the supreme power in the Church and the great European forum where the ideas of the Hussite revolution could be brought into focus, took upon itself the responsibility for the negotiations. This unprecedented advantage to the Hussites had also its disadvantage. Bohemia opened itself to the Council's diplomats who did their utmost to bring about by peaceful means what arms had failed to accomplish. With the support of powerful internal reactionary elements, they broke down the unity of the Hussite camp, crushed its radical wing and deprived the revolution of many of its dearly bought achievements. The peace negotiations thus became even more destructive than the wars and confronted the Hussite statesmen with situations more difficult than those which they had so far faced.

One problem was the December 1430 Polish-Lithuanian offer to host a disputation. It brough the Taborite expedition to Silesia to a premature end. The invitation from the only neutral neighbor was a momentous event which induced Prokop Holý and his captains to convene the

Bohemian diet at Kutná Hora for three weeks beginning at the close of December 1430.[1] The diet went on until February and only two facts are known: that it decided to send delegates to Cracow and that it elected a committee of twelve men to maintain good relationships within the Hussite movement and among the priests of the various parties.[2] Similar efforts had been made in the past but had failed. The last dangerous split following the fall of Korybut in 1427 had been patched up, but not healed, by the triumphant Glorious Campaign in 1429-1430. The diet of Kutná Hora, 1431, could look back to the attempt of January 1426 but its participants found the contemporary crisis much more deep-seated and dangerous. The committee[3] certainly fulfilled, at least indirectly, the demand that Litomyšl, in accordance with the peace of Vršovice, should be returned to the Prague association, by handing the town to William Kostka of Postupice,[4] one of its members. His family thus became one of the most important in the kingdom.

The work of the committee was made easier by the reduced tension between the brotherhoods resulting from the Polish invitation.[5] It was the outcome of lengthy negotiations between Polish diplomats and the papal court. To show his displeasure with Sigismund's lack of cooperation and his designs upon the crown of Rome as well as his undue interest in the Council of Basel, Martin V had established contacts with Cracow. Encouraged by Korybut's overtures of 1426, the pope was hopeful that King Wladyslaw's talks with the Hussites would go smoothly. In October 1428, the pope had sent his nuncio, Andrew of Constantinople to Cracow with full powers to negotiate with the Hussites. On his arrival, however, the nuncio had to intervene in the dispute between Wladyslaw and Grand Duke Witold who coveted the royal title which Sigismund had promised him. When Witold's death on 28 October 1430 put an end to this difficulty, the court of Cracow was at last free to comply with the pope's wishes and invite the Taborite leaders. The Polish gesture was not entirely selfless because Svidrygiello, the new ruler of Lithuania, also wanted the royal crown just as Witold had. The Poles began to regard the Hussite forces as potential allies in the war which threatened to break out. The group of Polish nobles who maintained friendly relations with the Hussites and had started Korybut on his mission to Bohemia had to work hard to make King Wladyslaw change his orientation. Its leaders John Siafraniec, the Chancellor, his brother Peter, the royal vice-chamberlain, with his son, and Wladyslaw Oporowski, the vice-chancellor, eventually overcame the opposition of the powerful Bishop of Cracow, Zbygniew Oleśnicki and his prelates who controlled foreign policy. The Siafraniec brothers even hoped, now that Witold was dead, that Korybut might be pardoned and allowed to return to Bohemia. And indeed, sympathies for Korybut were re-emerging among all those who could not put up with the return of King Sigismund, especially in Moravia, and there were signs that the pro-Polish party was rising from its oblivion.[6] The friction between the two brother-hoods subsided and the diet of Kutná Hora accepted the Polish invitations even though clear-sighted men such as Prokop Holý may have had mis-givings after their experience at Bratislava in 1429.

The delegation to Poland included William Kostka, Prokop Holý and Frederick of Strážnice.[7] On their way to Cracow they called at Gliwica now held by Korybut, who joined them, and they all received Polish safe-conducts. King Wladyslaw himself opened the talks on 19 March and the theologians of the Cracow university began by refuting the Four Articles of Prague, which they most probably knew in Peter Payne's Bratislava version. Because of the presence of court officials and promin-ent politicians, the ensuing discussion was largely conducted in Polish and Czech and did little to get the opposing sides together. In fact, the Cracow masters felt sure they had silenced their opponents. After a week the talks were interrupted and the Czech delegates were made to move to the Kazimierz suburb because Bishop Zbygniew threatened to stop the Holy Week services, an action which might have caused unrest in the country. The Czechs were offended and further talks were reduced to investigating the terms on which the Hussites would attend the Coun-cil of Basel. They presented their Bratislava formula which the king, on 4 April, countered with the demand that they should bind themselves in advance to accept the Council's findings. The delegates presented a polite excuse and a request that the king should send messengers to the next Bohemian diet, the only forum competent to deal with that matter. The king promised to do so and assured the departing messengers of safe-conducts to Basel. In Korybut's absence, Gliwica was betrayed and fell into the hands of Conrad of Oleśnica. The delegates and Korybut were completely unaware of this and narrowly escaped capture when warned by fugitives.

The result of the mission did not attract a great deal of attention at home because Prague and the rest of the country were engrossed in the forthcoming disputation where it was hoped a consensus would be reached between the Prague and Tabor priests, in response to the mandate of the diet.

On 30 April, the Carolinum was filled with priests from Prague and the provinces so that the gathering appeared to be a synod of the Hussite clergy,[8] The presiding Committee of Twelve created a calm and serious atmosphere. Příbram was absent and there was no occasion for sensationalism. John Rokycana, the head of the Prague clergy, who a short time before had received a masters degree, bestowed by Martin Kunšův,[9] an old disciple of Hus, summed up the differences between the Prague and Taborite tenets. He expressed his regret that the Taborites had deviated from the liturgy of Jakoubek whom he repeatedly mentioned as a consistent advocate of the middle course against the right-wingers who had seceded in the critical year 1427. Nicholas Biskupec presented an analysis of the Taborite stand on dogmatic matters which was rightly acknowledged as a confession of faith and was to appear in two more editions, 150-200 years later, in Protestant countries.

Nicholas, the ablest writer of the Taborite brotherhood, spoke with utmost restraint and made a sincere endeavour to reach an understanding, bearing in mind Tabor's uneasy situation. In addition Rokycana introduced an exposition of the sacraments, and in the most complex matter of the Lord's Supper identified himself with Jakoubek's tract of 1428.[10] The meeting ended in a polemic between the two main speakers on the question of the Eucharist.

Both sides stated their points-of-view but failed, as in 1420, to reach a consensus. A pronouncement in favor of either party would have wrecked the diet which was already sitting, and the presidium resorted to the customary suggestion of written exchanges of views in Latin, reserving the right to supervise them. The disputation which was conducted in a dignified manner made a powerful impact. It influenced the attitude of Peter Chelčický and was the first step towards the amalgamation of the Orphans with the church of Prague. The political situation also contributed to the latter development: on 20 March a new and the largest crusade against the Hussites was declared at Nürnberg.[11]

The imperial diet had opened on 20 February but a month passed without any progress because both Sigismund and Frederick Hohenzollern favored the "daily war," that is, defending the districts bordering on Bohemia. On 11 March the king declared himself in favor of a postponement and admitted that his jouney to Rome in quest of the crown was of paramount importance to him. Meanwhile, in had become known that Martin V, who had staunchly opposed Sigismund's candidature, had died on 20 February. This raised the king's hopes but at the same time a new man was already on the Nürnberg scene making arrangements for the crusade. He was the new nuncio, Cardinal Julian Cesarini, aged thirty-three, to whom Martin V, as one of his last acts, had given a mandate to lead a new campaign. Cesarini owed a debt of gratitude to the late pope for his promotion, and the challenging task spurred him on to maximum effort. Having been the secretary of Cardinal Branda, the organizer of two crusades, he knew many prominent personalities in central Europe and in the empire, in Poland, in Hungary as well as in France and England.[12]

At Nürnberg, Cesarini was faced with the crucial question of who is going to pay for the crusade. The imperial estates laid claim to the money from Cardinal Beaufort's collection which had disappeared in the pope's bottomless coffers. Cesarini made clever use of the death of Martin V and promised a full refund by the new pope whoever he might be. Within ten days he won over everybody including King Sigismund who quickly calculated that the powerful cardinal would prove valuable in his own quest for the imperial crown and so promised to take part in the crusade. The elector, Frederick, who felt he had stained his reputation by the treaty of Beheimstein, was similarly persuaded to crusade. On 18 March, summons were sent out to rally in preparation for a crusade and on the 20th the cardinal had the appropriate bulls solemnly proclaimed. Before the end of the month the diet carried out a thorough revision of the imperial register for determining war contributions on money, men and equipment, and issued new military statutes which were modelled on the Hussite ones.[13]

By the beginning of May, when the general assembly of the Hussites from Bohemia and Moravia was preparing measures for the defence of the country, a great deal of information on German plans had found its way into Bohemia. Multiple attacks from Saxony, Franconia, Bavaria and Austria were anticipated but there was no hint as to the place at which the enemy armies might join.[14] Both the king and Elector Frederick may have been hoping for last minute concessions to the Hussites which would be far-reaching enough to justify the disbandment of the crusading armies. Indeed, the Hussite assembly in Prague had to consider King Sigismund's request for a meeting at Cheb at the end of May because it was backed not only by the king of Poland but also by the new bishop of Olomouc, Kuneš of Zvole, who was anxious to show the Czech public that he was not toeing the hard line of his predecessor, John Železný. Nevertheless, the Orphans were against receiving Sigismund's messengers. Prokop Holý, however, provided them with safe conducts so that they could deliver their message to the assembly and show the Czechs a letter which the king of Poland had written to Sigismund.[15] Thereupon the assembly delegated captain Matthew Louda and the priest Markold for Tabor, William Kostka and a few burghers for Prague, and the old Orebite Beneš Mokrovousky[16] who were to meet Sigismund at Cheb. The powers of the delegation were restricted to the terms that had been previously presented at Cracow and laid down by the diet of Prague in 1429.

The failure of the negotiations was, therefore, a foregone conclusion although Sigismund was trying to take advantage of Cesarini's absence. Sensing this danger, the cardinal sent three theologians to Sigismund to make sure that he persevered in preparing for war. They were two doctors of the university of Paris and Dr. John Stojkovic, the cardinal's one confidant. Having seen the havoc caused by the Glorious Campaign, they rejected out of hand any concessions to the Bohemian heretics. Since the Hussites could not give an unconditional pledge to accept the Council's demands, in advance, they left for Prague[17] and were home in time for the traditional festival, "showing the insignia," which was now replaced by a procession to the church of Corpus Christi, since Sigismund had had the insignia removed from Bohemia. The delegates told the assembled crowds the result of their mission and that the Germans were preparing to invade the country.[18]

Simultaneously with these events, the field armies of the brotherhoods had been active since February in Lusatia where they could rely on the loyalty of the rural Slav population, and in Silesia which they used as a source of provisions with the tacit support of the court of Cracow.[19] In the first phase, in the second half of February, the combined Taborite and Orphan armies made unsuccessful inroads into Bautzen and Žitava but succeeded in capturing Löbau, and turning towards Görlitz, stormed Luban about the middle of March. In the same month they took Zlotoryja (Goldberg) and Lubin in Silesia after which they concentrated on amassing and transporting the booty all through April and May, having a free hand because nobody dared to stop them.[20]

While they were still in Silesia, Lusatia was preparing to take Löbau back. Görlitz, the richest and most populous town of the six, with a large army, wide-ranging international contacts and an efficient spy network, appealed unsuccessfully to King Sigismund for help. The Görlitz troops were sent to Löbau and launched a powerful attack on the Hussite garrison.[21] This induced Prokop Holý, without waiting for the outcome of the Cheb talks, which despite his own scepticism, he had helped realize, to leave the diet and intervene in Lusatia. He moved from Žitava towards Reichenbach and Löbau where the enemy in the meantime had raised the siege after receiving information that Prokop had crossed into Lusatia. Moving farther, towards Bautzen and Görlitz, Prokop burned the latter's suburbs at the end of May and returned to Bohemia via Silesia in record speed. On 7 June his army reached Česká Skalice.

On this campaign, Prokop had the chance to assess the situation in Lusatia, especially the efforts of John Hoffmann, the militant bishop of Meissen (he published the papal bull announcing the crusade on 24 April) and consider the plans for a possible clash in Silesia although it was not officially included in the overall crusading plan. From Česká Skalice Prokop and John Kroměšín summoned nine Moravian allies to set out for Plzeň where all the Hussite forces were beginning to rally to meet the crusading forces.[22]

The Taborites reached Plzeň on 28 June and were soon joined by the forces of Prague, the Orphan army and detachments from all Hussite towns and nobles. As there was no evidence of enemy action, The Hussite army advanced against the royalist frontier outposts, Horšův Týn and Planá, in order to be able to assist Tachov which had been keeping watch over the frontier since 1427.[23] At last, at the end of July, after the Hussites had withdrawn towards the interior of Bohemia, the crusading forces were on the move. In fact, the crusaders had idled away a whole month on the German side because of deep disagreement between their two leaders.

Cesarini had ceremoniously opened the fifth crusade on 29 June in the Church of St. Sebaldus at Nürnberg by investing Elector Frederick with the banner and the sword which King Sigismund had given to him.[24] Only the initiated sensed the depth of the enmity between the nuncio and the commander-in-chief which simmered beneath the glittering pomp.

The crusading army, as it marched out of Nürnberg, comprised the troops of Dietrich of Mörs, the archbishop of Cologne, of Frederick, the young elector of Saxony, of several Bavarian dukes and of a few bishops from the vicinity of Bohemia, such as John Hoffmann and the bishop of Würzburg.[25] Cardinal Cesarini had also been promised substantial contributions from Philip, the Duke of Burgundy, and Louis, the elector-palatine, whereby he hoped to curb Elector Frederick's tendency to bargain with the Hussites. Frederick, before taking command, had obtained from Sigismund unqualified powers to negotiate. To the cardinal's dismay, neither Philip nor Louis honored their promises, and King Sigismund, pleading injury, turned back as soon as the army reached the outskirts of Nürnberg. The huge army filled the area between the ridge of the Bohemian Forest and Neustadt in Franconia, but it was low spirited, homesick and torn by frictions between the urban contingents, which were larger but were expected to defer to those of the overbearing princes.

Frederick Hohenzollern kept withholding the order for the army to cross the frontier and initiated, probably with the help of Czech royalists, negotiations with the Hussites, although on the same terms as those which Sigismund had demanded at the Cheb meeting. He demanded unconditional acceptance of the Council's decision. In reply, the Hussites on 21 July, sent off a manifesto in which they steadfastly clung to the Four Articles of Prague, recapitulated all their failures in obtaining a fair hearing and appealed to the secular powers in Germany to consider justly the Hussite cause faced with the arrogant clergy who set themselves up as judges of Christ and his apostles.[26]

The chief commander could not persuade the nuncio to make concessions. At last on 26 July, Cesarini, from his camp at Weiden, sent the Hussites a reply which could only serve to rouse them to indignation. His most ardent wish, he said, was to bring the once famous kingdom back to the bosom of the Church. He had taken up arms with tears and sorrow at the sight of the horrors the Hussites had perpetrated. He however carefully dodged the crucial issue: the acceptance of the Four Articles. Instead the cardinal tried to undermine the Hussite leaders' authority, wondering how the rank and file could pin their faith on soldiers, burghers and peasants rather than on the Church and its scholars. Cesarini's manifesto raised his standing in the German army and made the position of the supreme military commander very difficult. Pressured by the negative answer from the Hussites and the two electors in league with the cardinal, Frederick found himself unable to postpone the invasion any longer. The news that the Hussites had receded from the frontier clinched the matter and on 1 August the army at last crossed the border.

The Hussites' withdrawal to an area east of Plzeň was an emergency move but sound strategy. Instead of being between two lines of fire, from the crusaders in front and the Plzeň *Landfríd* in the rear, the Hussites chose the interior of the country where they could restock and gather fresh forces, and employ their well-tested tactics by luring the enemy army from the shelter of the Bohemian forest.[27] The only Hussite base in the borderland was Tachov which had been held by the Orphans since 1427. The commander, Buzek of Smolotely,[28] found that the discord in the enemy ranks greatly assisted the defence of the fortress. While the impatient cardinal wanted an instant attack, the supreme commander decided that the exhausted men needed a day's rest. The next day the fortress put up such effective resistance that Count Palatine John, who claimed Tachov as his property since before 1427 and wished to get it back intact, managed to stop the shelling although Cesarini had offered the artillery high rewards for smashing the ramparts.[29] The siege was abandoned and instead, the crusaders started to slaughter indiscriminately and destroy far and wide. Their victims were mostly Catholics and subjects of the Plzeň *Landfríd*. Stříbro, however, was avoided because it had a Hussite commander and the memory of the last defeat was still fresh. Within a week the whole area was plundered and depopulated, and about 200 villages were razed. The crusaders decided against advancing further inland when they heard that the Hussites were assembling fresh troops near Karlštejn and because even the *Landfríd* was shocked by the atrocities.[30] By that time, Frederick had received the Hussites' final refusal to negotiate.[31] They offered to talk with King Sigismund but only if he came to their camp. Under the circumstances, this was a hopeless prospect and the supreme commander ordered a retreat to the frontier.

The war weary crusaders were glad of this decision. Only Cesarini protested but became assuaged when told that Domažlice, a Taborite bastion, was the next target. About 11 or 12 August the crusaders encamped near the town and laid siege to it. After part of a suburb was burned and the bombardment started the Taborite command offered to surrender on condition that lives and property were spared. Firing ceased and five knights were sent to the town to negotiate the terms, but part of the crusading army deliberately opened fire in order to prevent the truce talks and avoid losing the booty. In the ensuing confusion one man got away and reached the Hussite camp, informing it of the quarrels among the crusaders and of the situation at Domažlice. By 14 August the Hussite reinforcements had arrived.

By that time the tension between the commander-in-chief and the nuncio had reached a breaking point and Frederick decided to act on his own without taking either the nuncio or the elector of Saxony into his confidence. Knowing that the campaign would be lost in an open field he ordered a line of battle to screen an orderly retreat via Kdyně to the passes of Všeruby and Nýrsko.[32] The rumble and the direction of the departing wagons gave Frederick's plan away and both Cesarini and the elector of Saxony asked for an explanation. Frederick answered that these were his orders as the supreme commander and that they should act accordingly. The incensed cardinal accused Frederick of treason and raised the alarm.[33] To placate him, Frederick fortified a nearby hill with a replica of the Hussite formation of wagons which the cardinal manned with his Italian bodyguard, about 200 mounted knights. In the meantime, the general confusion precipitated a panic among the crusaders which spread like wildfire.

At two o'clock in the afternoon the thundering noise of the Hussite wagons and the loud singing of "Ye Warriors of God" and other war songs was heard in the distance and before long the Hussite cavalry rushed in and drove the crusaders before them in headlong flight. Only mounted soldiers and the carriages of the German princes and towns reached safety; the last of them was the Strasbourg batallion.[34] The infantry jammed the roads littered with the baggage which the cavalry had discarded to lighten the most valuable carriages. The rest of the foot soldiers straggled through the forest, perished or were captured. Most of the cardinal's bodyguard fell in desperate flight but a small residue with the cardinal were escorted in a roundabout way to the frontier by Henry of Plavno. After a nightlong journey he reached the troops of the bishop of Würzburg who accompanied him to Nürnberg in disguise to save him from death at the hands of his fellow soldiers.[35] The shattering experience had a profound effect on Cesarini and gradually induced him to work for the negotiations with the Hussites with almost the same zeal he had applied to their extermination.

Apart from the Italians, who fell in the hastily fortified hill, there were relatively few casualties in the battle of Domažlice. Most crusaders saved themselves but the booty they left behind them meant for the Hussites a gain almost as large as that from the Glorious Campaign. Out of the 4,000 vehicles laden with provisions, war equipment and chattels, only 300 escaped to Germany. Cesarini's carriage with his robes, cardinal's hat, crucifix and bell, was also captured by the Hussites and kept at Domažlice until the beginning of the Thirty Years' War.[36] King Sigismund expressed satisfaction at the safe return of the army "by the Grace of God."[37] The cardinal derived comfort from the hope that there might be another war for which the Knights of St. George had offered their services, more in consideration of the cardinal's ducats[38] than with the genuine religious zeal. Privately, the nuncio could not but realize that he had suffered a crushing defeat nor could he avoid feeling the pressure of public opinion that the Hussites were invincible. No doubt he felt pricks of conscience about the loss of his distinguished bodyguard and blamed himself for having neglected his mission to Basel. At the same time the pope had after all designated him for a task which he believed to be the speedy annihilation of the heretics with a crusade.

Cesarini therefore left Nürnberg immediately after King Sigismund's departure for Rome, and arrived in Basel on 9 September. The Council which his plenipotentiaries had opened on 23 July was still struggling with the initial difficulties. The cardinal soon swamped Europe with invitations and urgent appeals for help. He was anxious to make up for lost time and build a new barrier against the Hussites. He received ample support both from the Council and the ruling houses of Europe but was at the same time forced to compromise with a new current of public opinion, desiring negotiations rather than war, which spread to Basel before his arrival and had sprung from a curious incident.

On 10 August, four days before the collapse of the crusade, the members of the Council received the Hussite manifesto of 21 July to which Cesarini had given a feeble and disingenuous reply, doding the main point that the Hussites had been consistently denied a public discussion of their religious program. Now he had to take the consequences. The commander of the Basel contingent which formed part of the crusade had sent a copy of the Hussite manifesto from the front to his native town. Its content amazed both the Council and the population, and was widely discussed as a hopeful sign that war might be terminated. When, on 29 August, the commander instead sent a report of the catastrophe the people of Basel began to fear a Hussite invasion of their city,[39] and wondered who it was that had prolonged and lost the war by denying the Hussites a fair hearing. It came to light that the responsibility rested on two deputies of Cesarini who had wrecked the agreement between King Sigismund and the Hussite messengers at Cheb in May 1431. There must have been vehement clashes between some members of the Council on the one side and the town council and its liaison men on the other. At the end of 1431, Jean Baupére, the representative of the university of Paris, commented that the citizens of Basel were contaminated with Hussite heresy and sworn enemies of the Church and of the clergy whom they dared to treat in the worst possible way.[40]

Cesarini's arrival at Basel may have reduced the tension. It is uncertain when and whether he changed his mind completely on the question of inviting the Hussites to Basel. Whatever his opinion he had to tread lightly and not provoke to open revolt those who favored a conciliar discussion with the Hussites. There was always the possibity that the Council might be wrecked and that his share of the responsibility for the disastrous crusade be exposed. He was also aware that most members of the Council, coming from universities, had a special liking for lively discussion, and he could not avoid the challenge. Besides, inviting the Hussites to the Council of Basel offered him an opportunity to display his consummate diplomatic skill, to vindicate his reputation and reassert the position with which two popes had invested him.

To begin with, he put on the agenda of the conciliar meetings the question, whether the Hussites should be invited. After two weeks' deliberation, on 28 September, the Council passed a resolution that the Hussites should be granted a fair hearing. On 5 October, Cesarini and his confidants submitted a draft of the invitation which was debated, amended and approved, but Cesarini received the powers to edit it. The date of issue was 15 October.[41]

The result was almost a masterpiece of diplomacy. The attitudes of the two sides were poles apart. To the Hussites, the Four Articles were absolute truths, and the Bible their only authority; the Council regarded itself as the supreme authority in the Church. Cesarini could not afford to put this view on paper because the Hussites whose confidence had risen after their victory would not have come. Therefore he evaded the fundamental theses of the Hussite manifesto and inconspicuously introduced the idea that the Council was infallible because it was inspired by the Holy Spirit, the sole judge of the Hussites and the Council. This silenced the argument that inviting the Hussites would compromise the Council's authority. For good measure, the nuncio lavished courtesy on the Hussites and made bold to admit that the Church had erred by turning down their request for a discussion.

His vague phrases did not deceive the Hussites but they made it impossible for them, including the Taborites who had bonds of solidarity with the Orphans and with Prague, to refuse the invitation. At most they could demand various guarantees against deceit or circumvention and indeed they were to receive them during the meeting at Cheb in 1432. In the end, however, Cesarini was to shirk the obligations resulting from the Cheb talks, and remain the same slippery diplomat, justifying the severe judgment which Martin Lupáč later pronounced on him. Nevertheless, the invitation to Basel marked the beginning of peaceful exchanges between the Hussite revolution and the Council of Basel albeit in the face of serious obstacles. The main difficulty was Pope Eugene IV who dissolved the Council immediately after the invitation to Bohemia had been dispatched. He called once more to arms. It seemed that neither side was yet ready to lay down arms.

CHAPTER SIX

THE ROAD TO BASEL

The battle of Domažlice threw the enemy camp into confusion but did not altogether stop the war. It caused the Saxon army, which had over-run northwest Bohemia as far as Žatec to retreat hastily beyond the bor-der. But it was too late to help the Hussite garrison at Löbau which had been under siege by the Lusatian Six Towns since 17 July. In the end, it escaped without losses during a heavy thunderstorm on 12 August.[1] Albrecht of Austria held out considerably longer. Since the end of July he had been ravaging and scorching the land of the Moravian Hussite nobles in a manner reminiscent of the savagery of Pipo Spano ten years earlier. He seized the relatively unimportant Kyjov, defeated the Hussite nobles near Brno and laid an unsuccessful siege to Přerov, after which, at the beginning of September, he retreated from Moravia.[2]

Simultaneously, Prague held a festival of thanksgiving for the great victory of Domažlice. The enemy standards which the Prague soldiers had brought from the battlefield were displayed in front of the Týn church from which immense crowds marched in procession to the castle.[3] Laurence of Březová composed a special Order of Service which was in-cluded in his long "Song of the Illustrious Crown of Bohemia,"[4] an ex-pression of thanksgiving for 14 August. John Rokycana, the newly elected deputy of Archbishop Conrad who was then at death's door, celebrated

73

a solemn mass in the cathedral of St. Vitus. The festival, unfortunately,
ended in tragedy. Part of the returning procession, about one hundred of
them, fell to their deaths when one of the castle bridges collapsed under
them.[5]

This misfortune seemed to cast a shadow on the following Hussite campaigns which had been jointly planned in Prague by the commanders of
both brotherhoods. Prokop Holý led the Taborites to Silesia and the
Orphans, under Prokůpek and Čapek of Sány, went to Moravia. Both
were to join later in Upper Slovakia. Prokop Holý and the Taborites first
reinforced the Hussite bases in Silesia, especially Niemcza, and reached
a truce agreement with Přemek, the old Prince of Opava, who promised
that he, or his sons in the event of his death, would accept the Four
Articles of Prague within a year. From there, the Taborites went to Slovakia where they seized Likava on 27 September, joined forces with the
Orphans and throughout October pillaged the valleys of the Turiec and the
Nitra, proceeding as far south as Trnava and Levice.[6] Towards the end
of the month, a fateful dispute broke out between Prokop and Čapek.
Prokop undoubtedly sensed the risk of a prolonged stay in a country
with large forces at its command and urged Čapek to turn back before
the autumn rains set in. A disagreement on the division of spoils made
things worse and Čapek stayed while Prokop took his force safely home.[7]

On 7 November, when the Orphans too were almost ready to go home,
they were attacked by a large Hungarian army and forced to retreat and
fight back for ten days running. Their superhuman effort in the face of
terrible losses became rightly known as the anabasis of the Hussites, one
of their greatest feats of arms.[8] Exhausted and famished, they trudged
through the mire in closed formation until their wagons stuck in the mud
and 120 of them had to be abandoned to save their vital equipment. This,
however, lightened their load so that on 19 November they could seize
Ilava after which they had to ford the Váh because the Hungarians were
holding the bridges. Once on the right bank, they advanced for six days,
still fighting, towards a Carpathian pass near Bánov where the Hungarians
laid ambush, made a feint of retreating and put the first Orphan unit to
flight. Prokůpek opened the barrier of wagons to let in the fugitives but
the Hungarians got inside too. Their cavalry struck at the same time from
the rear and completely deranged the Orphan army. Some straggling warriors fell into the hands of Wallachian bandits or drowned in the Morava.
Prokůpek managed to cross the Moravian border and reach Uherský Brod.[9]

It was one of the most disastrous defeats a Hussite army had ever suffered. Worse still, it was immediately followed by an ominous upheaval in the Hussite camp which shattered the precious cooperation between the Taborites and Orphans. After the defeat, Čapek tried to clear his name by recriminations. He had sent a message to Prague alleging that Prokop had caused the defeat by having a bridge across the Váh pulled down behind him. The relief force which the New Town promptly sent to Moravia was too late to help the remainder of the Orphans who suffered from the severe winter conditions. Their pitiful appearance further aroused the feeling against Prokop and culminated in a slanderous campaign which spread even to the Old Town where he had many devoted friends.[10]

Tabor had also come to grief. A section of the Taborite nobility from the Pelhřimov area, led by Nicholas Sokol of Lamberk, misjudged the strength of the Austrian army and thought that the track was clear after Albrecht's September withdrawal. The Taborites spent a fortnight pillaging the surroundings of Pernegg. On their return, they were waylaid by the reorganized Austrian army and crushed near Weidhofen. The Austrians captured all the Taborite wagons and 500 soldiers; about 1000 were killed. Albrecht had the pick of their standards hung in the court chapel in Vienna. Another Taborite force carried out a retaliatory raid on Litschau in December but failed to free the captives who later perished in Vienna jails. It seemed that the Hussite camp was in utter confusion and on the verge of internecine war. At this grave moment, the invitation to Basel came almost as a relief.

The sound and dominant elements in all the three revolutionary parties regarded the offer as one of their greatest victories. Martin V's stubborn refusal to consider any discussion of their program had convinced the Hussites that the Four Articles were irrefutable truths revealed by God himself to the nation of John Hus for its unwavering faith and sacrifice.[11] It was generally believed that, once a free defence of the Hussite program was granted, the Church would give up the war, and the peace which had for so long been fervently desired would be almost within reach. The graciously sounding words of the invitation appealed to most and left doubts in the minds of some. But unity was imperative if the Hussite camp was to pass the historical test before the eyes of the whole world. These great expectations helped the Czechs overcome the crisis within three months.

The memorable invitation was issued in triplicate and sent to Sigismund who was on his way from Germany to Italy, to Nürnberg and to
Cheb. From Cheb the original copy was forwarded to Prague shortly
before 15 November where it was favorably received. The city council
replied immediately and the messenger from Cheb was generously rewarded and taken to the Týn church were Rokycana read out the invitation and expressed his satisfaction. He was then authorized by the Old
Town to correspond with the Council and its messengers.[12] The brotherhoods also received the invitation but their response to the king is unknown.

An assembly of the Prague and Orphan alliances met in January 1432
at the New Town hall because the Taborites refused to attend and the
Old Town hesitated to be the host for fear that it might embarrass Prokop
Holý and the Taborites.[13] The memorable achievement of this assembly
was the rapprochment between Prague and the Orphans. The simultaneous
synod of their priests reached a complete agreement on matters of faith
and liturgy. Rokycana, once the invaluable intermediary between Prague
and Žižka, was now head of the Prague clergy and, furthermore, the death
of Archbishop Conrad had removed the last traces of the ideological rift.
Through the intervention of Peter Payne the representatives of the Orphan
priests as well as Jacob Vlk, the superintendant of the New Town clergy
were admitted to the consistory. The agreement was summed up in 23
paragraphs and Rokycana wrote a special paper in its defence.[14]

Just as there was a coalition of the priests, so the statesmen of both
Prague and the Orphan brotherhood cooperated to deal with its political
implications. The unity of the whole camp was an absolute necessity in
view of the imminent talks at Basel. The problem was not so much the
periodic question of an elected chief administrator of the land, which in
any case could not be solved without the Taborites, as it was the con-
solidation of the country by administrative reorganization, so far resisted
by Tabor. The assembly decided that each region should elect its chief
and his council which would supply, at short notice, a peace keeping force
in the area as well as organize for its recruitment, mobilization and requisition while not burdening the other parts of the country, especially its
poor.[15] The stress was on humanizing war in accordance with Žižka's regulations of 1423. It seems that the new measures worked in the territory

controlled by Prague and the Orphans[16] but may have come up against
political immaturity elsewhere. The Taborites did not like the new group-
ing nor its policy, but the assembly gave the arbitration committee the
power to call a diet to which the Taborites were invited. The fact that
they accepted was a sure sign of relaxed tension; the alternative would
have been their isolation. Prokop Holý certainly used his influence, un-
affected by the attacks on his person, and although he had not attended
the New Year's assembly, he declared that Tabor would accept the ruling
of the majority.[17]

The diet meetings (10-27 February) therefore took place in the Old
Town at the University, in the presence of Prokop Holý with Otík of
Loza (Jacob Kroměšín's successor) representing the Taborites, and Čapek
of Sány and Prokůpek the Orphans.[18] Prokop was cleared of the charge
of having caused the calamitous end of the Orphan expedition to Slovakia,
and harmony between the two brotherhoods was restored. The Taborites
yielded and agreed to go to Basel, stipulating that the terms of the January
diet of Český Brod (1429) should form the basis of negotiations. Delegates were elected for the meeting with the Council's negotiators at Cheb,
where these terms were to be presented. The unity of the Hussite camp
being reestablished, a new joint campaign was planned.

The armies set out in mid-March 1432 and split into two flanks, the
western one heading for Lubań and Boleslawiec in order to disrupt the
concentration of enemy forces in the Glogów district.[19] This task accomplished, the western army divided into two streams, one moving west
towards Gubin, the other one returning to Lubań where it was joined by
the Taborites of the eastern flank. Together they laid waste the surroundings of Görlitz in order to hinder it from joining the Silesians, and to clear
the path for the Hradec Orphans,[20] the other force of the eastern flank.
Both flanks closed up on Gubin about 6 April, and forced it into a truce
for two years. The truce included Hanuš of Polensko who signed on behalf
of the whole of Lower Lusatia. Having secured the rear, the Hussite army
entered the Mark of Brandenburg ruled by the Margrave John of Hohenzollern, the eldest son of Frederick who had bought the territory from
King Sigismund twenty years earlier and separated it from the Czech
crown lands; the country had been acquired by Charles IV in 1373 and
the forty years of Czech domination were still fresh in mind despite the
efforts of both new rulers to cut the personal links with Bohemia.

Margrave John was much better prepared than the Hussites expected. The large fortified town of Frankfurt on the Oder and even the smaller Bernau resisted their attacks. Only some open towns succumbed, among them Lunsko whose former Bishop John of Buřenice,[21] had been a bitter enemy of Hus. He had applied for a transfer away from there as early as 1420. Some other towns saved themselves by paying ransom. Ulrich of Bieberstein, the lord of Friedland, saved Forst, his Lusatian estate, and Kamenz in a similar way after his mother had received a friendly warning from the priest, Frederick of Strážnice.[22] The Hussites did not achieve all their aims during the two weeks in Brandenburg but they gathered a large booty even thought it cost them dearly. Their heavy casualties arose chiefly from too many risks taken. Still, it was not a mere provisioning raid, as a captured Hussite said in the Görlitz torture chamber; it also yielded strategic and political results. It was timely in that it pressured the Basel negotiators at the coming meeting which the February diet of Prague had asked for in its acceptance of the invitation.[23]

The negotiations had their ups and downs. The Taborites had caused the first delay by not attending the New Year's assembly. The setbacks the campaigning armies had suffered in Slovakia and Austria, and the dissensions among the Hussites led the Catholic party to believe that its enemies who had been invited to Basel on the strength of their Domažlice victory were shattered and that the Hussite revolution could be disposed of by civil war in Bohemia.[24] At the same time the Council's conflict with the pope had suddenly sharpened. Acting on the hopes for Hussite disunity, Eugenius IV transferred the Council to Bologna on 12 November and dissolved it on 18 December, arguing that the invitation of convicted heretics to Basel was an insult to the papal see and the holy Councils of Constance and Sienna, as well as contrary to the decrees of the Holy Fathers and to Imperial statutes. The Council of Basel of course defied the argument and so did King Sigismund who had found in Italy that the pope opposed his coronation. Cesarini wrote two justifications for the Council's meeting, stressing that continual war with the Hussites was detrimental both to Germany and the Church, the clergy being exposed to the pernicious effect of the Hussite manifestos because of the endless delay in Church reform. Cesarini went so far as to resign his chairmanship of the Council, announcing it in the second, otherwise purely theological defence.[25]

The echo of the conflict between pope and Council caused anxiety in Bohemia about the fate of the invitation. After a month's wait for an answer to the diet's letter of acceptance, Prague lodged a complaint warning all and sundry that unless the hearing at Basel took place war was unavoidable. This letter passed the announcement that the meeting with the council's messengers would begin at Cheb on 27 April going in the other direction. The consultations did not get under way until 9 May, owing to the delayed safe-conducts.[26]

In the first place the Council sent out the two theologians who had been communicating with the Hussites from Nürnberg. They were John Nider, prior of the Dominican monastery in Basel, previously based at Nürnberg, and John Geilhausen, a monk freom the Cistercian monastery at Maulbronn. Both were dedicated servants of the Council and Nider had prepared a tract against the Taborite manifesto.[27] The most important personality was Henry Toke, the author of the bold proposal of a meeting of German and Hussite theologians which he had submitted, in accord with the Elector Frederick, to the Nürnberg diet two years earlier. Also two Nürnberg parsons, Albrecht Fleischmann of St. Sebaldus and Henry of St. Aegidius came. The elector may have influenced the choice of the latter three. The other ecclesiastic was Henry Parsperger, a canonist and the dean of Regensburg.[28] Nider and John Maulbronn knew what was at stake and requested the presence of the Elector Frederick and the Count Palatine John, as well as the town councils of Nürnberg and Cheb.[29] The success of the negotiations was vitally important to these parties since they had been affected by the Glorious Campaign in 1430. Nürnberg sent its foremost diplomat, Peter Volkmar, and its legal advisor, Conrad Konhofer[30] who had begun his studies in Prague and taken part in the trial of John Hus as an auditor in the papal court. He also had the writings of John Milič and anti-Hussite tracts in his library.

The Hussite theologians were Rokycana, Peter Payne (English) and Martin Lupáč for Prague, and Nicholas Biskupec and Markolt for Tabor. Nicholas of Humpolec, the chief city clerk, John of Krajnice for the Old Town, John Velvar for the New Town, Matthew Louda, the captain of Písek, Beneš Mokrovouský and Gregory of Dvůr Králové for the Orphans, Jacob of Vřesovice[31] for Žatec and Prokop Holý for the campaigning armies made up the lay delegation. The talks took place in the house of Elector Frederick and were opened tactfully by Henry Toke on the theme

"Peace be with you."[32] This was answered by Rokycana who stated that the Hussites had been driven into self-defence by the wars which the Church had unleashed, but that they were very glad of the friendly hand extended to them. All the same, the ensuing debates revealed that the two sides were poles apart.

In the first round of talks, the theologians were grappling with the task of establishing the basis for the hearing at Basel. The controversy concerned who or what would be the ultimate arbiter between the Hussites and the Council in the event of disagreement which could well be expected. The Hussites insisted that it should be the Bible and those ecclesiastical fathers and teachers who immovably based themselves upon it according to the formula adopted by the diet of Český Brod. This demand had already ruined the proceedings at Bratislava (1429), Cracow and Cheb (1431).

Both Nider and John Maulbronn knew that it was John Stojkovic, the Council's expert on Hussite matters, who had wrecked the negotiations at Cheb in 1431 by his express instructions that no concession whatever be granted on this most fundamental point.[33] Therefore on this occasion the heated controversy threatened to end in a deadlock. The situation was saved by the lay delegates who had the most to lose from the failure of the talks, especially Elector Frederick, the Count Palatine and their colleagues. As a result of their pressure the controversial paragraph was entered into the agreement as follows: "In the dispute about the Four Articles which the Bohemians advocate, the Law of God and the practice of Christ, the apostles and the primitive Church, together with the Councils and doctors truly founded on this practice, shall be accepted at the Council of Basel as the truest and indisputable judge."[34]

With the main stumbling-block out of the way, the political talks could begin. Elector Frederick and Prokop Holý followed up their confidential talks of Nürnberg, February 1430, after the conclusion of the Beheimstein treaty. Their problem was to establish who would be responsible for the safe conducts for the Czechs on their way to Basel and back, with so many lands to cross, some of whose populations had unpleasant memories of Hussite warfare. Recalling the Bratislava precedent, the Hussite delegates first asked to be given prominent personalities as hostages who would be kept in Bohemia until the safe return of their messengers. They were not forgetting that the Council of Constance had issued, for the protection of those who had sent Hus to his death, a decree based on existing canonical law, that promises given heretics were not legally binding. Nor did the presence of Prince John fail to remind them that he had had Jerome of Prague brought to Constance in chains.[35] "If you have the right to break every word given to heretics, what guarantees can you give us?" Yet in the end the Hussites accepted the explanation that their original demands were hardly feasible, and contented themselves with the personal guarantees of Elector Frederick, probably in return for his concession in the matter of the supreme arbiter. The Count Palatine and the towns of Nürnberg and Cheb made a similar undertaking which was later honored. The guarantees were incorporated into an appropriate charter and similarly a conciliar decree was drafted, specifying that the contrary decrees of the Councils of Constance and Siena were annulled and announcing that any transgressor would incur punishment according to divine, human and customary law. The Council also undertook these guarantees and promises on behalf of the pope, King Sigismund and other spiritual and secular powers.[36] In the end, not to insist on hostages was a significant concession on the part of the Czechs.

On the other hand, the representatives of the Council showed a certain amount of good will. According to the original instructions from Basel, the Hussites were expected to sign a general truce for the duration of the negotiations, a point raised by Sigismund at Bratislava in 1429. As opposition was anticipated, the delegates were free to act at the discretion of the princes. In the following debate, Prokop Holý declared that the diet, the only authority competent to deal with the matter, would scarcely allow a general truce because wars against the enemies of the revolution were fought for various reasons, and pointed out that new truce agreements had been signed in Lusatia and Silesia and others were about to be signed pending a favorable outcome of the Cheb talks. He recommended that all interested parties should approach the Bohemian diet. On 18 May 1431 the agreement was summed up in eleven paragraphs and texts were exchanged and sealed by both parties. A Hussite spokesman thanked the Council's delegates and Henry Toke closed the session with a moving speech which brought tears to the eyes of many listeners.

The agreements of Cheb are hailed by some as the greatest achievement of the Hussite revolution.[37] This is perhaps true in theory. The delegates of the Council were compelled to recognize the great Hussite principle, the supremacy of the Bible over the pope and the Council, but a number of participants merely yielded to temporary political pressure and did not feel bound to adhere to the letter. This negative attitude to the "arbiter of Cheb" (iudex in Egra compactatus) was to become the guiding principle of the conciliar leadership in its further dealings with the Hussites until the very end. At the moment, all this remained hidden in the confidential documents of the Council and came to light only by degrees undermining the Hussites' confidence, especially as men like Toke, who had a deep sympathy for the moral efforts of Hussitism, were superseded by diplomats without consideration or even shame.

The parting moments of Cheb were in no way troubled by whatever may have been looming ahead. The Hussite delegation left on 18 May, and three days later Prokop Holý was already in Prague where the forces of all three associations were waiting for their marching orders. Prokop sent a brief report of the meeting to King Sigismund and requested him to come to Basel at the time the Hussite delegation would arrive, and to empower the noblemen of his party who had taken the Hussite messengers to Bratislava, to escort them now to Basel.[38] Very soon the allied forces moved to Moravia where the local Hussites were in temporary difficulties. Early in May, they had seized a large fortified monastery, Hradiště near Olomouc, which induced Albrecht of Austria, who had been lord of Moravia for years, to move there and relieve the threatened Olomouc. The Hussite expedition forced the duke to retreat but in the end the Hussites lost the monastery[39] and turned to Silesia where a fairly large Hussite convoy had been captured on its way to Niemcza. This was a matter of extreme urgency and the Hussite cavalry arrived on 14 June. Reinforced by the garrisons from Niemcza and Otmuchów, it scattered the Silesian camp outside Strzelin and on the next day was joined by infantry and wagons. Strzelin surrendered and the Hussites took many prisoners and a large amount of booty, as they spread like a flood all over the surrounding country. Their progress was halted near Scinawa where the bellicose brothers of the bishop of Breslau, Conrad Kantner and Conrad the White occupied the bridge across the Oder. Yet they asked the Hussite leaders for safe conducts for the purpose of negotiating peace. Before they could make up their minds whether to accept the terms or not, the Hussite cavalry succeeded on 29 June in crossing the Oder, outflanking and chasing away the enemy, clearing the bridge and gaining access to the

right bank. The Hussites seized a number of rich monasteries and towns including Oleśnica. When the latter fell the Silesian princes and towns that
were still at war with the Hussites were induced to sign a new truce agreement. This included not only the house of Oleśnica, but also the principalities belonging to the Bohemian crown, namely Breslau, Swidnica and
Jawor, and with them the military bishop Conrad himself. The defeated
side paid 96,000 groschen for the truce which was to expire on 24 June
1434, and in return, Otík Loza for Tabor and Čapek for the Orphans
gave assurances that the dangerous neighbors on the Bohemian side of
the border would also observe it. The Hussite garrison of Niemcza, Klucz-
bork and Otmuchów undertook a similar promise. Smil Holický of Šternberk, Aleš Vřešt'ovský and John Černín of Vysoká were appointed guaran-
tors of the truce agreement which was to extend beyond its term even if
it was not formally renewed. Shortly before the two years were up, the
campaigning armies were to bleed to death at Lipany, making its renewal
superfluous.

The victorious armies returned to Bohemia but their commanders
went on to Poland where they had been invited for a meeting. They met
the Polish court at Pabianice.[40] Poland was preparing for a war which was
to be fought in 1433 against her inveterate enemy, the Teutonic Knights,
who had invaded and ravaged Kujawsko in 1431. Although the two years'
truce with the Teutonic Order was still in force, the contending parties
were mobilizing and Poland was glad of the Bohemian allies. This time,
the Hussites were treated with overwhelming hospitality and allowed by
the Polish bishops to attend church services which was made easier since
the Cheb agreements had practically suspended the interdict on the
Czechs. They were coming to Poland not only as triumphant campaigners
but also as full-fledged members of the Christian realm. And they were
soon to conclude a military alliance with the Poles against all nations,
especially the Germans but excluding the Hungarians. The Polish nobles
were anxious for the Hungarians to know that they disapproved of the
recent seizure of Trnava by a Hussite warrior.[41]

He was Blažek of Borotín who had taken advantage of the general
attention directed at the Hussite exploits in Silesia in order to take Trnava
by ruse. He allowed his men to mix with the noisy crowds during the
annual fair and got in touch with local clandestine Hussites who by night
opened the gates for his soldiers. The fall of this important stop on the

"Czech highway" to the Bohemian heretics came as a shock to the king of Hungary who had retained Trnava against a strong Orphan force two years before. It also dawned on him that the Czech-Polish alliance was directed at him as the king of the Roman empire and of the German nation. To be sure, the treaty of Pabianice had yet to be ratified by the Bohemian diet.

The diet which met on 30 August 1432 was the last to sit at Kutná Hora, the joint possession of the Taborites and Orphans. Its first task was to prepare to send a large delegation to Basel. A letter had arrived from the Council, radiating kindness and joy at the Hussites' return to the fold, announcing that the Cheb agreements, "an act of the Holy Ghost," had been ratified on 6 June. There was no mention, in this verbose effusion, of the safe conducts the Hussites had been promised at Cheb. One safe conduct from the Council was enclosed and another from Sigismund promised. It had already come to be known in Bohemia that the Cheb agreements had been reached only after hard bargaining. The letter from the Council, with only one safe conduct, confirmed the suspicion and made the Hussites reluctant to go to Basel. A general truce was again rejected and individual truce agreements were offered to those German states which would guarantee safe passage to Basel. The recent truce agreements with Silesia, Lusatia and the Elector of Saxony were poignantly mentioned. Nevertheless, the diet elected eighteen delegates and stipulated that two special messengers should call at Basel in advance to make various arrangements for the rest.[43] The Council had to put up with this further delay because it could not afford to jeopardize the negotiations. It was sitting in defiance of the pope's explicit prohibition and for the sole purpose of terminating the war with the Hussites. In fact, having recently failed to persuade the Hussites to accept the mediation of the court of Cracow, Eugene IV was now keeping the Council alive by his earlier hostility.[44] The fate of the negotiations and the survival of the Council were thus inextricably linked and concessions had to be made, if only as an expediency. A vast majority of the members, including Cesarini, who resumed the chairmanship on 12 September, struck to their original design to crush the revolt in Bohemia but hoped this time to be more successful. The events at Kutná Hora sustained this hope.

The diet meeting there was fighting over the ratification of the Pabianice treaty. Despite their pro-Polish sympathies, most Hussites accepted the return of Sigismund to the Bohemian throne because he had been the

initiator of the negotiations with the council. An armed alliance with Poland would have been an attack on Sigismund as the king of Germany and
a natural ally of the Teutonic Order. There was considerable opposition,
even from some Taborites, to the ratification which was passed by a very
narrow majority, probably because its movers could reassure their col-
legues that the outbreak of war was by no means inevitable and that the
threat of the invincible Bohemian armies might ward it off. The diet
actually, on 8 September, sent a threatening letter to the Grand Master
of the Teutonic Order, which was signed by the chief captains of both
brotherhoods, Otík of Loza and Čapek of Sány.[45] It was a victory for
the Orphans who unanimously supported the move, but it upset, and
later rent, the relationship between the brotherhoods, very much to the
enemy's advantage.

On the same day, the same chief captains acknowledged receipt for the
payment of the first half of the 5000 florins ransom due to the brotherhoods from the elector of Saxony.[46] This was part of the truce signed
in August outside the Fridštejn castle which had surrendered when support from Saxony did not materialize. It came in connection with the
military operations of the brotherhoods and Hussite towns against a few
royalist castles, some of which were able to hold out until February.[47]

The truce agreements with the countries east, north and west of Bohemia reduced the scope of Hussite campaigns abroad. Austria was the
only possible target.[48] Duke Albrecht had consistently refused to negotiate with the Hussites, relying on the success of his armored wagons,
built on the Hussite model. The university of Vienna stood solidly behind him. Hence the Taborites set out from Moravia in the direction of
Lau and began to plunder the Austrian side of the Moravian border in late
October 1432. The Austrian stand-by forces collapsed and the duke sent
an urgent appeal for help to the Council. It was not until early December
that the Taborites were thrown back to the Moravian border, after which
they made another raid at Christmas. This time, Albrecht's ablest captain,
Leopold Krajíř forced them to retreat in a bloody battle near Znojmo. By
that time the whole of Europe had turned its attention to Basel where the
great encounter had already begun.

CHAPTER SEVEN

THE TOURNAMENT AT BASEL

The Hussite threat to break off the negotiations with the Council if there was any further delay with safe conducts, had an instant effect. This was largely due to the efforts of John Maulbronn (Geilhausen). In response to his pleadings, Elector Frederick decided to risk the damages he might incur by issuing safe conducts. John Maulbronn was assisted by Herman, the Cistercian abbot from Ebrach who maintained contacts with the Bohemian monasteries of his order. Strangely enough, help was also forthcoming from the bishop of Regensburg, Conrad of Soest, a former master of the Heidelberg university and participant in the first crusade in 1421.[1] Whether his hostility to the Hussites had lost its edge or, whether he was worried about Regensburg which was almost within the range of Hussite guns, is difficult to say. Thanks to these men, everything was in order on 29 September when the advance Hussite messengers were escorted to Basel, received in ceremonial session of the Council and returned to Prague early in November well pleased with what they had seen. On 6 November Prague sent a message to Cheb that the Hussite delegates would meet at Domažlice on 6 December, and asked to be met there by their escort. It was incumbent on the Hussites to be ready for the decisive spiritual struggle with the Council which was to involve greater effort than any of the many military battles of the long war.

86

Of the eighteen men elected by the diet of Kutná Hora, fourteen had been at the Cheb meetings, the rest were two lords and two knights. Now, however, the two lords, Menhart of Hradec and Wenceslas of Strážnice, refused to go and so did Přibík of Klenové, a Taborite captain, who liked to cultivate contacts with the nobility. This was a deliberate move to prevent Prague and the brotherhoods from representing the entire Hussite camp; the first step by a small group of nobles, who had joined the Hussites under compulsion, towards forming a party of their own, which later joined the royalists.[2] The fact that Moravia was unrepresented strengthened the suspicion that all Hussite nobles had reached a secret accommodation with the Council.

Charles university was much more forthright and declared its unreserved adherence to the Four Articles.[3] Its rector, Křišt'an of Prachatice, nominated John Rokycana as his deputy. The university delegation was made up of Peter Payne, three Bachelors of Divinity who had been sent to Cheb in 1432, Ulrich of Znojmo, the parson of Čáslav, Peter of Žatec and three former lay participants of the Cheb meetings.[4] The defectors reduced the number of delegates, so that William Kostka and Jíra of Řečice could also join. Each of the fifteen delegates, ecclesiastical or secular, had a clerk or secretary, of whom only Laurence of Reichenbach, the clerk of Prokop Holý, is known by name. It is possible that Matthew of Hnátnice, commonly known as English, did similar service for William Kostka; he had been in England about the same time as Master Jerome and was employed on important diplomatic missions before and after.[5] The main delegation, including the clerks, numbered thirty and had seats reserved at the Council. The chief responsibility rested on the shoulders of the theologians who had been selected by the diet of Kutná Hora to defend the individual articles. The whole expedition with retainers totalled ninety. Because of financial reasons, this was fewer than had been originally planned.[6] The delegates left Prague on 6 December and were accompanied by Zdislav of Buřenice the burgrave of Karlštejn, who for ten years had maintained friendly relations with the Hussites. Protection was necessary because they had to traverse the land of royalist nobles. The rest of the Hussite messengers were waiting at Domažlice.[7] The delegates crossed the Bohemian forest with an escort supplied by Elector Frederick and Count Palatine John who welcomed them at Kaube and saw them off to Nürnberg. Before entering the city of 21 December, Matthew Louda

unfurled his banner displaying the motto "The Truth conquers all," proudly showing the cause for which the revolution, especially the Taborites
were fighting.[8] From Nürnberg, the Hussites followed the busy road which
had led John Hus to Constance eighteen years earlier.[9] The association of
the Swabian towns which had fought the Hussites in the past, undertook
to see them off from Ulm to Saulgau in Würtemberg where Jacob Truch-
sess of Waldburg took over until 30 December when the Hussites reached
Stockach in Baden. From there they proceeded to Schaffhausen with the
men of William, the Duke of Bavaria and Sigismund's deputy, a former
well known visitor to the court of Prague, while his sister, Sophia, was
queen. He had also attended the Bratislava talks in 1429 and knew the
leading Hussite figures.[10] At Schaffhausen the party had to divide up. The
duke and his guests went down the Rhine by boat but some wagons,
owing to their excessive weight, could not be shipped and were taken over-
land to Basel by the duke's retinue and arrived after dark. By accident or
design, this provided the Council, which had been scandalized by the display of the Hussite motto at Nürnberg, with a handy excuse for not afford-
ing the heretics the customary courtesy of meeting them outside the city.
The late arrival of the wagons was officially described as a dispensation
of Providence.[11]

The principal delegates disembarked at Lesser Basel early in the afternoon and received a ceremonial welcome from the city representatives
with whom they crossed the bridge into Greater Basel. The news of their
landing spread like wildfire. Everybody wanted to see the Bohemian
heretics whom their city force had been sent to fight. They especially
wanted to see the legendary leader Prokop Holý, who to the general
amazement, walked in the procession of priests singing familiar Latin
hymns and said a prayer for peace among them.[12]

Next day, the Hussite delegates went on a sightseeing tour of the city
in which they were to spend three months full of excitement, struggle and
disappointment.[13] Basel, then an autonomous part of the Empire, was a
great international center; a large part of it had been rebuilt in stone after
the great fire of 1417. The city council was a forward-looking body including men of international repute. Its liberal leanings prepared the ground
for association with nascent Switzerland in 1491. They were men who
might well have read and even distributed Hussite writings. The city council also provided the stimulus for the convocation of the Church Council

and prepared itself by getting information from Constance as to needs in communications, accommodations and economic conditions. At the time of the Hussites' arrival the city was flooded with new arrivals from far and wide so that life looked like a blend of a continual annual fair and international congress. All languages of Europe were heard and the book trade flourished.

The first few days were spent making various arrangements. Members of the city council brought the customary offerings of fish and other foods. Two special confidants of Cardinal Cesarini, John Stojkovic and Juan Palomar, the cardinal's former junior colleague as auditor at the curia, called to present their master's apologies for not extending to them the customary welcome. Other visitors were the bishop of Regensburg and even G. Landriani of Lodi, who had been making trouble for the Hussites at English universities only six months earlier.[14] On the fourth day, the Hussites moved to less costly lodgings available to delegations with many retainers. They rented four houses one of which was occupied by Prokop Holý and William Kostka. On the same day, Prokop asked Stojkovic and Palomar to dinner which was followed by a lively exchange of words between the guests and the Taborite and Orphan priests led by Peter Payne.

On 8 January, the cardinal entertained eight of the foremost members of the Hussite delegation to discuss the formalities of their entry into the Council, on which occasion Cesarini and Prokop met for the first time. Rokycana made an introductory speech. Ambrose Talaru, the archbishop of Lyon, called with two Parisian doctors to deliver a personal message from the king of France, who expressed his pleasure at being related to the Bohemian ruling house and offered his services.

On 10 January the thirty Bohemian delegates were introduced to the plenary session of the Council which took place in the refectory of the Dominican monastery in the presence of prominent secular personalities including the protector, Duke William. The cardinal delivered a very long speech which was a masterpiece of homiletics blended with diplomatic subtlety. Addressing himself mainly to the guests from Bohemia, but anxious to impress the rest of the audience, he spoke in the name of Mother Church welcoming her estranged sons back to the fold. The studied courtesy and blandness could not disguise the fact that the Church, or the Council, were convinced that they had truth on their side. At the end of the session, Matthew Louda asked for the text of the speech; evidently some listeners were sceptical.[15] On behalf of the Hussites, Rokycana thanked the Council for the invitation and for the help extended to the delegates on their journey. But he stressed again as he had done at Cheb, that the Hussites had not caused the wars which made peace negotiations necessary, and that the apostolic Church of Christ, from which the contemporary Church was far removed, was their ideal. Cesarini closed the session without reference to Rokycana's main point, and merely granted that a date should be fixed for the beginning of the Hussite defence. This was to be 16 January 1433 as the Hussites suggested.

The Council had begun to prepare to meet the Hussite challenge in March 1432,[16] as soon as it had learned that the Hussites were coming. In confidential disputations, the Four Articles of Prague had become the subject of intensive study and theologians from various universities of western and central Europe had been trained in countering Hussite arguments. The trial disputations yielded a fairly large number of tracts. A select committee of four theologians had been picked by Cesarini to face the Hussites in February 1433. Another committee had been set up to work out a code of dignified conduct eliminating anything that might offend the visitors. This had been somewhat pruned in October, but on the whole, the result seemed to serve the purpose so that, indirectly, the Hussites raised the standard of the Council's conduct.[17] Just before the arrival of the delegates, the Council had been panic-stricken with fear of heretical contagion, as if the Trojan horse were about to enter the city gates. The incident of the displayed Hussite motto was blown up all out of proportion and anti-Hussite zealots came up with measures to protect the public. About forty to fifty men were appointed to prevent any contacts between the laity and the Czechs. In the tumult after their arrival, things had probably gotten out of hand, and the committe for matters of faith elected two members to urge the city council to impose heavy penalties for any contacts with the Czechs, and to prevent the delegates from encouraging them. No unauthorized member of the Council was allowed to call on them or talk to them. On 13 January, the city and the protector issued an edict prohibiting any participation in the Hussite church services, in which the population was very much interested. Private conversation with the Czechs on anything but practical matters was also forbidden. The Council appointed two observers for secret reports on the movements of the Hussites. They were not spared insulting behavior. During a courtesy call to the presidium of the Council, they were not offered seats and Capra, the archbishop of Milan, and the patriarch John Mauroux, remained seated so that the Hussites soon left and protested against the discourtesies. After that, matters improved and on 16 January, the Hussites were introduced to the plenum by city representatives and by three members of the Council whom they had met at Nürnberg.[18]

John of Maulbronn who was daily entertained by the Czech delegates and had done much to smooth away their difficulties, arranged for Matthew Louda to be the first speaker, probably because he was a layman with command of the Latin. Louda thanked the Council, reiterated, like Rokycana, that the Church was responsible for the wars and read out three documents relating to the legal basis of the Hussites' presence at the Council: the safe conduct issued by the Council, the agreements of Cheb and the credentials given to Rokycana by Charles University. Peter Payne very briefly introduced the Four Articles, likening them, as in Psalm 104, 22 to the sun which would bring forth the unity and reform of the Church. Rokycana opened the defence of the Chalice, on behalf of all his fellow speakers, with a solemn protestation that they were presenting a discussion in the spirit of the agreements in Cheb. However, his contribution was so encumbered with the scholastic method and with quotations, that it took too more days to deliver,[19] and the main point that communion in one kind was a fairly recent introduction and contary to the practices of the primitive Church, was lost. Rokycana may have been too anxious not to offend the Council's susceptibilities but Prokop stepped in with an appeal that the Council should reintroduce the chalice after the convincing evidence supplied by Rokycana.

This remained unanswered and other Hussite delegates were allowed to speak. Nicholas of Pelhřimov (Biskupec), the head of the Taborite party, felt the tension rise when he defended the article concerning the punishment of public sins.[20] This quickly turned his defence into an unsparing attack, listing all punishable sins: simony, indulgences, anathemas, corrupt practices in veneration of images and pilgrimages, luxury, usury, visiting taverns and houses of ill-repute. Soon the spiritual leader of Tabor passed on to other topics, such as the deaths by fire of John Hus and Jerome, the ban of the chalice by the Council of Constance and the wars of extermination. The cardinal was hard put to keep the noise down and let Nicholas finish.

The third speaker, the Čáslav pastor and Bachelor of Arts, Ulrich of Znojmo, was more moderate in tone. But when he defended the article on the freedom of preaching the Word of God,[21] he felt it was his duty to pay tribute to John Hus. Ulrich had accompanied Hus to Constance and witnessed his trial and death. He refrained from commenting that he recognized, in the audience, participants in Hus' trial, but he severely criticized immoral priests and declared that Hus had become their victims. To which he added: "The whole kingdom and especially his close associates knew his blameless life, honorable character and fame as a scholar." Ulrich's speech caused indignation and led to stricter measures directed against the Hussites. The members of the Council had to swear that they would not lend the texts of the Hussite speeches to anyone.

This precaution was also taken in view of the next speaker who was Master Peter Payne. His speech[22] on the revolutionary theme of the poverty of the clergy was expected with some trepidation, but the four days during which he spoke passed more quietly than his adversaries expected, partly because of his accent and partly because of his consideration for Rokycana. On the whole, he confined himself to reading out quotations from authorities supporting his thesis, and only once, in passing, he mentioned the names of Hus and Wyclif. It was in answer to the chairman who, wishing to destroy the unity of the delegation, had produced a list of quotations from Wyclif and challenged the Hussites to declare whether they held these extreme views. The Hussites refused to commit themselves at this stage but Payne, probably when questioned by a listener, responded that in England he had been pressed to abjure Wyclif's views but that the king had absolved him from that. He added that he had not known Hus but had heard him praised and found no heresy in his writings. This was a prelude to a concentrated attack on Payne which was to reach its peak with the arrival of the English delegation.

On 31 January, the Council got the long-awaited chance to respond to the Hussite criticism and attacks. The first speaker, Stojkovic, a Croatian Dominican, was Cesarini's special advisor on conditions in Bohemia with exceptional knowledge of Hussite writings. He worked himself into a fury against the hated Hussites, so much so that Rokycana, Prokop and William Kostka stopped coming to the meetings at which he spoke. On 7 February, Prokop said that he would not have come at all if he had foreseen these ends. Both Cesarini and Archbishop Talaru tried to calm the storm but Cesarini shielded his protege and let him go on for another four days, after which the three remaining speakers refrained from using insulting language.[23]

As the Council's replies were drawing to a close, the question arose what the Hussites would do. The Council knew about the doctrinal differences among the Hussite parties, and the attitude to Wyclif was a touchstone of orthodoxy. Cesarini tried again to sound the Czech delegates on the subject but they refused to be drawn into such a debate and declared that they had been sent to Basel to defend the Four Articles and would prefer to answer the points from the doctor's speech which they were bound in honor to do. Their prolonged stay in Basel admirably suited the Council's purpose. While the Hussite wars were still being fought, important military leaders such as Louda, Kostka, Jíra of Řečice and above all, Prokop Holý, were being kept from their country. Also, the Council was still waiting for the promised arrival of King Sigismund.

On 2 March, the Hussites had the opportunity to speak again, this time almost without disturbances. The protest against the violation by the Council of the Cheb agreements and Prokop's remark on 7 February, not to mention the impact of a recent insolent attack on Rokycana by a bishop had not been lost on the Council. Even Stojkovic was more subdued when Rokycana reacted to his invective and advocated communion for children and enlarged upon the Hussite concept of the Church, referring to the revolutionary writing, *Defensor Pacis,* by Marsilius of Padua.[24] The second appearance of Nicholas, the bishop of Tabor, started more peacefully. He was only interrupted by his official opponent, Giles Charlier, nephew of the famous chancellor, John Gerson. Charlier had already clashed with the Hussites at Bratislava in 1429[25] and had written two tracts in preparation for another encounter with them. He was probably piqued by Nicholas' condemnation of capital punishment, having been implicated in the trial of Joan of Arc. Nicholas[26] brushed aside Charlier's references to ecclesiastical authorities and the Old Testament, declaring that only the New Testament was binding on a true Christian. Supporting his argument by quoting from the Holy Fathers, he said, on the question of executing criminals, that the principles of the Old Testament and human laws were contrary to the Gospels.

He particularly protested against executions of thieves which the Hussite priests were successfully opposing in Prague. He was equally uncompromising on prostitution.[27] Some years later, in his "Net of Faith," Peter Chelčický heartily agreed with Biskupec and thundered against Charlier's views on prostitution and the death penalty. Again, Nicholas rejected Charlier's great authorities, Thomas Aquinas and Augustine. "Christianity must not be content with a rotten compromise with the world," he said, "but must strive to change it according to God's laws." From historical evidence Nicholas supported what he had said before, that in its first three centuries the Church and its servants were subjected to the State. For Rokycana's sake, Nicholas tried to moderate his statements and for the sake of moderation did not mention Hus' name even when he was quoting from him. In the end, however, he could not restrain himself and said that Hus and Jerome had been wrongly executed and that the Hussites would never accept that their deaths were justified. The ensuing uproar did not stop until the meeting was broken up although the presidium did its part in trying to placate the Hussites.

The respondent to the next speaker, Ulrich of Znojmo, was Henry Kalteisen,[28] a German theologian from the University of Cologne. As an inquisitor, he was versed in dealing with heretics and familiar with the Hussite tenets. In 1430 he had written a tract against them for a disputation which in the end did not take place. In spite of his zeal and academic rank which later earned him the archbishopric of Trondheim, his performance at Basel was disappointing. No doubt, he gave an impeccable account of the teachings of the Church on all controversial questions, but Ulrich of Znojmo demolished his arguments step by step, even though he had to deal with details in which controversial issues were sometimes lost. But it was exactly what stimulated the listeners' curiosity. Kalteisen hotly argued that even an unworthy pope should be obeyed; accused the Hussites of rejecting the Holy Fathers and ecclesiastical doctors; insisted that only priests had the right to preach, and the rest of the clergy only when authorized by a priest or a bishop. Ulrich reminded Kalteisen of the deposed John XXIII and of the fact that the Council of Basel was sitting in defiance of the pope's orders; that the Hussites rejected only those fathers and doctors who were in conflict with the Bible, and that the Bible was the basis which the Council's representatives had accepted at Cheb; and pointed out that recent doctors, such as Thomas Aquinas or

Thomas Netter could not agree on immaculate conception, and had embroiled the Franciscan and Dominican doctors in the dispute. He then asked, who had preached before priests existed. Quoting the holy father, Jerome, Ulrich deduced that episcopalism was the outcome of a period of decadence of the Church and that ecclesiastical hierarchy was a mere copy of a pagan model. So far, Ulrich's performance was strictly academic and gentle. But when Kalteisen interposed, rather foolishly, a casual remark that if Emperor Constantine had surprised a priest in sexual intercourse, he would have covered him up out of respect for his office, Ulrich replied: "With us I am afraid, the priest might have lost his male organ!" The incident which caused laughter in the assembly undoubtedly made Aeneas Silvius generalize in his *Historia Bohemia,* that this was the custom of the Orphans. Ulrich disposed equally well of Kalteisen's assertion that Hus had been sentenced for his heresy, not for his virtues or opposition to simony, as Charlier had supposedly proved. Ulrich produced the solemn protestation which John Hus had prepared for the Council of Constance but had not been allowed to deliver. While Ulrich was reading out the relevant passages nobody in the audience dared raise his voice.

The last Hussite speaker, Peter Payne, was matched against Juan Palomar.[29] As the star performer of the trial disputation of 1432, in which Cesarini had keenly participated, Palomar had written two tracts against the expropriation of Church property, the highly inflammatory article of the Hussite program which had been widely disseminated by the manifestos and regarded by the Church as the quintessence of heresy, cutting at the very roots of the power of the Church.

Palomar felt sure that he could force Payne to come out of his shell by criticizing his January speech. To his unpleasant surprise, Payne at first restricted himself to providing evidence that the priests of the primitive Church had lived in poverty. The auditor, as Palomar was called, thought that his opponent was hedging because he feared that he could not match him in debate. In point of fact, Payne did not wish to embarrass Rokycana who had never been a keen advocate of expropriation, bearing in mind the position of most university masters whom the confiscation of property might have driven into the opposite camp. Then Palomar came to his aid by associating Wyclif and Hus. The English Wyclifite eagerly seized the chance to show his loyalty to the evangelical doctor and quote from his writings. Again he had to speak with the self-restraint that he had acquired in Bohemia, his adopted home, and to consult Rokycana who allowed him to quote from Hus' university decree of 1412 whithout naming the author. Payne[30] was thus quoting Hus' defence of Wyclif to his countrymen who had been sending his coreligionists to their deaths. At this point, the skirmish with Palomar gave Payne the opportunity of showing his mastery of repartee and trenchant comment which made the audience laugh and reminded some of his fellow delegates of Master Jerome before the tribunal of Constance.

Within a week the indignant English delegates tried to deprive him of the immunity he enjoyed as a member of the Hussite delegation.[31] They claimed that the excommunication which had been pronounced on him in England was still valid and that according to English law he was a traitor, implicated in the assassination attempt on the King of England in connection with the revolt of Lord Cobham, to which several members of the Council testified. The Czech messengers took him resolutely under their protection. William Kostka reminded the Council how kindly an English diplomat had spoken to Payne at Bratislava, and Rokycana testified to his upright character. The accusations were referred to the Bohemian diet and that was the end of the incident which aroused a great deal of attention. Prokop Holý's clerk, who recorded the incident was surprised to find that the English could tell lies, very much unlike "our magister" as he called Payne.

After 1 April, when Payne ended his speech, the disputes of the theologians went on for another six days. The conciliar speakers had the last word while the Hussite delegates occasionally objected, embittered and wondering uneasily whether they had been deceived.[32]

The outcome of the discussions showed that the Hussite speeches had been of no avail. The Council usurped the supreme authority, yet it could not afford to let the negotiations break down. The return of the Hussites to the Church and the prospect of peace in Bohemia furnished it with the most effective weapon in the struggle against the pope. King Sigismund's prospects in Italy[33] were now very promising, but a conciliar agreement with the Hussites was essential to his return to Bohemia. He urged his deputy, Duke William, to do his utmost and tried even direct negotiations with the Hussite delegates who of course had no powers to speed up his journey to Prague for crowning.[34] The protector of the Council was also under pressure from the German princes who had no truce agreements with the Hussites and feared the consequences. When the Czechs applied for a safe conduct home there was general consternation at the Council. On 6 March Duke William produced a solution which was probably inspired by the cardinal's entourage, that the Czechs should be persuaded to cancel their application and give up the results of the Cheb agreements. The prime mover in the matter was Nicholas Cusa,[35] a doctor of canonical law and an ex-pupil of Cesarini who had recommended him to the protector as an interpreter and secretary. He had arrived in Basel at the beginning of 1432 and started a brilliant career by writing his famous book, *De Concordantia Catholica*, dedicated to Sigismund and Cesarini. On Cusa's initiative a select committee of sixteen members of the Council and fifteen Hussites were set up.[36]

Its work began on 11 March with a prayer. Cesarini made a moving speech, after which he disclosed that the Czechs were invited to join the Church and thus church unity would be achieved. In other words the Czechs were to lose their only real gain, the agreements of Cheb which put the Bible above the Council. The Czechs demanded the text of the proposal, and after it had been read out by Cusa, they put a stop to the negotiations. The committee of sixteen survived merely as a body of experts on Hussite affairs.

Aggrieved by the failure of the action whose causes he did not quite comprehend, Duke William arranged, on 19 March, for another committee to be set up, consisting of four members on each side. In the Czech group were three laymen and Prokop Holý. After a week of confidential talks whose contents has not survived, the Council authorized a delegation of its own to go to Prague and try to have its proposal accepted by the Bohemian diet.[37] The committee on Hussite affairs worked out appropriate instructions. The deadlock was broken although the Czechs could not help feeling that they were forfeiting their costliest achievements while the Council was gaining unfair advantage. The scheme to seize upon the weak points and divisions within the Hussite movement and exploit them to the utmost had long been worked out. The Hussites consistently resisted the urgent request that at least their theologians should stay a little longer and the parting date was fixed for 13 April, Easter Monday.

All went according to international etiquette.[38] Rokycana expressed the delegates' thanks to the Council and to the city of Basel. William

Kostka delivered a political declaration in favor of the King of Poland in his conflict with the Teutonic Knights and asked the Council not to believe the accusers of Poland which was not represented at the Council. A spokesman for the Order promptly asked the Czech delegates to explain themselves. Prokop answered that the Bohemian diet had been requested by Poland to mediate in the conflict with Lithuania. He then asked to be allowed to speak for himself because so far he had not had a chance. He refuted the charge that he had been killing people in war, and then urged the Council to carry out church reform in the spirit of the Four Articles of Prague and of the New Testament Church. He did not hesitate to defend the Waldensians who had caused uproar in France and elsewhere by collecting money for the Hussites in 1432.[39] The cardinal made another futile appeal to the Hussites to stay and wait for King Sigismund and then delivered the fairwell speech on the biblical topic of the day, likening the Hussites to the disciples going to Emmaus and made no scruples to say that Jesus appeared to them when the Council was speaking. He thanked Rokycana affably and Prokop courteously, referring to his appeal for reforms with the usual circumlocution. He dismissed the messengers with the benediction and offered to shake hands which a few delegates avoided.

They were taking home good wishes from several quarters. An unsigned Franciscan monk wrote to them that he wished at least Rokycana and Payne had been able to stay to enforce the article concerning poverty of the clergy, which was dearer to him than the Czechs. Referring to their lavish returns of hospitality, he criticized their way of life and recommended that they should live in absolute poverty at least for a time. The sender was very probably the eminent French preacher, Guillaume Josseaume who had long been imprisoned at Constance and persecuted by Michael de Causis, the notorious advocate at the time of Hus' trial, and by various inquisitors. Rokycana had a fine letter from an anonymous Council member who regretted that the Council had not accepted Rokycana's argument in favor of the chalice, and spurred him on to further effort by subscribing to the motto "Truth prevails." A German theologian called Rokycana the Czech Achilles because of the eloquence and readiness to defend the chalice.[40] The heartening tributes from his opponents could indeed fortify Rokycana for the remaining thirty-eight years of his fruitful life. After Basel, Prague was his next battlefied.

CHAPTER EIGHT

BETWEEN BASEL AND PRAGUE

On 14 April 1433 the Hussite messengers left Basel and were joined by ten delegates the Council was sending to Prague.[1] They were Henry Toke, the provost Parsperger and John of Maulbronn who had all attended the Cheb meetings; Charlier and Palomar chosen for their vigor; Bishop Philibert of Coutance and Peter of Schaumburg, the bishop of Augsburg, whose function was mainly representative; Thomas Ebendorfer from Vienna, Martin Berruer, the dean of Tours, and Archdeacon Alexander Sparrow of Oxford. The five first-named were charged with the chief responsibility for the mission and Palomar soon assumed the leading position. The instruction from the committee for Hussite affairs merely outlined the extent of their powers. The main purpose of their presence in Prague had been privately worked out with the cardinal. It was, in the words of a well-informed Council member, "to sow among the Czechs the seed of blissful war and disrupt the baleful peace in which they had been living."[2]

The two delegations made a stop at Nürnberg where the delegates from Basel spent four days in consultations with the city council. Elector Frederick had his political friends. The Hussites reluctantly allowed more delegates to join them. These represented the elector, the count-palatine John, the bishop of Bamberg, and even Amadeo, the Duke of Savoy,[3] the future Pope Felix V. The messengers of the German lands welcomed the chance

99

to renew the truce agreements in Prague which were due to expire when the Hussites returned home. The delegates from Basel wished to appear as peacemakers and avail themselves of their associates' knowledge of the situation in Bohemia. The next stop was Cheb, where more delegates were added. Jakoubek of Vřesovice provided the escort from Žlutice to Prague where the delegations arrived on 8 May. The festive welcomes they received on the way were not so much meant for the foreign delegates as for the returning Hussites, disillusioned and embittered as they were.

The Basel diplomats were a month too early for the diet which was to begin in June. Using an interpreter from Cheb, they passed the time paying and receiving courtesy calls at the university and both town halls,[4] and gaining safe conducts not only for German princes, but also for Czech royalist lords under the pretext that Prokop Holý's veto of a general truce made them necessary. The diplomats also did their best to secure access to the Bohemian diet for the foreign envoys in order to coordinate with them the strategy against the brotherhood armies, the main obstacle to the kind of peace the Council wished to attain. The lodgings of the delegates became hotbeds of espionage which was conducted with almost incredible crudity, if not shamelessness. Jacob Vlk voiced a sharp protest on behalf of the population of the New Town in his sermons and continued to do so disregarding the prohibition which the New Town council issued under pressure from the Basel visitors.

The diet opened on 12 June at the Carolinum, with Rokycana in the chair and Peter Payne and Nicholas Biskupec on either side. *Veni Sancte Spiritus* was sung and then Rokycana welcomed the Basel delegates giving an account of the activities of the Hussite messengers at the Council. Bishop Philbert and Palomar delivered brief formal addresses but made no concrete peace proposals.[5] It was not until two days later that Palomar disclosed what turned out to be Cesarini's original suggestion that the Hussites should submit to the Council by giving up what they had achieved at Cheb and for which they had gone to Basel to fight. This sounded almost like mockery. The Council was putting before the diet something that the Hussite delegates had already rejected, as if expecting it to repudiate what its select members had done on its behalf. The diet appointed sixty members to work out an answer and they, in turn, empowered Rokycana and Prokop to show the Council that they identified themselves with the stand their messengers had taken in Basel. On 18 June, Rokycana explained with the utmost courtesy that the proposal was utterly unacceptable. Prokop dealt only with the responsibility for the wars against the Hussites. It is the only preserved speech of the great statesman and the last one he delivered on an international forum.

"The God who knows all things, knows that it was your party that started the war and ravaged the kingdom with fire and sword. We, with the help of God, have risen against the unjustified violence and up to now have had to defend ourselves. These wars, cruel as they were, produced many a spiritual gain and will produce others as we believe. Many obdurate enemies of the sacred Four Articles have in the end, through word and deed affirmed their faith in them and become their voluntary defenders unto their deaths. And a great multitude of the faithful, guarded by these salutary truths, have been saved by these wars from the fury of enemies. Otherwise they would have become frightened of the terror and forced to abjure these truths, or even fight against them and sin against the Holy Ghost, the greatest teacher of truth. And it was this war that has led to the convocation of the Council of Basel and to a fair and open hearing for us. That these truths which bring salvation to all the faithful have come to the knowledge of so many people, we accept as a special gift from God. And we fear, these wars will not cease unless the Church accepts these truths in good faith. We can assure you that we condemn the abuses of war, that we deplore them from the depths of our hearts and that our ruling bodies prosecute them. We truly bear the burden of the war only in order to bring about the recognition of these holy truths by the Church of God, and to live and see the blessing of peace and good days from which unity, brotherly love, moral reform and everything else will come to the Church, with God's help."[6]

Palomar was not yet ready to give in and responded with a militant speech which provoked a sharp protest from Prokop, Rokycana and Biskupec. Realizing that he had gone too far, Palomar stopped and changed the subject suggesting that the Council delegates be given the wording of the Articles on which all Hussite parties agreed, and that the diet committee should be reduced to a third. To his intense annoyance, two-thirds of the new committee were members of the brotherhoods and included Prokop, Louda, Ambrose, Kostka and Simon of the White Lion, not to mention the four theologians who had spoken at Basel. On 23 July, he

complained to the plenum about the attitude of its committee and provoked a clash with Rokycana and Prokop which Henry Toke tried to
pacify.[7] On the morrow, five members of the diet committee called on
Peter, the Bishop of Augsburg, and demanded emphatically that the
negotiations should not return to what had been finally settled at Basel,
but move from there and reach some conclusions. The Council delegation
had to admit that some concession was necessary to prevent a breakdown. This time, the moderates such as Toke got the upper hand over the
implacables, such as Ebendorfer.

The Basel messengers felt an obligation to the extreme right-wing Hussite lords, hence they were the first to hear of their momentous decision
to compromise. A few of them were called to a meeting in the Týn parish
and told that the Council might grant communion in both kinds if the
Hussites submitted to the Church on all other points.[8] This was an eventu-
ality Cesarini and his circle had already considered and one which Duke
William advocated. The difficulty was that the matter should have been
fought out in the plenum of the Council with those who opposed any
concession whatsoever, especially the Germans. Under the circumstances,
the recourse to the Council had to be abandoned because the Bohemian
diet might disperse, in which case the Basel delegates would not have been
able to prevent the collapse of the negotiations. After these deliberations,
the committee and then the plenum of the diet were informed of the
compromise. This removed the impasse but the Hussites remained sus-
picious. Even at this time, Palomar behaved with his habitual impetuosity and worked hard on the barons, hoping to sway them into direct
action against the brotherhoods. When the lords, on 1 July, announced
to the delegates that they had to go with the brotherhoods, not against
them,[9] the delegation had to acquiesce to the diet's decision to send three
messengers to Basel with powers to sign a peace treaty on condition that
it meet the diet's demands summed up in a precisely worded statement.
As the Basel diplomats could participate in the preparatory work of the
diet, they could surmise what the document would contain but they were
kept in the dark as to its final shape, probably in return for being so
secretive in their own negotiations. This they did not mind very much,
as long as they could hope to return to Prague to accomplish their real
mission, the destruction of the brotherhood armies.

On 3 July the diet broke up, but the men from Basel overstayed their official welcome by a week, profiting from the hospitality of the city and gaining confidants among malcontents who wished for the return of the good old days. Some influential people, certain Hussite and royalist nobles and university masters,[10] called spontaneously on the delegates. John Smiřický who, six years earlier, had promised to seize Prague for the Elector Frederick, again offered his services. The delegates found the man who would coordinate and lead the forces of reaction. It was the Czech magnate, Menhart of Hradec who had been in secret agreement with the Council and had therefore not gone to Basel at the end of 1433 although he had been delegated by the diet of Kutná Hora. He had paid the delegates a visit as a member of the diet, on the eve of the opening session, to invite them to a banquet, and called on them again on 7 July to say farewell and to coordinate the plans which were to lead to the destruction of the field armies. Perhaps he also named the traitor from the Taborite ranks.

The diet which had just dispersed, attained historical importance not only for its negotiations with the Council, but also for the fateful military decision which was probably made by Přibík of Klenové, the Taborite captain of Stříbro, who wanted to create the appearance of innocence while plotting treason. His position in the Hussite council of war was shaken because he had failed to go to Basel. Now he proposed, with considerable eloquence,[11] that the campaigning armies should strike at the leading town of the powerful royalist alliance, Plzeň, which had become bloated with pride after having three times thwarted Hussite sieges and refused to buy a truce. Přibík's proposal was passed despite the misgivings of seasoned Hussite warriors, because there was nothing better to suggest. The large number of truce agreements with those willing to pay for them, left only Austria and Slovakia open. While Prokop Holý was at Basel, near the end of February, the Taborites, under John Pardus and Frederick of Strážnice, had gone first to Austria.[12] Having met very strong resistance there, they turned to Raciborz in Silesia and gathered a large booty which they sent to Moravia. The main army was heading for Slovakia via Poland. The Poles needed their Czech allies against the Teutonic Knights and so reluctantly granted them passage. The field armies went on through Slovakia with such vehemence that it paralyzed the country's defence. The Hussites took Kežmarok almost without fighting. Having given up Kremnica which was too well fortified, they returned via Turiec valley and Trenčín, and reached Prague just before the diet opened. All this happened under favorable but unstable political conditions and another such campaign to Slovakia could not be contemplated. This silenced the objections to a new siege of Plzeň. Přibík knew that it would be the beginning of the end of the field armies. The siege began on 13 July, after Plzeň finished what was an early harvest.[13]

The siege had been planned as a joint enterprise of the Taborites, Orphans and the Prague alliance. For a long time, the Taborites fought alone. The Orphans had left Bohemia towards the end of April to fulfill the obligation of the Treaty of Pabianice which the diet of Kutná Hora had ratified in September 1432.[14] Led by Čapek of Sány, they went to Poland where they received fine equipment and a cavalry escort led by Peter Sziafraniec, the old and loyal supporter of the Czech-Polish alliance. The allies took twelve towns in the New Mark and advanced towards Prussia, receiving more reinforcements from Poland and the Pomeranian duke, Bohuslav. Their progress was halted outside Chojnice, the great fortress of the Teutonic Order, which they could not encircle even though the main Polish army had in the meantime arrived. After six weeks, at the beginning of August, they raised the siege and turned east burning down the Pelplin monastery, and then moved north towards Gdansk, another very strong base of the Order. The well-fortified Tczew guarded access to it. Surprisingly, Tczew fell at a stroke on 29 August, yielding rich spoils and many prisoners of war. Čapek asked for the extradition of the Czech captives and had them burnt alive as traitors to the Czech nation, apparently thinking that they discredited him in the eyes of the Polish allies. Gdansk was shelled for four days from the top of a nearby hill but the lack of heavy artillery forced the allies to cease fire and plunder the surroundings, attempting to enforce a truce agreement. But Gdansk, possibly having found out that the formidable Orphans were wanted at home, refused.

Before leaving, however, the Czechs held a valedictory celebration on 4 September. A number of warriors, Čapek among them, were dubbed knights, following the custom of the Teutonic Knights who used to confer distinctions on their foreign allies after successful wars. The Czechs organized equestrian games and jousting in the shallow waters of the Baltic where they had the first glimpse of the sea.[15] The campaign had been a success and ended in a peace treaty due to expire in eighteen years. The Hussites received the agreed upon payment and the king of Poland lavished presents on their leader. Everybody was going home in high spirits. Nobody thought then that it was the last Hussite campaign.

In September, the same month in which the most celebrated Hussite campaign reached its climax at the Baltic, the revolution at home suffered a tragic blow by the fall of its greatest statesman, Prokop Holy. Over a period of time, his political activities had been running into difficulties. They demanded great sacrifice from the Taborites who had thought from the beginning that his journey to Basel was a grave mistake and that it had turned out to be a considerable material loss. It stopped their raids into southern Germany and, after the Hussites' stay in Basel, resulted in a truce for which the enemy paid nothing. The outcome of the June diet proved a failure, and all that the Council delegation had to offer, and with reservations at that, was so meagre that it sounded to the Taborites like sheer mockery. The propaganda and espionage against the campaigning armies made them furious and when it turned out that not one of the numerous German diplomats[16] who had come to Prague with Prokop's consent signed a truce, it became clear how much things had changed since the year of the Glorious Campaign (1430) when all the neighbors of Bohemia were trembling with fear and paying heavily for their safety. Prokop lost considerable prestige in people's estimation. In fact, at the June diet, an unknown nobleman demanded of him, rather brusquely, that he return the Church property which he had, like the other delegates to Basel, accepted to defray the cost of the journey.[17] These were the circumstances when he returned, after a year's separation, to his brethren. One way to regain their respect was by hard work on the battlefield. Unfortunately the time was short and the task before him brought him ruin instead.

The siege of Plzeň did not go well.[18] At the beginning, the Taborites fought a lone battle, receiving detachments from the towns of the Tabor and the Žatec associations. Prokop brought more men in mid-August. On 1 September, the Plzeň garrison carried out a highly successful nocturnal sorties against the besiegers. The relief force from Prague arrived just after that event. Plzeň was receiving help from various quarters: the *Landfríd* had by then become a virtually independent state within a state, fashioned after the German urban republics[19] with the full backing of the Council which identified Plzeň's interests with its own. On their way from Prague in July, the delegates arranged a loan to be sent from Nürnberg to Plzeň for the purchase of victuals. Since the beginning of January, the town had had an inconspicuous envoy at Basel, the Franciscan monk, Nicholas,[20] who had undoubtedly heard the disputations before he returned home. On 18 September, he was back in Basel bringing with him two burghers as eye-witnesses to the siege. He gave the Council a glowing account of the herosim of the defenders and details of the sortie, volunteering the tale that the Hussites had sworn to fight to the bitter end. The effect was a large collection of money and appeal for donations.

Shortage of food forced the Hussites to send a provisioning expedition to Bavaria which was virtually at war with them by its overt support of Plzeň. The raid under the Taborite commander, John Pardus of Horka and the Domažlice captain Řitka of Bezdědice penetrated fairly deep into the Upper Palatine. On their return, they were waylaid at Hiltersried near Waldmünchen and crushed by Hyncík Pflug, a Czech by birth. They lost the booty, all the wagons and well over a thousand men. A small number of horse and foot soldiers cut their way free.[21]

Even more catastrophic than this fiasco was its sequel of which details will probably remain obscure forever. Pardus had been blamed for the defeat at Hiltersried. Although he and Řitka had escaped from captivity they faced trial at home. At this time the captains rose in revolt against Prokop Holý. He was criticized for having replaced Otík of Loza with Pardus. There was a scuffle in which Prokop was wounded and then put in prison by Captain Tvaroh, his successor. He was soon released but he left the army.[22] The damage was irreparable. The only man who could guide the brotherhood and the whole Hussite camp unscathed through the critical transition from war to peace, was stripped of power. He was a Taborite without a trace of fanaticism who knew how to deal with extremists and handle disputes between the Hussite priests.[23] Officially, he was the leader of the extreme left but he acted, like Žižka, as a man of the center, experienced and tolerant, placing the common welfare above that of the individual parties. More than at any other time the revolution needed him. In spite of his fall as the commander he stayed with his brotherhood and was soon sent to the diet, the other battleground of the great struggle where he was to meet his adversaries returning from Basel well pleased with the havoc they had helped to create.

Having gained sufficient insight into conditions in Bohemia and secured support from certain Hussite nobles and university masters, such as Příbram and Prokop of Plzeň,[24] the Basel diplomats found it easy to come up with a clear-cut program. They would make a concession which would satisfy the moderate or conservative Hussites; they would grant the laity the right to the chalice. Once the Council of Basel had granted the chalice, the Prague association would close the ranks with the Catholic and Hussite nobles and crush the rule of Prokop Holý and the field armies on their native soil. With some money from the Council, these Czech allies would succeed where the crusades had failed.

The Council messengers were aware that unless they conceded in the matter of the chalice they could not win over the Prague association and another journey to Prague would then be fruitless. However deeply divided the Hussites may have been at times, the chalice had become the unifying force of all shades of opinion. As the symbol of their faith, it was more easily understood by everybody than the learned theological formulae at the time of Hus' trial. Because the chalice was a sign of revolt, the Church since Constance had solemnly condemned it and stubbornly resisted any concession as an encroachment on its supreme authority.

This put the Council of Basel in a very difficult position. Rokycana's reasoned argument that the chalice for the laity had been common practice until two hundred years before, was about as useless as trying to squeeze blood out of a stone. Between outbursts of ugly temper and polite reserve, the Council remained adamant. Its German members in particular regarded any concession to the Czechs as an insult to their national honor; the university of Vienna ordered its delegates to walk out rather than relent in the matter of the chalice.[25]

The Council heard the reports of Philibert of Coutance, Palomar and Henry Toke, after which, on 11 August, the Hussite delegates were admitted to the assembly. Prokop of Plzeň said that the chalice had been revealed to the Hussites, and stressed that their wars were fought out of the necessity to defend it. He urged the Council to carry out a strict reform of the Church and to lend a favorable ear to the Hussite requests, whereby it would earn the gratitude of all peace-seeking peoples, especially the Germans. After him spoke Martin Lupáč, a priest of the Prague association, who was generally believed to be an Orphan owing to his forthright views.[26] His performance at the Counil was seen to be harsh as long as he criticized the way its delegates had been conducting themselves in Prague, or as long as he avowed his unflagging devotion to the chalice and to the memory of Hus and Jerome (whose commemoration the Basel delegates had witnessed in Prague). His assurance at the end, that the Hussites sincerely longed for peace and harmony with the Church, mitigated the initial unfavorable impression he made.

Next day, the plenary session elected a committee of eight men, all from the Romance language countries, with the apparent intention of excluding the Germans. These immediately protested, after which the committee was declared open to anyone who wished to join. The total now rose to the unwieldy number of fifty which Cesarini, Palomar and Nicholas of Cusa managed to keep under control with difficulty.[27] The Germans were passionately opposed to any compromise until they received assurances from Palomar and Cusa that the concession would be temporary and liable to cancellation in altered circumstances.

The heated discussion on the subject started on 13 August and continued for three weeks. The talks were conducted behind closed doors. Palomar converted quite a few members of the committee through an exhaustive analysis of the Bohemian situation and through his conclusion that the granting of the chalice would throw the tripartite Hussite camp into confusion and result in internecine war. Duke William and the representatives of the Elector Frederick, the Count Palatine John and the city of Nürnberg then joined the assembly. Conrad of Soest, the bishop of Regensburg, urged the Council to work for peace with the Hussites. John of Lübek, a sincere advocate of Church reform and Sigismund's confidant, seconded this appeal on behalf of the Council. This voice from Bohemia's neighbors, supported by the Emperor, could not have been more welcome to Palomar; Sigismund had been crowned Roman Emperor on 31 May. When the theologians decided, after long and probing deliberations, that it was permissible to grant the chalice to the Czechs,[28] and to them alone, the final solution was referred to a confidential meeting of 160 doctors and hand-picked prelates for fear that information might leak to Constance where a papal delegation was staying. On 26 August, Palomar stressed again that only the dictatorship of the field armies stood in the way of the Hussites' absolute submission, and announced the theologians' findings that the Council of Constance had not banned the chalice in principle but condemned its arbitrary introduction by the Hussites as a revolt against the authority of the Church. What the Church had prohibited in 1415 for the stated reason, it could permit now on the strength of its supreme authority and sanctify what would be criminal heresy if turned against the Church. Palomar ended up with the following characterization of the Czechs: It is an untamed but thoroughbred nation, which must be handled like a horse or mule of similar temperament, very calmly, and kindly, until the bridle is over the head and it can be tied up in the stable. After Cesarini's speech to the same effect, yet another committee was set up with the inclusion of members of the "German" or central European curia to scrutinize all the major problems which were then summed up by Cesarini as instructions to the future delegates to Prague. In the final stage, the celebrated Nicholas of Cusa, who was then a lawyer by profession, went one better than Palomar. He introduced a clause reducing the freedom of the chalice in a way to which any German could have subscribed: it was to be available only to those who would submit to the Church by accepting all its other rites.[29] This meant that the Taborites and Orphans would reject the clause and internecine war in Bohemia was a certainty. This silenced all objectors.

On 2 September the Czechs were summoned to the assembly and told that Bishop Philibert, Palomar and Toke and Martin Berruer had been chosen to carry the Council's answer to Prague.[30] Although they had not been informed of the contents of the answer, the Czechs must have gathered that their demands had been rejected. They were so disconcerted that even the moderate, Prokop of Plzeň found it hard to adapt his prepared farewell address to the new circumstances. On 11 September, both delegations left Basel and did not reach Prague until 22 October, the intervening time being spent in consultations at Nürnberg, and then at Cheb were safe conduct passage through the Hussite territories had to be negotiated. The messengers from Basel were delighted to hear of the disastrous end of the Taborite raid into Germany and the fall of Prokop Holý. They hastened to report to Basel that the Hussite parties were on the verge of mutual destruction.

This rosy assessment was somewhat exaggerated but not far from wrong. The siege of Plzeň went on and the Orphans, back from the Baltic, arrived in the middle of October. The overbearing Čapek, puffed up with success, soon caused trouble among his fellow commanders and the campaigning armies were becoming increasingly unpopular because they had to requisition food and engage in hazardous guerrilla warfare. Rising prices, disease and wide-spread fear of the plague, a name for any epidemic, multiplied their problems.[32]

In these circumstances, the diet met as late as November and the reactionaries took advantage of the turmoil. After a meeting with the diplomats from Basel, the Czech aristocracy, led by Menhart of Hradec, which functioned, then as before the revolution, as an indepedent estate, usurped the leading position at the diet. Following the political line of the diet of Čáslav (1421), it proposed the election of a regent and his council. This was a recurring and so far unrealized idea because it was difficult to find a man acceptable to all three Hussite parties. Now it appeared that Aleš Vřešt'ovský of Riesenburg possessed the specified qualities. He had been a joint founder, with John Žižka, of the Orebite, later Orphan brotherhood, and was a capable soldier as well as political leader. In 1434 he had been elected the chairman of the arbitration committee of twelve and had gradually acquired more power than he was, strictly speaking, entitled to. In any case he was elected, on 1 December, and his council was partly chosen from the old committee of twelve with the nobles occupying at least a third of its seats.[33]

The nervous atmosphere in which the diet worked suited the diplomats from Basel. Again they had a month to spare in which to forge plans with the Catholic and Hussite lords. When their spokesmen told the diet, on 21 November, that the Council had granted the freedom of the chalice as long as the Hussites promised submission and obedience to the Church in every other respect, there was an outburst of grateful acclamation. After the long and protracted negotiations, peace suddenly appeared within reach, peace with so many blessings which the sorely tired country had not known for years. The delegates from Basel struck while the iron was hot and pressed for a speedy signing of the treaty. Only the lords and the conservative masters accepted the Council's terms without reservation. The rest of the parties were beginning to suspect a hidden trap under the undue haste and polished manners. In the end the leadership of the diet gave way and put pressure on the Taborite, Orphan and Prague priests so that on 30 November, they assented and shook hands over the Council diplomats' draft of the agreement as amended to take account of the various wishes expressed by the clergy.[34]

When the delegates came forward with their precise demands like the immediate signing of the general truce, a termination of the siege of Plzeň and disbandment of the field armies, the Hussites at once sobered down. With pain and bitterness they had given up the dream that the Council might be persuaded to reintroduce the chalice in the whole Christian realm. Now they realized that after all their sacrifice, Bohemia would have a strong Catholic minority whioh would take the offensive after Sigismund's accession to the throne. What the Council was demanding was complete disarmament and abject surrender.

This realization rallied all Hussite parties except the defeatist masters.[35] After a short adjournment, at the beginning of January 1434, the diet unanimously demanded that the chalice should be made binding on the whole of Bohemia before the treaty was signed, claiming rightly that a permanent division of Bohemia into Catholic and Hussite areas would destroy the unity of the state. This fell on deaf ears. The Council rejected the diet's demand as contravening the November agreement and reluctantly allowed one Czech delegate to go to Basel to present the diet's request. The Council was adamant and insisted on a cessation of hostilities which meant disarmament of the revolution, before agreeing to further negotiations.[36]

This was the end of two years' parleying with Basel. The Council was now utterly indifferent to peace in Bohemia. Its sole concern was to save Plzeň, the bastion of Catholicism, and to seize the unique chance of destroying the dangerous, hated brotherhoods.

CHAPTER NINE

LIPANY

It was obvious from the brusque ultimatum by which the Council broke off the negotiations that it was on the way to achieving what it had set itself to do. According to the frank admission of Matthew Döring, a member of the Council, the seed of blissful war had been sown and the baleful peace in which the Hussites had been living had been disrupted. It was left to the Czechs to begin warring among themselves and destroy the field armies. On 12 January, the Council heard the optimistic but out of date report of Martin Berruer who had left Prague on 20 December. It was thought then that Emperor Sigismund might go to Nürnberg, assemble his adherents as well as those who were satisifed with only granting the chalice, and persuade the latter to prevent bloodshed by returning to the Church which would automatically lead to the disintegration of the field armies and the lifting of the siege of Plzeň. Sigismund was then staying at Basel. When approached by Cesarini, he took fright, crossed himself and presented all sorts of excuses for not going to Nürnberg, claiming that he had already hired 1200 soldiers to engage the besiegers and enable Plzeň to get supplies. This was his usual idle talk.[1]

Soon after this bubble had been pricked the rest of the delegates returned from Prague on 12 February and reported the failure of their mission. The Council authorized immediate action and appointed Palomar as its leader. He took charge with true Spanish impetuosity and carried out the Council's instructions within three months. At the end of February

he set off with the Count Palatine, John and a load of ducats[2] provided
by the Council. He had more money than the Elector Frederick had had
at his disposal in 1431. It was enough to field quite an exceptional army.
For this particular purpose, Palomar wanted the Czechs rather than
Germans.

The Czech lords were already waiting for him at Kaube in Bavaria, close
to the Bohemian border, where war plans were discussed and money for
recruitment distributed The dangerous and most urgent task of taking
supplies to Plzeň was undertaken by a traitor. He was the Taborite captain,
Přibík of Klenové[3] who carried out the mission within days and made it
possible for Plzeň to hold out for another two months. All the final details of the campaign were however not worked out at Kaube.

Having provided for the safety of Plzeň, Palomar went on to Austria
to meet Duke Albrecht, the most implacable enemy of the Hussite revolution. The duke had exhausted his resources in previous wars and could
not be expected to contribute materially but was able to prevent Moravia
from aiding the field armies. The brotherhoods still held Třebíč, Moravský
Krumlov and Ivančice and had allies among the Moravian nobles.[4] Nevertheless, the Hussite aristocracy in Moravia could, like their Bohemian
counterparts, welcome the freedom of the chalice and at the same time
remain loyal to Albrecht, to whom resistance was pointless because he
had no rival.[5] As a soldier, the duke did not understand the intricacies
of the Council's secret diplomacy and was, like his university, ill-disposed
towards the chalice. But Palomar could cope with him. He found the duke
in council with the Moravian nobles, some swearing allegiance, others
signing truce agreements. Palomar had powers to receive expressions of
loyalty and, in return, grant amnesty on Sigismund's behalf. Palomar
departed for Regensburg about the beginning of April where he decided
to wait for the outcome. He knew that the avalanche which was to sweep
away the enemy was in motion.

The antagonism against the brotherhoods was as old as the brotherhoods themselves and periodically reemerged since the time of Žižka.
This was a manifestation of the fact that all social classes contributed to
the revolution. But Žižka's great achievement had made Hussitism so
secure that in recent times Prokop Holý and men of similar calibre were
able to bridge the sharp social divisions by cultivating a consciousness of
national solidarity. As a result the Basel diplomats almost had to resurrect

the old enmity.[6] Besides, Prokop had carried the war mostly to foreign countries while in some parts of Bohemia the brotherhoods had established peaceful, even friendly relations with the Catholics which protected the brotherhoods just as well as did their military prowess.

This spirit of tolerance had started to collapse since the beginning of the ill-starred siege of Plzeň in July 1433. Although the incorporation of the Plzeň territory was in the interest of Hussitism as well as national integration, the siege at that point of time taxed the country's resources to the utmost. War returned to Bohemia and the field armies, once so popular, became gradually the object of general hatred. They were blamed for everything: requisitions, famine, and disease. They were accused of having brought infection from Poland and the hostile propaganda called them the foreign rabble because of the sprinkling of Poles and Germans who had joined them from abroad.[7] The antagonism against the field armies was rapidly reemerging and driving the country towards reaction.

Emperor Sigismund to whom credit was due for starting the negotiations with Basel, now was claiming the gratitude of the Hussites, and was looking forward to reaping a reward. The wrongs he had done to the Hussites were being forgotten. More and more it became clear that he would be the future ruler. This was especially important to those who had appropriated some church property in the name of the revolution. Almost all the lords were personally involved. Since church possessions were then regarded as crown property, which only the sovereign could dispense, the lords were rushing to the royalist camp and Sigismund derived a great deal of malicious pleasure from the sight of certain Hussite nobles hastening to fight the brotherhoods.

The turmoil also pervaded the regent's council which, from the beginning had been the arena for both parties, and in the end Aleš Vřešt'ovský himself succumbed to the reaction. How it could have happened to a man with his past behavior can only be conjectured. He was scarcely very much better than other men of his class although he was to get only four villages out of the final settlement.[8] He may have felt threatened as Žižka's former fellow fighter and as an advocate of Czech-Polish friendship. The Orphan captains such as Beneš Mokrovouský, John of Rušinov and John Královec followed his example which seems to suggest that the leadership of the Orphan army had influential adversaries in the brotherhood itself. These may have become disillusioned in the brotherhoods because of their antagonism towards the domineering Čapek of Sány who had usurped the command of both field armies after the fall of Prokop Holý and was absolutely unfit to lead the siege of Plzeň when the struggle was a matter of life and death.[9]

At the end of April the siege was nearing its climax. The field armies were losing heavily to the town and to the *Landfríd* of Plzeň which had excellent warriors in the surrounding castles especially in Radyně, where the name of young John Jiskra of Brandýs appeared for the first time. The records of the various phases of fighting are scanty. We know that Captain Tvaroh was killed, two other captains were taken prisoner and Menhart of Hradec defeated the Hussites near Horažd'ovice and Benešo-ov.[10] Each defeat worked up passions. Plzeň was short of food and its fall seemed imminent, and it was precisely at this moment that Přibík of Klenové broke through the blockade for the second time, on 5 May, bringing supplies to the besieged town. Three days later, the Hussite camp learned that war against the field armies had broken out and that Prague was in the hands of the enemies.

The attack on Prague was the outcome of long deliberations among the lords which ended at the beginning of April after Palomar had become sure of the neutrality of Moravia. The Catholic and Hussite nobles signed a document of armed alliance which proclaimed a general truce and appealed to all other noblemen and to the towns for signatures. They threatened that dissenters would be treated as peace-breakers and public enemies, and promised amnesty to those who would submit. The document has not been preserved. Corroborative records suggest that it contained a solemn declaration that the signatories adhered to the resolutions of the January diet in matters of religion.[11]

Before the capture of Prague, the document had to be kept secret.[12] The Taborites and Orphans still represented considerable military might and the lifting of the siege of Plzeň, which would have immediately followed after the fall of Prague, posed a dilemma. To aid Catholic Plzeň would have compromised the Hussite nobles in the eyes of the Hussite community. Such help was on the other hand, a prerequisite for further financial aid from the Council. The nobles had to conquer only the New Town (Prague) as it had severed its ties with the Old Town in 1429 and was now in league with the Orphans. It promised very rich spoils, housing Čapek's large fortune augmented by the recent acquisitions from the campaign to the Baltic. At the time when the lords were preparing for war the field armies were concentrated in the west leaving the large Orphan domain in east Bohemian unprotected so that the lords could carry out mobilization in the area and rendezvous at Kačina near Kutná Hora swiftly and inconspicuously.

On 5 May their army suddenly appeared outside the gates of the Old Town and was promptly let in. On the next day, the New Town was stormed before it could recover from the shock and summon help. Its defenders were pushed to the town hall and forced to surrender after which they were allowed to depart without hindrance. The conquerors obviously felt uneasy about the sudden victory and made haste to seize Čapek's fortune as well as the funds of the Orphan brotherhood, deposited in the parsonage of St. Mary's *ad Nives.* Prokop Holý, who was at this late hour restored to the leadership of the Taborites, escaped, as did Čapek of Sány.

After consulting Čapek, Prokop wrote a letter to the priest Prokůpek who was in command of the Orphans and sent it to the latter's camp outside Plzeň. The letter gives a unique insight into the dramatic situation details of which are lost forever:[13] Our omnipotent Lord who calms the storm and comforts the aggrieved, be with you, brother in Christ, who are dear to me beyond others. Know that, by the dispensation of God, the false lords and the citizens of the Old Town have attacked our dearest friends, the citizens of New Town, slain some and seized the town as we have seen. We think therefore that you should leave everything, and move from Plzeň to Sedlčany. Čapek is gathering many men and so are we, the Taborites, as we hope that it is better to die than not to avenge the innocent blood of our dearest friends which had been treacherously spilled. Be strong in the lord, knowing that He comforts those whom he had punished." Prokop Holý.

The letter was intercepted by the enemy but its message reached the camp. Přibík of Klenové's treachery made the siege pointless and the Hussite army left on 9 May heading for Prague with the relief forces of the Taborites and Orphan towns. They reached the outskirts in two weeks but failed to wrest the city from the lords because the vacuum created by their departure from West Bohemia was already filled by powerful Catholic armed troops, especially those of Ulrich of Rožmberk and the *Landfrid* of Plzeň. Increasing enemy numbers and a shortage of food forced the Hussite army to withdraw to Kolín.

The lords were close on their heels and struck on 27 May, at the Orphan town of Český Brod. After one day's futile shelling, the aggressors withdrew intending to force the brotherhoods into combat. The opposing armies occupied positions, the Hussites on a hill near Lipany, the lords lower down near Hřib, facing each other and feverish with tension.

In spite of their hostile feelings, neither side moved for two days. With so many seasoned warriors on both sides it was clear that it was going to be one of the bloodiest battles of the whole war in which nobody would yield unless forced to. Even at that late stage more prudent Hussites on both sides were exploring the slender chance of averting the battle.

Contemporary information is entirely derived from intelligence of the victorious side, especially its Catholic participants, and throws little light on the drama. It seems that in the many hours of talking, and then shouting, the extremists got the upper hand. Frederick of Strážnice, the Taborite priest and captain, arrived with his men too late to fight, and finding access to the Hussite army barred, he was admitted only to the negotiations and left when these broke down. The field armies, with Prokop Holý and other leaders, as well as the forces of the great majority of the Hussite towns (of which twenty-two were expressly named by a contemporary sources) marshalled for battle.

On Sunday, 30 May, when the last attempt at reconciliation failed, the brotherhoods opened fire from their vantage point on the hill at four o'clock in the afternoon. The lords would have preferred to wait for more reinforcements. But they were forced by their initial losses to open attack according to an ingenious plan drawn up, most likely by their chief commander, Diviš Bořek of Miletínek who had learned military strategy from Žižka, fighting sometimes at his side and other times against him.[14]

The lords and their Prague allies moved their wagons up the hill and spread them out in a long formation which in the end hemmed in the camp of the brotherhoods along two sides while dense smoke from continuous gunfire veiled the battlefield. Then the lords ceased firing and were seen, through spaces in the clouds of smoke, descending in an orderly manner, with their standards invisible. This was misinterpreted as a retreat and encouraged the brotherhoods to move their wagons from their impregnable position and give chase amidst thunderous shouting: They flee! They flee!

The army of the lords was indeed descending cautiously keeping the line of the wagons intact and gradually accelerating. When the two armies were about a hundred paces apart, the brotherhoods sallied forth from the interior of their wagon formation. Čapek and the cavalry rushed ahead full tilt to catch up with the front line of the enemy wagons which was left ajar to entrap them, while the Hussite infantry broke in through the rear. This was exactly what the lords and their picked warriors were waiting for. The real battle now began under ideal conditions for the lords so that the brotherhoods were already doomed.

Their trapped soldiers were fiercely attacked by the perfectly arrayed knights flying their banners which had previously deliberately been lowered. Čapek's cavalry was cut off and its leader decided to flee to Kolín leaving the foot-soldiers to their fate. For this unbecoming conduct Čapek was later ostracized and eventually compelled to leave the country in disgrace ending up in Poland. His flight clinched the defeat of the brotherhoods.

The fate of the foot-soldiers was decided in a few minutes. They were slaughtered or trampled to death by the horses of the heavily armored knights. The Hussite formation of wagons became a death trap, the enemy pouring in through the front, the rear and then the broken sides. To enable some of his soldiers to escape, Prokop Holý gave his last orders to force apart the wagons so that they could jump to safety and run towards Český Brod. He himself did not take advantage of this opportunity and was killed with Prokůpek and the Taborite priest, Markolt of Zbraslavice.[15]

The carnage is said to have gone all through the night. There were few prisoners. Roháč of Dubá and Jíra of Řečice, Žižka's fellow captains, as well as Peter Payne were fortunate enough to be captured by the Hussites of the opposite side. Those who fell into the hands of the Catholics, mainly the Rožmberk force, were herded into barns and burned alive. The number of these victims is said to have run to a thousand.[16]

CHAPTER TEN

FROM LIPANY TO THE PEACE OF JIHLAVA

The Catholics broadcasted the news of their triumph while still on the battlefield. Emperor Sigismund, the Council, Plzeň and Nürnberg were the first to be informed. Sigismund, who was then at Ulm, ordered a special mass in the cathedral and invited the Basel fathers to celebrate the great victory. This the Council did with great pomp; about one hundred mitres were counted in the solemn procession. Many years later, a conciliar historian inscribed his account of the celebration as a "triumph of believers in the kingdom of Bohemia over the armies of the Taborites and Orphans."[1] The Council could rightly rejoice and so could Palomar as the chief planner and executor of the action and as the one who had provided the money which had won the battle on Czech soil with Czech weapons against the armies which had once been led by Žižka and had wrecked five crusades.

The jubilation of the Catholics was in sharp contrast to the depression which the catastrophe wrought upon the Hussite allies. A, contemporary chronicler expressed the anguish in the final sentence of his account of the Lipany battle: "Dear God, what a grievous loss, these Czechs and valiant fighters for Thine Holy Law." He was obviously thinking mainly of Prokop Holý who was universally respected. A German humanist who was born in Bohemia wrote: "He died chivalrously like the heroes whom the wise heathen Aristotle calls brave and even worthy of an everlasting

119

memory. They remained steadfast in good and ill fortune, even in death."[2] Many genuine Hussites, Rokycana among them, were rightly worried that the defeat of the field armies had left the country open to attack from abroad. Rokycana was bed-ridden during the Lipany crisis and unable to exert his restraining influence on the rival parties. After the battle, all the troubled Hussite moderates were flocking to the great preacher in tribute to his strenuous effort over the past three years in dealing with the Council diplomats, maintaining cooperation between Prague and the Orphans, and curbing the dangerous controversy with Tabor.

The Hussite military and political circles also realized that it was time to close the ranks. The towns of both brotherhoods and their allies among the nobles were not yet brought to their knees. Immediately after the battle of Lipany, some detachments were sent farther, probably to the besieged Kolín. A few days later, an agreement was reached that the siege be raised, and the victorious party accepted the word of honor from Čapek and Ondráček Keřský[4] that they would not try to reconstitute the field armies, and would submit to the resolutions of the next diet. The main concern of the Hussite towns was to retain their representation at the diet and thus help decide the fate of their country. Prague was ready to support their claim as it could help the city regain the leading position in the realm which it had enjoyed at the beginning of the revolution. The siege of Plzeň, with its sinister shadow, was over and the bonds between Catholic and Hussite lords loosened. The manner in which the Catholics exploited their victory, especially the Rožmberk atrocities, shocked those Hussites who had been manoevered into the unnatural alliance mainly by the adroit Basel tactics.

The new situation was reflected in the proceedings and resolutions of the Prague diet which was in session between 23 June and 3 July.[5] The powerful impact of Lipany was still very fresh, many members having fallen in the battle. Almost everybody missed Prokop Holý. His absence was a poignant reminder of all he had done for the revolution and the state. The diet declared a general truce between the Catholics and the Hussites for a year and set about repairing the damage done by inter-Hussite wars and the battle of Lipany. It arranged for the release of prisoners-of-war, for the return of banished citizens and the restitution of their property, an act which restored peace between the Old and New Towns. Undesirable persons were given the chance to sell out rather than have their property confiscated. Aleš Vřešt'ovský and his council, supplemented by new members, were entrusted with peace-keeping duties and the administration of the land court. Security in the country was placed in the hands of regional captains and their elected councils. The renewal of the old and traditional regional institutions, which had been previously successfully adopted by the Orphans but shunned by the Taborites, was now to apply to all Hussite areas and was enforced not without some harshness. It meant that the brotherhoods ceased to exist. Čapek and Nicholas Padařov[6] (in lieu of Ondráček Keřský) appeared in the diet and declared submission on behalf of the brotherhood armies, whereby these disappeared from the diet as one of the estates. But the members for the brotherhoods were incorporated within the estates of the towns and the gentry.[7] This group thereby retained overall majority over the barons. The diet thus preserved the power of Prague and of the gentry, their chief gain from the revolution, which remained in force until 1627, the year of the issue of the "Renewed Ordinances." By accepting the new administrative changes and political measures, the revolution lost the stigma of military dictatorship and overcame the Lipany crisis making the June diet of Prague an historic landmark.

The diet also elected messengers to the meeting with Emperor Sigismund at Regensburg. They were Menhart of Hradec, Ptáček of Pirkštejn and Wenceslas of Strážnice for the lords,[8] William Kostka, Sokol of Lamberk, Beneš Mokrovouský and Čapek of Sány for the knights, four burghers of Prague and one each for the towns of Žatec, Tabor, Klatovy and Hradec Králové. Two ecclesiastics, John Rokycana and Martin Lupáč were also sent.[9] In preparation for the expected encounter with the Catholic theologians, the synod met in Prague at the end of July to unify all currents of Hussite opinion. This failed as before, in the face of opposition from the Taborite priests and even more, from the right wing consisting of Příbram and most of his university colleagues[10] who intended, under the tacit protection of the emperor and the Catholics, to bring to an end the negotiations with the Council of Basel which were based on the so-called first Compactata of November 1433. This was an obvious attempt to oust Rokycana by obstructing his great unifying effort.

On 22 August, the meeting at Regensburg was opened by Sigismund's bombastic speech.[11] He claimed his hereditary right to the Bohemian crown as a descendant of Přemysl the Ploughman and expected to be rewarded for his efforts. The talks had no sooner begun than they ended. William Kostka and Rokycana declared that there was no objection to Sigismund's return as long as the negotiations with the Council were satisfactorily completed and communion in both kinds made compulsory in Bohemia. The team from the Council, twelve strong,[12] was indignant to see that Lipany and the death of Prokop Holý had not reduced the Hussite spokesmen into submission. The Hussites who had helped to save Plzeň and defeat the campaigning armies were hoping that the Czech Catholic lords who were also present would declare themselves in favor of the crucial demands of the Hussite delegation. This was refused. The Czech royalists had come to Regensburg to cultivate contacts with the Council and to earn money from its funds. The talks ended in an impasse and ill will on both sides. The Council delegates showed their implacability by prohibiting the funeral of a Prague delegate who died at Regensburg, and his body had to be taken to Prague. Furthermore, William Kostka was forcibly removed from the Dominican monastery where he was worshipping. It was only with great difficulty that the emperor was able to persuade the Czech delegates to promise to give an account of the Regensburg talks to the Bohemian diet and to see that a response be sent to him and the Council delegates at Cheb.

Developments in Moravia, of which the leading circles must have had inside knowledge at the time of the Regensburg talks, help explain the unyielding attitude of the Basel diplomats, and Sigismund's reluctance to put pressure on them. Three Hussite delegates,[13] went from Regensburg to Brno where the Moravian lords, including the Hussites, were setting up a *Landfríd* with Duke Albrecht. The appropriate document, issued on 9 September, was a counterpart to the resolution of the June diet of Prague, with one difference: the first two signatories were the ruler of Moravia and the bishop of Olomouc, and the barons were the only representatives of the people of the land. There was no mention of Hussitism or the towns which were to wait for their representation at the diet for another six years. This was the continuation of Palomar's intervention, aiming at suppressing Hussitism in Moravia and all elements of social and religious progress in the towns and among the lesser nobility. The *Landfríd* of Brno was mainly directed against the Taborite garrisons at Třebíč and Ivančice and the remainder of the Hussite nobles who refused to surrender.

The Hussite conquests in Silesia, the other Bohemian crown land, disintegrated in a different manner.[14] The truce between the Hussites and the local princes and towns had expired in June, at the time of the diet of Prague. The Silesian association first tried to obtain the best possible terms from the exodus of the Taborite garrisons through negotiations. But on 11 August, Frederick of Strážnice, the Taborite commander of Niemcza, was treacherously captured by Hain of Čornov, a Silesian who had joined the Taborites earlier but now, fearing for his life, after the battle of Lipany, tried to save himself through the capture of Frederick. The Silesian association laid siege to both Niemcza and Otmuchov but meeting with very determined resistance decided to resume negotiations. As a result, the Breslau prisoners of war, who had been kept at Homole castle since 1432, were released and Conrad, bishop of Breslau, met Aleš Vřest'ovský, the regent at Náchod, to negotiate peace with Bohemia. Contrary to all expectations, Aleš refused to sacrifice the Taborites and demanded the end of the siege. In December, the talks continued at Nysa where Vřešt'ovský was the bishop's guest and brought John Pardus of Hrádek, as a representative of the last Czech garrisons in Silesia at Niemcza, Otmuchov and Vrbno, with him. Both sides accepted Vřešt'ovský's arbitration verdict, that the three castles be returned to the Silesians for ransome, and that Frederick of Strážnice, as well as the former commander of Niemcza, be set free.

By that time in Prague, the October diet had ended in an atmosphere of gloom. The onus of renewing the negotiations with the Council and the Emperor which had nearly broken down at Regensburg, rested on Rokycana and the unified Prague and Orphan clergy. The consistory of Prague, its leading body, had the unqualified support of these priests,[15] and the Taborites who at first maintained the usual negative attitudes, became persuaded to accept Payne's arbitration and, at least outwardly gave up their opposition to Rokycana. Thus they gained two years' respite. At the diet, Rokycana's party reiterated its demand that communion in both kinds should be made compulsory in Bohemia. This had the support of the majority of the estates and the towns and the lesser nobles. Then the lords stepped in and killed the motion. They took advantage of the established revolutionary custom which had become part of the unwritten constitution of the Czech state, that a diet resolution should be carried only if voted for unanimously. They overruled the majority and spared the Council of Basel the trouble of concerning itself with the chalice.

The request of the dissenting parties was nevertheless included in a memorandum for the Council diplomats which admitted the possibility that it might not be met in full, in which case additional requests were made. These were summed up on the second part of the memorandum declaring that the Hussites would give up further wars if given certain guarantees: the right to partake of the chalice on request and in all parts of the country where it had been common practice; the freedom to discuss the question of whether the chalice had been ordered by Christ and the primitive Church, as well as the other three articles, and to dispense the chalice to children, until the time the Council had debated these problems and reached a solution corresponding to the Cheb agreements. They asked further for protection against the charge of heresy and for the recognition of an elected Hussite archbishop and two suffragans who would promise obedience to the Council on condition that they could defy anything contrary to the Law of God even if ordered by the pope or any prelate. The elected archbishop should be in control of all clergy in the country and nobody should be allowed to appeal to any authority abroad. Foreigners should be barred from holding prebends in Bohemia. These demands were to ensure the Hussite sovereignty in matters of faith as well as their supremacy over the Catholics in Bohemia, and independence from Rome.

To deal with the departure of the Hussite garrisons from Slovakia, the October diet sent negotiators to meet the emperor at Bratislava. Redeeming the territories under Hussite occupation was a slow and costly business for Sigismund[16] but a speedy return to Bohemia was even more urgent. As this could not be accomplished without a final agreement between the Hussites and the Council of Basel, the emperor pressed for another meeting between the representatives of both sides. Hankering for the crown of Bohemia had become his morbid obsession which was further aggravated by his vindictiveness and his failing health. The revolution was thus about to enter upon a particularly dangerous stage as legalization of its achievements and constitutional changes over the past years was at stake.

Another meeting of the Bohemian diet was contemplated early in 1435, to study the expected response from Basel to the requests of the October diet and to prepare the terms of Sigismund's recognition as King of Bohemia. For a country with so much bitter experience at the hands of the iniquitous monarch it was going to be a difficult test of statecraft.

The news of these preparations greatly alarmed the members of the former brotherhoods, especially the Orphans, the true heirs of Žižka, who had the worst to fear from Sigismund's return. They found a new spokesman in John Roháč of Dubá, a Taborite whom Žižka had appointed as the captain of Čáslav. Roháč called an assembly of both brotherhoods in order to restore their unity, and became their joint captain. On 21 December 1434, members from most Tabor and Orphan towns gathered at Tabor and rallied against "the sworn enemy of divine truths and his wily and deceitful helpers." In a solemn and fervent manifesto[17] the members vowed to observe the Four Articles, to do penance, to help one another regardless of sacrifice and to maintain unanimity among the communities and at the diet. Many manifestations of support arrived from Moravia and Bohemia, especially from the nobles and towns of the Žatec group.

The only record of consultations which preceded the issue of the manifesto is the colored information from Rožmberk spies which names two opposing speakers. Václav Koranda[18] laid the blame for Lipany on the lords who had infiltrated and betrayed the brotherhoods, and proposed that the field armies should reform and launch a ruthless war on traitors. Simon, an alderman from Tabor, warned against new wars because things had vastly changed since Žižka's time; the overtaxed masses had defected from the brethren and the lesser nobles had been bought by the Council of Basel. When pressed for concrete proposals Simon suggested that all contributions available from the Hussite towns and castles should be assessed, and if found adequate an army should be gathered and should try its strength against the enemy. If found too weak, the brotherhoods should save their resources until the Council of Basel dissolved completely and the decrepit emperor died, which might well happen within a year. Then the Germans and the Hungarians would have worries enough and that would be the moment to strike at the lords, call the diet and subdue the world as the ancient Romans had.

There was a mixture of truth and exaggeration in his account. The Hussite towns were confused and partly estranged from their original cause. Reconstituting the brotherhoods at this moment would have required superhuman effort. As time went on, no action was taken[19] and the towns which had not sent representatives to the Tabor assembly probably decided to wait and see what was going to happen at the new diet which was to meet in Prague early in March 1435. Among them was Kutná Hora, formerly the joint property of the brotherhoods, now administered by the regent.

The chief aim of the diet was to negotiate the terms for the recognition of Sigismund and to establish the supremacy of the Hussites in the country making sure that the Catholics who had not come to the diet should never be powerful enough to upset it. This time, the political preponderance of the gentry and the towns, the pillars of the revolution, was treated as a matter of minor importance. This happened partly for tactical reasons, and partly because the two estates felt confident that their constitutional positions had become firmly established.[20]

In the sphere of religion the diet demanded that the emperor as well as his court and chaplains should receive communion in both kinds and that public sins, from gambling to prostitution, should be prosecuted; the regular clergy should be allowed to return only with the permission of the town concerned; the demolished churches, monasteries and castles should not be rebuilt. The council of state, land court, and the office of the emperor's deputy in his absence should be open to the Hussites only. Rents collected on behalf of church offices were not to be renewed. Bishops in Bohemia and Moravia should be elected by the estates and no priest should be summoned abroad by an ecclesiastical court. The Hussite lords who during the war had come into possession of crown castles would keep the tenure as officers of the crown unless the chalice were introduced in the whole country. The towns should have the right to resist the emperor and his officials, and those towns which had renounced the chalice. To prevent inroads into the domain of the chalice, all places that had adopted it should be registered.

The political demands concerned protection against Germans. No German or any other foreigner should become an official or a landowner. Catholic burghers should not become aldermen even if they sympathized with the revolution. The emperor should return the imperial insignia, the Bohemian crown jewels as well as the land records which he had removed from the country. Without their return the legitimacy of war-time transfers of property would have been questioned. Moravia which had been ceded to Duke Albrecht should be reunited with Bohemia. The emperor was asked to refrain from pawning the crown castles until approval by the council of state was given. This would have appreciably reduced the funds from which he paid his adherents. The land court which had stopped sitting during the revolution should be reconstituted on the lines of the revolutionary diet by the admission of the representatives of the gentry and the towns. The royal towns asked that they not be pawned, nor administered by regional captains or burdened by additional taxes without their consent. The royal vice-chamberlain, to whom they were subject should be a citizen of Prague. The university appealed to the lords to support its claim to the restitution of its property in return for services rendered to the reactionary cause.

These terms were generally well devised. Their goal was, above all, the Hussite control of the council of state which had been the most powerful body in pre-Hussite Bohemia.[21] Whether the vindictive and crafty emperor could be expected to dismiss his all-Catholic council which he had maintained during the revolution to delude himself that he was still king of Bohemia, was questionable. He was, however, ready to make time serving concessions and then cancel them on his accession to the throne as the near future was to show. Tabor with Roháč, its captain, and three other Taborite towns rejected the resolutions of the March diet and preferred war. The rest of the Hussite towns that had attended the December assembly accepted them and escaped the coming attack.

Its planner, Ulrich of Rožmberk, had already struck in January in order to earn more money from the Council of Basel. On his behalf, Prokop of Plzeň, Menhart's confidant, wrote a patriotic proclamation warning the Hussites[22] not to expose the Basel achievements to risk, and containing a veiled attack on Rokycana and those Taborites who opposed the March diet. As soon as the diet session was over, Ptáček of Pirkštejn with his regional forces and the men of several other nobles laid siege, on 17 March, to Ostroměč castle in the Sedlčany area guarding a ford across the Vltava.

Its lord was the Taborite captain, Philip of Padařov, who came of peasant stock and was unusually well educated having been originally intended for the priesthood. He had become so fond of art and Bible reading that he had a Czech Bible especially written for himself and so beautifully illuminated that it could have graced a king's collection.[23] Philip was also a good soldier and defended his castle for two months until compelled to surrender on 22 May when the enemy received reinforcements. The garrison was allowed to leave for Tabor and Ostroměč was demolished, never to be rebuilt. Almost simultaneously the Rožmberk forces laid siege to Lomnice and Božejovice in south Bohemia and probably captured Přibĕnice which the Taborites had taken in 1420.[24] At the end of April a Prague force marched out against Kolín, now held by Frederick of Strážnice who recently had been set free in Silesia. Diviš Bořek of Mile-tínek, now the burgrave of the castle of Prague, was in command and received help from John Hertvík of Rušinov to whom Bořek had sur-rendered Kolín eight years earlier. The siege was soon abandoned because Frederick knew people in high places. Hence in June he could depart for Brno, where the Hussites and a delegation from Basel were to meet the emperor to complete the negotiations which had broken down at Regens-burg in 1434.

The invited parties gathered very slowly.[25] The delegates from Basel had stayed in Vienna for a long time. From there they went to Bratislava for two consultations, in March and April, with the emperor to discuss the date of the Brno meeting and possibly also the ambiguous tactics which were to be employed there. They reached Brno on 20 May. Duke Albrecht and the Czechs arrived in June and the talks began the day after the em-peror's arrival on 2 July. The composition of the Council delegation was inauspicious for him. The men who embarrassed Cesarini by their dislike of Palomar's tactics and bearing were missing: the bishops of Augsburg and Lübeck as well as Henry Toke, John of Maulbronn and John Nieder. Those six[26] who did come, brought very rigid instructions and a negative answer to the terms of the Prague diet. This was partly a retaliation for Regensburg where the Czechs had offered resistance instead of abject capitulation and partly a sign of fear that any concession to the Hussites might further antagonize the pope.[27] The long stay of the Basel delegates in Vienna and the contact with its strongly anti-Hussite university had hardened their attitude even more. At the very beginning they refused the Czech request that the talks should open before the emperor came; they had probably been cautioned by him and waited for his support.

The Prague delegation was unusually strong consisting of ten members of each estate and led by Aleš Vřešt'ovský. Among the lords were Menhart of Hradec, Wenceslas Strážnický, Ptáček of Pirkštejn and George of Podĕbrady, then only fifteen years old. The towns were represented by equal numbers of the burghers from the Old and New Towns, headed by John Velvar and Nicholas Humpolecký, the city clerk; the leading gentry were Kostka, Smiřický, Carda, Nicholas Sokol, Hertvík, Louda and others. The clergy included Rokycana, Wenceslas of Dráchov, Jakoubek's successor at Bethlehem chapel, Martin Lupáč and Ulrich of Znojmo, the parson of Čáslav. Frederick of Strážnice, Koranda, Nicholas Biskupec and Peter Payne were briefly present. Menhart of Hradec brought Křišt'an of Prachatice and Prokop of Plzeň as observers. Even Ulrich of Rožmberk and other Catholic lords attended as did the duke of Savoy and the archbishop of Magdeburg [28]

The emperor displayed his talent for intrigue and deception to the full. Pretending that the Czechs mattered more to him than did the Council, he invited Rokycana to speak first. Rokycana reiterated the three most important demands of 1434 to which the Czechs had still not received an answer. The Council maintained that the Hussites had not fulfilled the alleged obligations of the First Compactata of November 1433, namely that they would submit to the Church in liturgy and church order. Palomar challenged them to comply. Rokycana nevertheless insisted on an answer to the diet's demands. After some equivocation, Palomar declared that the Council had rejected all of them. Rokycana decided that the Czechs had better go home if that was the final answer. Then the emperor intervened, pretending ill will towards the Council diplomats with whom he was in secret understanding, and pretending friendship to the Czechs, he generously granted what Basel was denying. On the fifth day of the meeting, he signed a great charter granting Prague practially all its religious demands and had an extensive document drawn up for the benefit of Bohemia as well as for Moravia, fulfilling all the demands of the October diet and promising to plead with the Council towards that end.[29] The seals, however, were withheld. Yet the deadlock was broken and on 15 July the Hussites were persuaded to reopen the talks. These yielded two valuable results: the document confirming that the Hussites were entering into a union with the Church, and the acknowledgement thereof by the Council. After this, the old altercations broke out again without positive results; at the end of July, there were so few Prague delegates left at Brno that they refused to seal the document, and the final agreement on Sigismund's return to Bohemia had to be put off for a year. Nevertheless, Sigismund had gained the devotion of Prague and was soon to have a stroke of luck in different quarters.

War flared up between the Teutonic Knights, allied to Swidrygielo, the grand duke of Lithuania, and Poland. The Poles ignored Sigismund's attempt to arbitrate and went on with the war which ended in their victory at Ukmerge on 1 September. Sigismund accepted the result with relief because one of the war victims was Korybut, the erstwhile candidate to the crown of Bohemia.[30] Ever since he had left Bohemia in 1428 and lost Gliwica in 1431, he was plagued with misfortune. The Hussites, in vain, pleaded with King Wladislaw on his behalf at Pabianice; he did not benefit from the King's death on 31 May 1434, and when he eventually threw in his lot against the Poles among whom he had grown up he incurred the fierce hostility of the Polish prelates. They brutally had him put to death after the battle in which he was wounded and taken prisoner. His tragic end calls for human sympathy. In spite of some grave errors which had brought about his fall in 1427, the two brief periods of his regency were of service to the Hussite revolution because they had ensured the neutrality of Poland without which the Hussites could not have stood up against so many enemies in the early crucial years of the long war.

Another piece of good news reached Sigismund after he had left Moravia for Hungary. At Brno, Ulrich of Rožmberk received another handsome subsidy from the Council, and anxious to please his paymasters, he struck at a Taborite relief force on its way to the besieged Lomnice.[31] In the gruelling battle near Křeč, 800 Taborites were reported killed. This induced Roháč to depart from Tabor, resulting in the complete transformation and reunion of the Taborite-Orphan brotherhood from which all towns by Hradec Králové had defected. Frederick of Strážnice took charge at Tabor and steered his policy in the direction advocated by Simon Kovář, to seek the renewal of the brotherhood.

Lomnice resisted the siege and its heroic stand lent moral support to the diet which met at the beginning of October[32] to sanction the modest achievements of the Brno talks and prepare the peace settlement. Since the Council of Basel persevered in stubborn silence the diet elected four priests who were to proclaim the Hussites' return to the Church. It also set about electing an archbishop, taking advantage of Sigismund's approval given at Brno and hoping for his intercession with Basel in the matter. Eight priests and eight laymen (two of these being lords, two squires and four burghers) carried out the revolutionary election with utter disregard for canonical law.[33] Rokycana was unanimously elected the archbishop of the Czech Church together with his suffragans, Martin Lupáč and Wenceslas of Mýto. The unique occasion was celebrated by bell-ringing and hymn singing all over the capital as if a peace treaty had already been signed.

The magnitude of the event was reflected in the conduct of the opposite camp. Rokycana's enemies, especially Sigismund's entourage,[34] attempted to invalidate the election by spreading rumors that the new archbishop was contemplating a coup in Prague. Knowing that Sigismund would be glad of Rokycana's death they made an abortive attempt on his life. The likely plotter was Caspar Šlik who sat in the diet as the emperor's chancellor. Sigismund had to content himself with telling the men from Basel that the populace nearly drowned the newly elected archbishop and was still seeking his life.[35] The probable background to the conspiracy was Rokycana's refusal to attend a new meeting with the Basel envoys because they had ostentatiously broken the promise to further the Hussite requests at the Council and failed to apologize as before.

The meeting which was to conclude a peace treaty between the Czechs and the Council took place at Székesfehervár in Hungary in the presence of the emperor.[36] The instructions from Basel were more severe than ever. The Council regarded Rokycana's election as a showy violation of existing agreements and urged Sigismund to declare that he would never again interfere in ecclesiastical matters, and to revoke the promises he had already made. Menhart of Hradec and Ptáček of Pirkštejn pointed out that a breach of promise at this stage might mean the end of the negotiations, and whatever was arranged in secret would eventually leak out and shatter the emperor's position in Bohemia.[37] John Velvar, a Prague burgher and Latin scholar, now and again uttered warnings that the Czech delegates would leave and the emperor declared that he would rather forgo the crown of Bohemia than to bow to any such threats. In the end he got the better of both sides. Behind the backs of the Basel envoys, he handed the Czechs the agreed Brno document granting the demands which the Council had rejected out of hand, and he appeased the Council delegates with a secret verbal promise made before three witnesses that he would not infringe on the rights of the Church. On 1 January 1436 he reassured them that the concessions made to the Hussites were nothing but a means towards the ultimate goal, the crown of Bohemia, which they would realize as soon as he set foot in Prague.[38] On that score he was of one mind with Palomar. After 6 January, when the Czechs received Sigismund's document the talks were switched to the question of where the peace treaty should be promulgated. The emperor still felt uneasy about Prague, the city which the Council envoys favored, and settled on Jihlava at the suggestion of the Czechs. The date was fixed for 1 May to give the emperor ample time to secure the Hungarian border against the Turks. The talks ended on 11 January. The celebrations at Székesfehervár and later at Buda masked the fact that the meeting had not effected its purpose and that it was necessary to call another meeting of the diet.

This was opened in Prague on 29 February 1436.[39] It approved the proposal that a new diet should be called at Jihlava and took the required measures to that end. A small delegation was sent to Hungary to consult with the emperor and to inform him of the resolutions of the Prague diet. Stress was laid on the stipulation that the Council should ratify the election of Rokycana and the two suffragens. The Turkish invasion into Hungary caused further delay and the diet of Jihlava eventually met at the beginning of June.

It was a unique event in the history of the Hussite revolution. One of the strongest German bastions on Moravian soil with scarcely ten percent of its population Czech and on which several Hussite attacks had foundered, opened its gates to the Bohemian diet with a Hussite majority and became the scene of the final struggle for peace.[40] At the very beginning of the talks it turned out that the Council of Basel had ignored the conditions stated by the Prague diet and refused to ratify the election of Rokycana and the two bishops. The representatives of the towns, including Prague, declared that they would not enter into any further negotiations unless individual towns wished to do so, and asked for permission to go to their home towns and sound out opinions. If Prague alone had disagreed the diet would have broken up. But the acquiescence of Prague was assured by the Brno privilege from Sigismund, and its deputies returned to Jihlava with an affirmative answer just when the Council envoys were beginning to fear another breakdown. Sigismund thus won the first round. There were some last minute clashes and on 3 July when the emperor and Bishop Philibert had donned their robes for the final ceremony, the Czechs refused to come because they had been denied their wish to speak, in four languages, on their struggle and the reasons why they were returning to the Church. The controversy caused two days' delay and the Czechs gave in again but remained embittered even on the festive day, 5 July.

The peace was promulgated in the main square of Jihlava in the presence of the emperor and Albrecht of Austria, the envoys from Basel being seated on their right, and Aleš Vřešt'ovský, Menhart of Hradec, Rokycana and the two bishops on their left. John Velvar, the spokesman for the Prague delegation, handed the Basel diplomats the document by which the Bohemian diet accepted the so-called First Compactata of 30 November 1433 and received from Bishop Philibert the first copy of the same with the signatures of the Council envoys. Then the clerk of the imperial chancery read out the letter on which the Hussites promised to live in peace and unity with the Church, and the statement of the Bohemian diet giving full powers to the four priests to promise obedience to the Church on behalf of the Hussite clergy and laity. The leading personality of these priests was Wencelas of Dráchov, the preacher at Bethlehem chapel.[41] The promise was formally received by both Bishop Philibert and by Archbishop Rokycana and his bishops, Martin Lupáč and Wenceslas of Mýto. In return, the Czechs received from the Council a decree ordering all Christian rulers and nations to live in peace with the Bohemians and Moravians and to refrain from reviling them for their faith. The Bishops of Olomouc and Litomyšl were cautioned not to hinder dispensation of the chalice and to ordain the Hussite priests.[42] This decree was read out by Rokycana, and the imperial clerk announced that it would be read in Czech during the service on the following day. The Catholics and Hussites went to separate religious services and the Basel envoys sent the Council a jubilant message.[43] The Czechs had every reason to remember Master John Hus; it was the eve of the anniversary of his martyrdom and Peter of Mladoňovice, the man who had witnessed and recorded it, was to appear on 6 July during the final phase of the solemn occasion.[44]

On that day, Bishop Philibert celebrated mass before the emperor and the Czech delegates who had just been cleared of the stigma of heresy. Rokycana presented the Czech version of the conciliar decree and before him, Peter of Mladoňovice read out in Latin the acceptance of the Compactata by the Hussites. He had taken refuge on Menhart's nearby estate where the was to stay for the rest of Sigismund's life; he had reasons to fear the emperor's vengeance, having exposed his part in the trial of Hus.

In 1427 he had parted company with Jakoubek and Rokycana, disagreeing with them on matters of church order. It must have been a heartening moment for the Hussites to see the former rivals reunited at the same altar at this historic moment when the unity of the movement was so vital. In this, Rokycana soon received an object lesson from Palomar who came running to the altar reserved for Rokycana who felt entitled to dispense the chalice there after the promulgation of the peace. Palomar objected and started a vehement quarrel which took eight days to simmer down, after which the emperor issued a document recognizing Rokycana's election, and assured him that he would obtain his confirmation by the Council or the pope.[45] Behind Rokycana's back he advised the Basel diplomats not to turn down the recognition outright but to temporize because the Czechs would kill Rokycana and dispose of the problem. This was one of the greatest blunders of the practised liar and intriguer who was to become the king of Bohemia.

CHAPTER ELEVEN

SIGISMUND'S RETURN AND DEATH

The promulgation of the peace of Jihlava fulfilled the fundamental condition for the recognition of Sigismund as king of Bohemia. It was now incumbent on him to grant the promised requests. At long last, he issued a great charter of twenty-five articles, an outstanding specimen of diplomatic cunning.[1] He dealt with most requests summarily, either omitting some altogether, as in the case of those touching freedom of religion, turning down others out of hand, or referring them to the council of state which had yet to be reconstituted either by election or by nomination, as he put it. Every reference to this important body which was to provide the principal constitutional guarantee of his rule, was made with a touch of irony. The towns got the worst of it. The emperor omitted any reference to their right to self-defense and to independence from the regional captains. It was quite a different matter for the lords and the gentry who had seized the royal castles and the surrounding land during the revolution. They asked that their tenure of royal castles be extended by six years and vigorously demanded compensation from church property for the royal property soon to be given up which was valued at 390,000 groschen. To his relief, this settlement was delayed until he arrived in Prague,[2] as was the reconstitution of the council of state which he was going to do in his own way, avoiding the controls to which he had been subjected in Hungary. All this being settled, John Velvar declared, on 25 July, that the diet would recognize Sigismund as the king as soon as he returned the crown jewels and the land records which he had taken to Hungary. To this purpose, the Czechs offered to call a new diet in Prague, which Sigismund rejected seeing danger in delay, and had the Bohemian crown jewels and the land records brought to Jihlava where he was proclaimed king on 14 August. Vřešt'ovský absolved the present members of the government of the oath they had sworn to him and resigned as the regent, after which Menhart of Hradec and John Velvar paid homage to the new king on behalf of his subjects. It escaped the official notice that some lords and gentry were missing but the absence of members for Tabor, Kolín, Hradec Králové and Stříbro aroused the emperor's anger and was recorded.[3] The government which had just resigned had guaranteed safety for the emperor's journey which took him via Německý Brod, Čáslav and Kutná Hora, the sites of his defeats by Žižka, to Prague where he was ceremoniously welcomed. On 23 August 1436, he siezed power over the largest fortress in the kingdom and was free to carry on systematic and premediated vengeance on those responsible for years of frustration.[4] Vengeance was his main preoccupation in the city of his birth which fourteen months later he hurriedly fled.

Ten days after his arrival, he introduced himself by dissolving the city councils and appointing his supporters to new ones. Thus John Velvar and many other convinced Hussites lost their positions. Matthew Louda of Chlumčany who had treacherously surrendered Písek, the second largest Taborite fortress, to the emperor, and John of Kunvald, the new vice-chamberlain, set about demolishing the privileges of the Hussite towns. These abuses as well as the continual merry-making and unconcealed dissolute ways of the court, scandalized public opinion, especially among the Hussites.[5] Tension increased sharply in September when the Catholic party came to the general diet for the first time since 1423, in such strength that it gained a majority among the lords and forced the Hussites to retreat in many ways. At this opportune moment, the emperor finally named the council of state which showed the real power of the Catholics.[6] He tried to appease the Hussite nobles with title deeds to church property. By that time, however, discontent all over the country erupted in an armed revolt led by Hradec Králové. On 27 September, the priest Ambrose, declared a state of emergency and appointed Zdislav Mnich,[7] a knight, the commander of the local forces. The war which Sigismund was able to contain for almost a year forced him in the end to flee the country.

For the time being, Sigismund was laughing because he could employ one of the ablest Bohemian warriors, Diviš Bořek of Miletínek, the victor of Lipany, who undoubtedly bore a grudge against Ambrose who thirteen years earlier had beaten him at Hradec, with Žižka's help. Both Diviš and his new associate, William Kostka had just received title-deeds to church estates which they had once occupied, and the emperor expected an easy victory. But months passed, and Hradec Králové not only resisted but also attacked. On 6 November Kostka fell in battle and Diviš, whose forces had scattered, fled to his Kunětická Hora castle. Sigismund had to acquiesce and seek rapproachment with Tabor which, like Kolín, was still opposed to him though not actively aiding Hradec. Tabor was now in the hands of Frederick of Strážnice, an advocate of Simon Kovář's wait-and-see approach. He believed that Sigismund would soon die and wished to establish a short-term truce to enable Tabor to survive. To attain this, he sought not only contacts with Sigismund but also with Ulrich of Rožmberk.

As the Council of Basel regarded Sigismund's return to Prague as the final victory over the Hussites, it stopped the flow of money for war on Tabor. After the severe blows Ulrich had sustained from the Taborites in the past, he did not feel like waging single-handed war against them. Rather he sought to take advantage of their difficulties by playing the role of mediator at court. The Taborites were not only concerned about consolidating their material gains of the revolution, but they also feared for their religious freedom more than did Rokycana's church. Their very simplified liturgy was under constant attack from the Basel diplomats who were still in Prague. Over the past two years, the Taborites had been somewhat protected from Peter Payne's arbitration judgement because he had postponed its proclamation with their consent. Now, the emperor forced him to write down his verdict which was sent to Tabor and answered by Nicholas of Pelhřimov in Prague on 22 October in the presence of the emperor and the Basel envoys. Rokycana also stated his point of view.[8] In the end, the decision on acceptable forms of worship was deferred until the end of February 1437 when a special committee of four was to meet. On 18 November, Frederick of Strážnice reached a favorable solution which the council of state had worked out for the emperor who had to admit his advisors' expert knowledge of conditions in Bohemia.[9] As a result, Sigismund conceded to the Taborites a

measure of religious freedom and tenure to the property they had conquered, while Frederick and other Taborite priests promised the obedience
of Tabor and Kolín and thus left Hradec Králové to its fate. A shame-
faced proviso stated that Tabor would not have to fight against Hradec
or its allies, namely John Roháč, John Kolda of Žampach and the Šárovec
brothers of Lanšperk. This was to lead to the fall of Hradec and to the
execution of Roháč. Despite this treachery, Hradec Králové was to help
the Taborite priests to retain their religious freedom even after 1437.

The proviso on the neutrality of Tabor was nothing his imperial majesty
could be proud of. He may have been amused at his heretical allies helping him against other heretics but he had to proceed with caution because he was bankrupt. He could no longer plunder the country as in
1402 or 1420, nor could he curb his extravagant spending or expect
more money from Basel. He had to call the diet to acquire the means
for war on Hradec. By reopening the land court, which was felt to be
overdue, Sigismund was able to exploit the grave political mistake of the
revolution which had failed to set up its own court of justice. He also re-
opened the land records so that it seemed as though restoration of legal
order had for seventeen years depended on the return of the king.

Sigismund therefore set to work and called the diet which met late
in January 1437.[10] At last on 26 January, he pronounced his verdict on
the composition of the land court, the point at issue being the representation of the lords and knights. The admission of the knights was
vehemently opposed by the lords as a revolutionary innovation and Sigismund would not and could not allocate all the associate court positions
to the Hussites as they demanded. In the end the lords gained twelve and
the gentry eight places, including the office of the chief notary. The total
was equally shared by the Catholics and the right-wing Hussites to the
complete exclusion of men like Smiřický and of course those of Rokycana's church, a fact noted with satisfaction by the emissaries from Basel.
On 28 January the land court set to work, with Aleš Holický, a Hussite,
as the chief chamberlain, Nicholas Zajíc of Hazmburk, a Catholic, as the
supreme judge and Aleš Vřešt'ovsky, the ex-regent, as the chief notary.
The court worked without stopping, having to approve or turn down all
the transfers of property within a year in order for them to be valid.
These achievements were much appreciated and Sigismund turned them
to his advantage by requesting authorization for an exorbitant tax[11]

amounting to the annual total of the peasant levy. This, he argued was in the state's interest and necessary, above all, to finance the war against Hradec Králové and Roháč. Most Hussites admired the heroic stand of the beleaguered town and regarded the issue as Sigismund's private affair, while the lesser nobles objected to the tax because of its enormity. The emperor secured the support of the lords by giving them control over the office of collection in the regions of the country, a profitable business and entirely exempt from control.[12] Because most of the gentry had left Prague before the end of the long diet the bill was safely passed without them.

Sigismund celebrated by granting a privilege to Kutná Hora whose gates he also opened to returning Catholics and Germans, and by having his wife Barbara belatedly crowned in St. Vitus cathedral.[13] His own perfunctory and hasty coronation in 1420 had allowed no time for Queen Barbara as people still remembered. On the whole, the outcome of the diet was a success for him. He was given a huge line of credit and was able to incur debts immediately for fighting Hradec Králové. The fate of the town was thus sealed but it did not give up and lodged a complaint with the diet about the violation of agreements between Sigismund and the Hussites. The complaint was supported by the gentry of the surrounding area so that the whole region stood up solidly against Sigismund. But his court won over Zdislas Mnich, the commander of Hradec, with promises and induced him to overthrow the rule of Ambrose and take his priests prisoner. Ambrose escaped with a broken leg. A deputation from the new regime soon arrived in Prague to sue for peace and probably obtained terms similar to those of Tabor and Kolín. The priest, Martin Prostředek and other enemies of Sigismund got away and joined Roháč's garrison at Sion castle. It seems likely that the removal of Žižka's relics from Hradec to Čáslav was connected with their exodus.[14]

While waiting for the first proceeds of the tax which would enable him to attack Roháč, the emperor turned on Rokycana whom he considered the more dangerous. The uncompromising disciple of Hus and Jakoubek stood like a rock against threats, attacks and intrigues in the unequal fight for a final victory. From the moment he had seized power, Sigismund joined forces with the Basel delegates and tried hard to deprive Rokycana of his high rank as the head of his Church which trusted him implicitly. To Sigismund, Rokycana was not only an odious censor on his loose

living but also the cause of his failures, first in 1424, when he had reconciled Žižka with Prague and then again because he had obstructed, as the
emperor believed, his return to Prague for three years. The Basel envoys
detested Rokycana because he had compelled the Council to allow communion in both kinds and because he had consistently opposed its policy.
The underhanded designs on his person, the attempt on his life and the
conspiracy charge further increased Rokycana's prestige. Palomar, who
was hoping to go back to Basel with tangible results, tried to undermine
Rokycana's authority by persistently remonstrating about the Hussites'
alleged failure to observe the Compactata and adapt themselves to the
Roman liturgy. This would have meant betraying the life-work of Jakoubek and forsaking Rokycana's adherents for whom the simplified order
of service had become tradition and an important link between Prague
and the Orphans since their amalgamation in 1432. As Rokycana resisted
the pressure, Palomar rudely told him, on 24 October, that his tenure
on the Týn parsonage was contrary to canon law. This was correct, since
the Hussite priests had been appointed by the revolutionary consistory,
not ordained by a Roman Catholic bishop. Palomar thus gave away the
envoy's intention to cancel all these appointments. When this was brought
to the emperor's notice, he and the council of state realized—because he
needed the neutrality of Tabor in his conflict with Hradec Králové—that
removing Hussite priests would be a more complicated upheaval than replacing the city councillors. They directed their attention then at Martin
Lupáč who was made the scapegoat. This was probably why he left
Prague on his own accord. But as soon as the treaty with the Taborites
and probably also with Jacob of Vřesovice was signed, the long-prepared
attack was renewed.[15]

On 21 November, Sigismund called a meeting of the delegates from
Basel and the lay representatives of the Hussites to discuss the implementa-
tion of the Compactata. The delegates heaped the usual accusations on the
Hussite priests whom they required to undergo examination showing that
they had abandoned all their devious views, and entirely adapted themselves to the Catholic ritual. The lords and the Prague councillors were
complaining that the bishops of Olomouc and Litomyšl had not yet been
instructed to ordain the Hussite priests and see to it that the chalice be
dispensed without hindrance. When Rokycana was admitted to the meeting and enumerated the places where the obligations were not observed,

the delegates answered with further accusations and challenged Rokycana and his clergy publicly to renounce Wyclif's doctrine on the Lord's Supper.[16] Rokycana presented the required declaration although it weighed heavily on his conscience but he resolutely opposed the examination of his priests and certain church assemblies. His university colleagues, however, failed to support him. In the end he was forced to resign the leadership of the clergy in favor of Wenceslas of Dráchov who, on 13 December, yielded to threats that otherwise the Basel delegates would leave Prague, and promised to submit to their demands. So after many years Prague saw a Christmas with full Catholic pomp and the restored rites, including the images of saints which Jakoubek had removed. Only communion for children, lesson reading and hymn singing in Czech were retained, the points which Rokycana wished to be raised at the Council. On 18 December, Palomar could triumphantly depart for Basel to report and to prepare for his last encounter with the Hussites. He hoped to meet Rokycana once more and to gain the final victory. It was not to be; he was never to see Prague again.

In spite of his painful retreat, Rokycana did not stop fighting.[17] Steeled by the memory of Hus and Jakoubek and by the seven years of struggle with the Council of Basel, he found the outlet for his energy in the pulpit of the Týn church where he hammered the enemies of the chalice as if he had learned the craft in his father's smithy. The January diet (1437) encouraged a brief resurgence of Hussitism among the ranks of the gentry and the towns, but as soon as the diet was over, reaction again raised its head coinciding with the coup at Hradec Králové. Palomar sent two bulls to Prague from the Council containing a *pro forma* ratification of the Jihlava agreements and requesting Sigismund to ban communion for children as well as to summon Peter Payne to appear before the court at Basel, that is, to certain death. The emperor could not yet afford to take such action in Bohemia. He withheld both bulls while Rokycana again pointed out which obligations the Council had failed to fulfill.

Nevertheless, the Basel delegation induced Sigismund, in return for the ratification, to call the synod of the Hussite clergy which was asked to suppress Rokycana's liturgy in the whole country as had been practically done in Prague in December. The synod gathered in Prague on 3 March, the day of the Hradec coup, and complied with the emperor's demands. Rokycana still obtained the reservations that the Council should discuss communion for children and the use of the vernacular during the service but Sigismund and the Council envoys remained unswayed. They felt so sure of success that Berruer was sent back to Basel as no longer needed, with only Bishop Philibert left in Prague.[18] He and Sigismund had plans to get rid of Rokycana as fast as possible, and decided to dispatch him to Basel whence he would not return. Having received the reports from Prague the Council felt strong enough to shake off the obligations to the Hussites and arranged a disputation on the chalice as promised in the Compactata of 1433. Sure of the emperor's support, it believed in the final Hussite defeat and treated the disputation as a mere formality. The invitation had been sent in February together with the two bulls and handed to the Hussites as a great favor. As Rokycana refused to go, Příbram and Prokop of Plzeň were delegated. When urged by Prokop to change his mind, Rokycana reminded him gently of what had happened to certain Czechs at Constance. The emperor exploded and said that he had given his word of honor and that he would not tarnish his reputation for Rokycana's sake. Rokycana refrained from naming John Hus but refused nevertheless and thus kept the spirit if revolt alive.[19]

This had just been brought home to Sigismund when none other than the mildest of the Hussites, John Příbram, presented him with the complaints from the councillors of Prague and the university. Some were directed against Philibert and concerned the violation of agreements. Sigismund was chiefly accused of condoning the aggressive behavior of Catholic priests, hindering the Hussites from their accustomed worship, and of tolerating prostitution and other public sins in Prague.[20] In private, Příbram added that the people of Prague were boiling with indignation at the steady influx of canons and monks who called the Hussites heretics. Sigismund and the court had just attended a militant sermon by Nicholas, the monk from Plzeň, that town's delegate to Basel in 1433. Sigismund denied and half admitted the charges adding that as lord of the castle he could do as he pleased. If he could not he would leave Prague. This frightened the councillors of the New Town so that they subsequently assented to the presence of the regulars at Hradčany castle which the Old Town had no doubt done before. Both Philibert and the emperor were stung by Příbram's remark and felt some concession to popular feeling was necessary. However, it never crossed their minds that they might stop welcoming monks to Prague so they tried a different course of action.

The festival of the "showing of the insignia" was imminent and Sigismund was to fulfill the promise that he would bring back the imperial crown jewels which his father had acquired. The plain fact was that he had them removed from the country for fear of the Hussites and had pawned or sold them to the city of Nürnberg where they were to be kept up to the end of the Holy Roman Empire of the German nation in 1804, and then transferred to Vienna where they are to this day. Instead, the Bohemian crown jewels were brought from Jihlava and put on display at the Corpus Christi chapel in Prague. On this occasion, the emperor and the bishop issued a proclamation saying that the Czechs who communicated from the chalice were Catholics and true Christians whom no one was allowed to call heretics.[21] This was read out, on 13 April in Latin, Czech, German and Hungarian, during a solemn mass. Plaques with corresponding Latin and Czech texts were placed inside the chapel.

On the same day, a synod was held in Prague on the initiative of Bishop Philibert and in the emperor's presence. To supplement the measures of the March synod and to improve the disciplinary supervision over the clergy in general, and of the Hussite priests in particular, the bishop reintroduced the office of dean which had fallen into disuse during the revolution. The newly appointed deans were given instructions to carry out the synod's resolutions.[22] Peter Payne and Koranda, a Taborite priest were among those summoned. Koranda who had found refuge in Žatec after the emperor's treaty with the Taborites, was ordered back to Tabor on pain of death. The English master was less fortunate. Sigismund could not extradite him to certain death at the hands of the Council; he had to give him a safe conduct which he dared not violate in Bohemia. When Payne refused to submit to the synodal resolutions Sigismund banished him from the country as a foreigner on the expiry of the safe conduct. Upon its expiry Payne disappeared from Prague and found refuge among friends.[23] Next it was Rokycana's turn. On 24 April the conservative John Papoušek got the Týn parish while Příbram was appointed to St. Giles and Prokop of Plzeň to St. Henry's. The emperor even came to the latter's induction.

Ignoring the ominous signs of revolt, at the beginning of May, Sigismund gathered forces for an attack on Roháč and called a new diet for 25 May in order to ask for more money. This time, his demands were strongly resisted by the gentry, who appealed to the barons on the grounds that the exorbitant sum was out of proportion to what they could afford and contrary to the traditional freedom which the ancient kings of Bohemia had granted to their ancestors.[24] They also implied that the tax was not in the national interest and demanded further that the diet sessions should not be unduly protracted and that the assent of the few who could afford to stay on should not be passed off as resolutions of the whole assembly. It seems that on this occasion the emperor did not overcome the gentry's opposition and that the net result of the diet was the election of the delegates to Basel.

The outcome of the session which ended in mid-June was disappointing for Sigismund because he had failed to persuade Rokycana to go to Basel and thus get rid of him. At the emperor's request, Rokycana had appeared at the diet where he again voiced the Hussite complaints that Philibert was still avoiding old obligations. The bishop could only present feeble excuses; he had committed the indiscretion of enlisting the help of Hofman, the bishop of Meissen and a well-known anti-Hussite zealot, who had probably come to Prague on business of his own.[25] In the increasingly tense atmosphere the diet demanded the removal of Philibert on grounds that he was a foreigner. The emperor retreated and seconded the diet's proposal that the Prague archdiocese should have an acting administrator, pending Rokycana's recognition. With the support of the lords and the university, the emperor decided that it should be Master Křišt'an of Prachatice, rather than Wenceslas of Dráchov, the candidate of Rokycana's party. On 16 June, Philibert invested Křišt'an, and on the same day, Rokycana and a friend went for a walk outside the city walls where Diviš Bořek and his mounted escort were waiting to take him to the safety of the Kunětická Hora castle whence he was to move to the congenial atmosphere of Hradec Králové where the forces for the defense of Hus' legacy against the faithless king were gathering.[26]

The manner in which Rokycana had slipped through his fingers brought home to Sigismund that fact that Bořek, the victor of Lipany, had now become his enemy. Sigismund's attention was, however, diverted to Germany where the conflict between Eugene IV and the Council of Basel was brought to a head as a result of the pope's determination to destroy the Council. To avert this, the electors urged the emperor to call the imperial diet at Nürnberg. The emperor however feared rebellion in Bohemia in his absence and after long negotiations the electors agreed to have it meet in Cheb. He arrived there on 2 July and although he accomplished little, returned home again on 7 August. Sigismund was welcomed in Prague with the enthusiastic but short-lived rejoicing of his party.[27]

His main concern was strengthening his position in Prague. Leaving the reliable Old Town councillors in office, he replaced the whole council of the New Town with accommodating ones. Now he had a free hand in reinstating monasteries which were the strongest support of his throne and which were increasing in importance as his health rapidly deteriorated and he became afraid of death. By November, he had returned no less than fourteen monasteries in Prague to various religious orders, including one, where Želivský used to preach, to the Carmelites.[28] Sigismund's greatest worry was the castle Sion, belonging to John Roháč, one of his more staunch opponents, and situated in the territory once controlled by the Orphans and Taborites. Its successful defiance of the king made it a rally point for the opposition. The nobles from the Hradec and Chrudim areas were beginning to assemble there and complain about the emperor who was not keeping his word. This was an ominous echo of how the revolution had started twenty-two years earlier. Sigismund was thirsting for the blood of the courageous captain who defied him with scarcely a hundred men especially because the long shadow of Žižka in the background recalled to Sigismund his own ignominious flight from Bohemia during which he had contracted the painful gout. The blind hero had long been dead but the emperor tried, but failed, to destroy even Žižka's small castle, Kalich.[29] Distrustful of the Czech commander in charge of the siege of Sion, Sigismund hired picked Hungarian troops at a high cost. By sheer coincidence, Sion fell as soon as the Hungarians appeared on the scene.

The young Czech commander did not seem to be in a hurry; he had camped near Sion for four months. He was Hynek Ptáček of Pirkštejn who was to become the founder of the Poděbrady party and a prominent Hussite statesman. The tunnel which had already been dug under the access to the moat would become fatal to the castle only if the wind blew in the right direction. This happened on 6 September soon after the arrival of Michael Ország and his Hungarians. A gust of wind blew gun smoke into the moat enabling the besiegers to scale the ramparts. In the fierce fight which went on till nightfall some men were killed and very few escaped. The rest, including Roháč, were captured.[30]

Aeneas Sylvius commented ironically that Roháč had derived the name
for his castle from the belief that it would bring forth the truth which
would liberate the Czech people, alluding to Isaiah's account of Senacherib
and the Jews. This great faith was not fulfilled but Roháč seemed per-
ordained to bring down the perfidious king in a different way.

On 8 September, Sigismund ordered a great celebration. He had the garrison of Sion brought before him to hold up Roháč to ridicule. Roháč
said he would rather have his eyes put out than to look at the vile king.
Sigismund had him so savagely tortured that his intestines fell out. He
then ordered him to be executed by hanging. A three-story scaffold was
erected in front of the Týn church where Roháč died clad in baronial
robes and hanging on a gold chain. Next below him hung Wyszek Raczin-
ski, a Polish nobleman, the priest Prostředek and Zelený, the best artillery
man of the garrison. Underneath swung the bodies of forty men of the
garrison, the emperor and the court watching the gruesome spectacle
which even after many years brought tears to peoples' eyes.

On the day before the fall of Sion, the emperor had doubts about his
victory over Roháč and revoked the diet which he had originally called
for Čáslav, choosing it as a site as if to rehabilitate himself in the town
where he had been dethroned. Because Sion was close to Čáslav, he
changed his mind and ordered the diet to meet in Prague where he felt
more secure. There he met solid opposition led by Diviš Bořek of Miletínek who had amalgamated the resistance of east Bohemia including
those whom he had defeated at Lipany. He was forgiven by them because
he had saved Rokycana's life. He brought to the diet an indictment listing eighteen instances in which Sigismund had violated the obligations
to which he had earlier agreed. Two-thirds of them concerned non-ob-
servance of the Compactata including his own guarantee of freedom
which he had frivolously signed although the Council of Basel rejected
them. The rest of the complaints dealt with secular matters. It stated
forthrightly, without threats, that the emperor had not returned the
imperial insignia; he had violated freedom, law and order in an unprecedented way; he had introduced foreigners to office, courts and to the
archdiocese, to the detriment of the Czech language, God's truth and the
agreements into which he had entered; he had failed to restore property
to the university and hospitals; he had reduced Kutná Hora to squalor and
degeneracy to the discredit of the crown of Bohemia; he had encouraged

the coinage of false money; he had excluded prominent Hussites, spiritual and temporal, from the council of state; he had installed into offices and the government of the country, people who were repugnant to them.[31]

This protest had the true ring of the old Čáslav which had deposed him twenty-six years earlier.[32] It seems that this time the emperor did not try to justify his actions or provoke his adversaries. Some of them, such as Beneš Mokrovouský and Hertvík of Rušinov, former Orphan captains, openly declared war on him and were soon joined by Frederick of Stráž-nice, the lord of Kolín, whose cavalry was already beginning to harrass Prague.[33] By then, the emperor's gout had become excruciating as the amputation of a big toe had brought no relief. The danger that he would be captured by his enemies, from whom he had narrowly escaped in the past, was now real. He knew that he was hated and despised. Fear of vengeance for his perfidy and the crime against Roháč drove him from Prague.

Early on 11 November, he left Prague, carried on a stretcher and ac-companied by his wife, the whole court, a large armed force and the in-dispensable prostitutes, and made for Moravia by the shortest rout avoid-ing Čáslav and Jihlava where he did not feel safe. In about a week he reached Telč in Moravia where he reduced speed and on 29 November arrived at Znojmo. He had Queen Barbara arrested on suspicion of plotting with his enemies and rejoined his daughter and her husband, Albrecht of Austria, the only persons he trusted. He died there on 9 December.

According to the story spread and possibly invented by his devoted biographer, Eberhardt Windecke,[34] the emperor, already on his death bed, ordered that he be attired in his imperial robes and crown. True or false, the story is in character. Many Germans were devoted to him. The Hus-sites' judgement of him had been inexorably summed up by Žižka as far back as 1421: "The heretical king, betrayer of the Lord God and his Scriptures, violator of unmarried and married women, murder, arson-ist and wreaker of destruction on the Czech language (nation)."[35] History pronounced a similar judgement.

The last phase of the Hussite revolt against Sigismund almost coincided with its final struggle with the Council of Basel. The diet of May 1437 sent off the fourth, and last, delegation to settle the remaining contro-versial questions and implement the Compactata.[36] The delegates were the theologians, Prokop of Plzeň and John Příbram; a knight, Přibík of

Klenové; two burghers, Matthew Louda and Wenceslas Březka, and Lord Peter of Zvířetice, the first man of baronial rank to be sent to Basel. On 26 August, the Czech delegates opened the disputations which they had been granted by the Compactata of 1433. It concerned the fundamental question of whether Christ had authorized communion in both kinds. It if had been answered in the affirmative the chalice would have had to be reintroduced in the whole Church or at least throughout the Czech lands. At once opinions clashed and the Council would not move an inch from the negative view that it had held from the beginning. The chief spokesman was Palomar, the successor to John Stojkovic, who had been sent to Constantinople to establish contacts with the Greeks. Palomar suited the Council as it was generally admitted that in the disputations of four years earlier, Stojkovic's conduct had gone beyond the limits of propriety.

As a matter of fact, there was not much to choose between the two. Palomar expected to face Rokycana who was in his, and the emperor's opinion, the most dangerous rival. Palomar had prepared himself by thoroughly studying the 1433 disputation and then rehearsing the subject matter with prominent theologians. It was well that he did so because Příbram had reverted to the fervour of his early speeches delivered at the time of the Council of Constance when he had earned his spurs at Jakoubek's side.[37] His criticism of the Constance fathers who had banned the chalice caused enough ill feeling. As a newcomer to Basel as well as one of the party which had helped the Council destroy the brotherhoods at Lipany, Příbram felt entitled to special treatment. It did not occur to him that he had possibly played out his role and was fading into insignificance, a fact which Palomar might have hurled in his face at any moment. When Příbram presented the bold demands of the Prague diet, Palomar accused him of transgressing the instructions from Charles University and produced, amidst loud clamor and even saber rattling, a different set of directives to the university masters which had been drafted by the extreme right wing in Prague and which undermined the instructions Příbram had brought to Basel. Needless to say Příbram was very angry about the underhanded dealings.[38] After him Prokop of Plzeň entered into the discussion more calmly, defending communion for children. The disputation went on until 20 October when the lay delegates in the name of the Prague diet brought forward requests which caused a storm of protest.[39]

The diet demanded an unequivocal statement that freedom of the chalice should be introduced all over Bohemia for all time and that all rulers, spiritual and temporal, should be notified of this by appropriate bulls. It also stated that the Council should confirm Rokycana and his suffragans as holders of the offices to which they had been elected. On the question of whether Christ had authorized communion from the chalice, the diet required the Council to adhere to the Cheb agreements and stated that it should permit communion for the children as well as the singing and reading of the Creed, Lessons and Epistles in the vernacular, a right which the Church had granted the Southern Slavs.[40] Furthermore, the Council should exercise its influence towards raising the University of Prague to its former status, and carry out church reform as promised by the Compactata and demanded by the fourth article. The Council was adamant as ever, denying the Czechs any right to make demands as long as they maintained their liturgical peculiarities, and refusing to recognize Rokycana as the archbishop. The bold language of the Czech delegation which the Council had been led to believe supported zealously the emperor's cause and which included two former Taborite captains, who had betrayed their brothers, and an aristocrat, a supposed pillar of reaction, startled the members of the Council. It made them wonder whether they had been misled by Palomar's celebrated knowledge of Bohemian affairs or Philibert's rosy prediction of recatholization of that country. It appeared that the thoroughbred stallion to which Palomar had likened the Czech people was not nearly ready to be tied up in the stable.

Apart from Příbram, Peter of Zvířetice made easily the most effective contribution to the debate.[41] A baron by birth, a Hussite by background, he was educated and knew Latin, and was a former candidate for the priesthood. He had signed the letter of protest to Constance and fought on the side of the Orphans. His elder brother, Zdislav, had lived in the Bethlehem College while Hus was its pastor. Hus had also conferred both bachelor and master degrees upon him. In 1417, Zdislav was elected rector of Charles University. Long after Zdislav's death, Peter took the same resolute stand at the Council of Basel as he had in 1415 when he had appended his seal to the famous protest. It was his task to present the demands of the Bohemian diet to the Council. For all its efforts, the Council could not convert the Czech messengers and had to find an appropriate formula to cover up the sharp conflict.

It instructed Palomar to work out a sharp answer rejecting all the requests outright but did not find opportunity to hand it to the Czechs. Cesarini did his best to calm the special committee entrusted with drafting a decree on the chalice by informing the Czechs of its rash conclusions that they should renounce the chalice altogether. It was hoped that the Czechs would be mollified by inclusion of a statement that the Council did not mean to violate the Compactata. The Hussite delegates declared proudly that this answer would not satisfy the diet. On 24 November, after a month of unproductive dicussions, the Council retreated and promised an answer after it had time to sort out its divergent views. Příbram's appeal for a few modest concessions was rebuffed in retaliation for the daring demands made by the Czech diet, so on 29 November the Hussites decided to leave. The parting ceremony went off with the customary courtesy and Příbram, in a dignified but emphatic speech, told the Council some home truths. He stated that for the sake of peace, Bohemia had given up many towns and contributions from territories far beyond its borders, that the Czechs had amply vindicated their right to the chalice, and yet none of their demands had been met. Unless the Council was willing to adhere to the criterion of the Cheb agreements, the Czechs would never accept its decision. He added that the manner in which they had been snubbed would encourage the wicked people at home to destroy the hard-won peace. Furthermore, he pointed out, it had been the Czech nobles who had wiped out the subversive elements which no foreign armies or princes could beat in the field.

Finally, the Czechs expressed their sincere thanks for the renowned hospitality of the city of Basel and requested, as a conciliatory gesture, the release of one prisoner according to Bohemian custom.[42] Despite the friendly farewell, the Council could not fail to detect threats in the valedictory address and issued, on 23 December (the day the delegation returned to Prague), an entirely negative decree on the chalice coupled with an ultimatum inserted in the draft of the bull, which was to replace the Compactata and make communion in both kinds available only to those who would accept the decree of 23 December.[43] That bull was never issued. Bohemia was not at all interested in the delegates who were about to be sent to Prague early in 1438. Having learned that they were not welcome in Prague, the conciliar messengers went to Vienna whence they returned to Basel. The main architects of the document of 23 December

1437, Cesarini and Palomar, joined forces with Eugene IV who dissolved and eventually brought down the Council by war. Palomar died in 1442[44] and Cardinal Cesarini fell in the battle of Varna in 1444 after having persuaded King Wladislaw to violate the peace which he had sworn to uphold. This was another outward sign of the moral taint which the cardinal had already revealed in his dealings with the Hussites, and which earned him the stern by just judgement of Martin Lupáč, who saw through him more clearly than others: ". . . he incited the Council against the pope with whom he was in secret understanding. . . and induced the king of Poland to commit perjury whereby he treacherously gave up innumerable Christian soldiers to the Turks."[45]

Cesarini and Palomar deserted the Council at the height of its struggle with the pope, and at a time when it was making an intense effort to carry out Church reform in a manner that would satisfy the yearnings of generations of enlightened churchmen. In the attempt to curb papal absolutism and extortionistic fiscal practices which had, for more than a century, been widely criticized as a source of moral corruption, the Council of Constance had decreed decennial meetings. This was not an adequate measure to control Martin V who had called the Council only because he had sworn an oath to do so, and then immediately dissolved it. In 1433, the Council of Basel, partly as a result of the negotiations with the Hussites, issued two comprehensive decrees[46] which, with some exceptions, were intended to restore to chapters and monastic orders the right to elect prelates by withholding from the pope the right to appoint them. The second decree introduced synodal control over bishops. If these reforms had been carried out at that time they would have saved the Church from the upheavals of the following century which were to give rise to national reformed Churches in some leading countries in Europe. In 1435, the Council of Basel abolished almost all payments to Rome in order to force the pope to make concessions. Eugene IV was resolutely opposed to these changes, a fact which in 1438 led to the outbreak of war between himself and the Council.

The Council held out for a long time as it had many inspired and dedicated individual supporters within the reform movement. England kept aloof from the struggle. In the previous century, Parliament had introduced measures to curb interference from Rome even though these were not strong enough to prevent some of its powerful rulers from coming to terms with certain popes. France also remained neutral in the armed conflict but in 1438, on the king's behalf, the general synod at Bourges declared the so-called Pragmatic Sanction accepting most Basel reforms. In this, the German electors followed France's example, recognizing the Basel decrees in the document, called the Acceptance of Mainz, issued in 1439. After the coronation of Albrecht' s successor, Frederick III, the situation deteriorated swiftly. At this time Henry Toke skillfully defended the Council's position in a paper written in German in 1442. It was soon followed by Matthew Döring's vehement *Confutatio Primatus Papae* (1443). The pope too had competent advocates, especially Nicholas of Cusa and Aeneas Sylvius who had deserted the cause of the Council and become a clerk of the Vienna chancery. Frederick III concluded the Concordat of Vienna, dealing a death blow to the Council and exacting a price of many ducats for it. Sylvius, as the mediator, earned for himself a handsome bishopric. The city of Basel was ordered by King Frederick to give the Council notice to quit, and on 28 July 1448, Henry Beinheim bade farewell to its members. They left for Lausanne ruled by Duke Amadeo of Savoy who had been elected pope by the Council in 1440 but resigned within a year after which the Council was dissolved.

Pope Nicholas V celebrated the victory by sponsoring a noisy festival in Rome during which he made a profit out of indulgences. Twelve years after that, Aeneas Sylvius, now Pope Pius II, could rejoice when the new king of France repealed the Pragmatic Sanction. Both popes were wrong in thinking that Basel was finished. It survived in its copious literature and in the *Gravamina Nationis Germanicae,* the frequent complaints from the imperial diet about the increasing exploitation of Germany by Rome which tried to compensate itself for the diminishing returns from France and England. With the age of printing, the propaganda of the opposition flourished prodigously,[47] especially at the beginning of the new century. New champions were rushing to the anti-Roman front, such as the humanists (Wimpfeling, Erasmus and Hutten) and the leaders or prophets of frequent peasant rebellions of the *Bundschuh* confederation which was largely inspired by the boldest piece of writing issued by the Council of Basel, the famous "Reformation of Emperor Sigismund" of 1439. It was modelled on the Taborite manifesto of 1430 and on the Pragmatic Sanction. Its author was almost certainly Dr. Beinheim, the foremost member of the Basel reform movement. The interaction of various tendencies and currents of opinion raised the feeling in Germany to such a degree that when in 1518 an almost obscure Dr. Martin Luther was tried in Rome for his stand against indulgences he could calmly face the wrath of the Vatican under the protection of public opinion. His militant challenge "To the Christian Nobility of the German Nation," a refurbished and more penetrating version of the program of the Council of Basel, kindled a revolt which lost Rome a great part of the German nation forever.

Bohemia heard only a distant echo of these turbulent changes after it had cut its ties with the Council of Basel in 1437. It was too preoccupied with its own problems as the revolution had not nearly achieved its ends. In 1438 the Hussites and their Polish allies fought, mostly in southern Bohemia, with the party of King Albrecht, Sigismund's son-in-law and successor. In October 1439, Albrecht died without male issue and his party had to try to come to terms with the Hussites who had the majority in the diet. At the beginning of 1440, on their initiative, the diet of Prague unanimously made into law a resolution embodying the agreements of Jihlava and Sigismund's concessions binding both the Hussites and the Habsburgs, Catholic parties and placing any future sovereign under obligation to have Rokycana recognized by the Church. The record of this agreement between the two parties known as the letter of peace (*list mírný*). It ushered in a period of calm, so that conditions now favored Hussitism. The kingdom was for years left without a king since Poland had lost interest in Bohemia, and Ladislav, Albrecht's son and heir, born posthumously in 1440, was in no position to intervene. The country governed itself for more than ten years as a defacto republic.

The Hussites skillfully utilized the regional constitution. Regional assemblies signed the letter of peace and issued writs for the election of regional captains and their councils. These captains had ample military resources to replace the former brotherhoods, especially the Orphans. While in western Bohemia the former Hussites had to share power with the Catholics, they established their decisive influence over a large continuous territory in eastern Bohemia, bordering on Prague and adjoining the Tabor area in the south, with Kutná Hora, Čáslav and Hradec Králové as its military and political supporting bases. This also included the regions of Boleslav, Chrudim, Kouřim as well as Klodzko (Glatz) territory. Within this sphere of influence the regional council had representation from the towns and from the lesser nobles in accordance with principles of Hussite democracy. The reorganized administration rendered the Poděbrady party, the new name for the determined adherents of Rokycana and young George of Poděbrady, so powerful that in 1448 it could seize Prague almost without a shot being fired. It obtained for George the position of regent in 1452, and finally had him crowned king after the sudden death of Ladislav Posthumous in 1458. The Hussite king[48] of course had to fight new bloody wars for the achievements of Jihlava but the strength of the revolution stood him in good stead against the reaction at home and the popes, and helped protect the work of the revolution for the future.

CHAPTER TWELVE

THE ACHIEVEMENTS OF THE HUSSITE REVOLUTION

We have been following the struggle through the last thirteen years of the Hussite revolution, one of the most dramatic and blood-stained epochs of Czech history. Let us now try to assess how much the enormous sacrifice was able to achieve and save for the future in the face of a hostile world.

The revolution summed up its program in the principles which became famous as the Four Articles of Prague. They were disseminated directly in the manifestos which reached even such far-off countries as England and Spain, and indirectly in the many polemics written against them at almost all universities in Europe.[1] They expressed the moral and religious yearnings of generations of reformers from Milič of Kroměříž to Hus and Jakoubek. Matthew of Janov described the reform movement as an endeavor to bring the Church back to its wholesome and substantial beginnings, that is the institutions of the primitive Church of Christ and of the apostles.[2] This revolutionary ideal which was tersely expressed in the famous Cheb agreements (1432) had earlier inspired the Four Articles. The first article, calling for freedom of preaching, also reaffirmed the obligation to protect Hussite preachers against the death penalty which the Church had inflicted on dissidents in the 12th century; the famous letter of protest to Constance against the burning of Hus had been the first pledge of its kind. The second article, demanding dispensation of the chalice to the laity which the Church had gradually rooted out in the 12th and 13th centuries, was a step towards depriving the clergy of it presumed superiority over the laity. The third article, preaching apostolic poverty of the clergy was aimed at breaking down the economic power of the Church by expropriating its immense property. Lastly, the fourth article demanded that the state should be the keeper of public morality and prosecute all public sins, especially prostitution, paying no regard to the priestly privilege of being tried only by ecclesiastical courts. It also rejected simony, that is any payments to priests for administering sacraments and for granting church offices whereby the Church had greatly enriched itself.

The Four Articles in this form originated from the moderate Hussites represented by Jakoubek in Prague and Žižka at Tabor. The right wing tended to tone them down to prevent a complete breach with Rome which would have wrecked prospects for peace. The Taborite extremists, on the other hand, introduced some radical modifications[3] while still adhering to the Articles at all times because they formed the basis of their alliance with Prague. In spite of their isolation, created by the alliance in 1432, between the Orphans and Prague, the Taborites stood united with the rest of the Hussites during the peace negotiations at Basel as well as in the Compactata of Prague (1433) and Jihlava (1436), on these Four Articles. These last two agreements, together with Sigismund's concessions, provided a legal basis for a kind of *Magna Charta* of the first church to achieve self-determination by a de facto separation from Rome, and set an example to the reformed churches of the world.

The Hussite church grew amidst ceaseless fighting and was not without shortcomings, nor did the revolution achieve all its aims. Its luminaries, such as Rokycana and Prokop Holý, who dreamed that the country of John Hus would reform the whole Church according to its ancient model, finally had to accept the fact that even in Bohemia and Moravia a viable Catholic minority and political reaction would survive. Rokycana was never confirmed archbishop by Rome nor did he acquire the right, either arbitrarily or with Constantinople's assent,[4] to ordain priests so that the desparate shortage of clergy had to be obviated by every possible means. Yet this Hussite church merited respect and admiration. Everywhere in its sphere of influence, even among Czech Catholics, the horrors like the inquisition, the burning of heretics and witch-hunts were unknown while in the surrounding countries thousands of women were sent to torture chambers and the stake in the second half of the fifteenth century.[5] The freedom of religion opened the Czech lands to individuals and groups of people who were in conflict with the Catholic church, including Andrew Galka, from Cracow, Gregory Heimburg, a diplomat in the service of George of Poděbrady, John of Lübeck, many priests from Poland and also to a large number of Waldensian families whom the Unity of Czech Brethren had rescued from Brandenburg and resettled as German confraternities near Lanškroun and Kravař in 1480.[6]

A very attractive feature of the new church was the popular character of its liturgy, the great heritage of Jakoubek and John Čapek. Rokycana successfully kept it alive although while he was in Prague he sacrified a number of Jakoubek's innovations, for the sake of peace with the emperor and the Council envoys. After escaping from Sigismund he found himself in the free atmosphere of Hradec Králové and immediately adopted the Czech mass which had become traditional since the time of Žižka and his Orphan preachers. He upheld this practice in Prague after his return in 1448, pointing out as a precedent that the popes had authorized St. Cyril and St. Methodius to use the Slavonic liturgy.[7] In 1462, Pius II unilaterally repealed the Compactata and thus freed Rokycana and the Hussites from observing those agreements of Jihlava which had been forcibly imposed upon them. The sixth of July was consecrated not only to the memory of Hus, but also of Jerome, Žižka and the martyr Michael Polák, Rokycana's worthy successor whom Wladislaw Jagiellon ordered to be executed in 1480. The memory of these great figures inspired enthusiasm for the ideals of the Hussite revolution and the strength to resist enemies abroad and at home.

The inner vigor of the Hussite church was demonstrated in that it gave rise to the Unity of Brethren which replaced the Taborites when these could no longer maintain an independent existence during the Poděbrady era. As the head of the united Hussite camp, King George could not allow Tabor free play especially when her politicians compromised themselves with the Catholics. The Unity strove to bring separation from Rome to a more far-reaching and consistent conclusion than the Taborites. It followed in the steps of Rokycana and his disciple, its founder Brother Gregory and his associates. It also followed in the footsteps of Peter Chelčický, its spiritual father.[8] Peter had grown up among the Taborites whose priests he avowed he had always loved. But he parted company with Nicholas Biskupec when he adopted Wyclif's scholastic theory of the Lord's Supper. Peter, himself remained faithful to Jakoubek's simple faith. When after the latter's death the tide turned toward the right, Chelčický drew closer again to the Taborites but later found himself in agreement with Rokycana when Nicholas veered toward the far left. Nevertheless, the ferment of Taborite militancy found its way into the young Unity and caused temporary discord, with some loss of life, and a parting of ways between the Unity and its Hussite mother church. Eventually both Hussite churches established a harmonious *modus vivendi* based on mutual understanding, disturbed by occasional skirmishes. These were usually provoked by the Catholic party whenever it thought fit to attack the Hussite church, censure critics of unilateral repeal of the Compactata or take arms against the Hussite king. Since King George warded off this danger and Wladislaw Jagiellon, his successor, was sworn to observe the Compactata, the Peace of Kutná Hora (1485) finally enabled the Unity and the Hussite church to develop side by side. In the last decade of the fifteenth century, the Unity admitted persons with higher education to its ranks and soon began to use the art of printing to the maximum advantage.

The apologies published by the Unity of Czech Brethren exercised a profound influence on Martin Luther, a young professor of the new University of Wittenberg and helped to shape the destiny of the founder of another large reformed church which broke away from Rome.[9] Encouraged by the pioneering work of the Czech Brethren, he launched an attack on the papacy which had already been severely shaken by the resistence of its grossly exploited adherents and by the growth of humanism. Luther not only drew strength from his Hussite forerunners but also knew that he would have found refuge in Bohemia if he had lost the support of his patron. Other national churches were formed after the example of the Saxon church, not only in other parts of Germany, but also in England, and inflicted shattering and lasting blows to the papal system. The struggle between the two camps went on for another century but in the end laid permanent foundations for modern European culture of which freedom of conscience and scientifice research are essential ingredients.

The Hussite revolution also had a far-reaching political and social program which was never officially summed up because it tended to be overshadowed by the widely know Four Articles. The political and social changes can only be pieced together from the records of contemporary public life, especially the minutes of the Hussite assemblies. Even this fragmentary evidence reveals the greatness of democratization of the Czech state and its institutions.[10]

All political power in pre-revolutionary Bohemia had been vested in a few baronial families that controlled legislation and the judiciary, and against whom there was no appeal. Of the four highest offices, only that of the clerk of the courts could be held by a commoner because it required expert knowledge. The aristocracy had acquired great power and wealth as a result of the revolt of 1394-1405, against the weak rule of Wenceslas IV which had thrown the Czech lands into disarray. The king succeeded partially in retaining control of the royal council and was thus able to counter-balance the lords who held the highest offices. Otherwise he could rely only on the royal towns and the officials whom he appointed, such as court nobles who performed military duties at the royal castles and the royal vice-chamberlain who was in control of the royal towns.

The calamity which the revolts represented for royal power, struck the gentry, who later supplied the revolution with its most valuable cadres, an even more severe blow. Yet the effect on it was comparatively mild in light of the effect it had on the very foundation of the nation, the dependent peasant population. Until then the peasant had had the right to appeal to the land court, a valuable right even though the judges were relatives of the defendants. In 1402, the right of appeal was abolished, giving free reign to the nobles' caprices. The villein was burdened by the corvée, tied to the soil and gradually reduced to serfdom.[11]

The revolution introduced many changes in the polity. Although the lords maintained, on the whole, their privileged position, for example they controlled the land court, they did have to give the gentry a certain number of positions. In 1437, eight knights were added to the twelve lords and during the revolution legislative powers were transferred to the diet the composition of which changed radically. In pre-revolutionary times, the diet was invoked occasionally by the king at his pleasure. The revolutionary diet met more frequently, even twice a year, and the main decisions were made by the spokesmen for the field armies.[12] After the battle of Lipany, their seats were awarded to members of the gentry (knights) and the towns. The division of the diet into these three estates, undoubtedly dating from the time of Žižka, became the fundamental institution of the state as well as an excellent training ground for statesmen of the Hussite democracy and survived for almost two centuries as one of the chief gains of the revolution. In 1502-17, when the lords attempted to dislodge the towns from the diet, they failed completely.[13]

This political advance of the knights and the towns was a just reward for the invaluable service rendered to the revolution in the first difficult years. The towns also benefited by the overthrow of the largely artificially maintained German minority and by their share in the distribution of church property which enabled them to repair heavy war losses and raise their standard of culture. Numerous and better grammar schools were founded under the guidance of the Charles University which helped rear a new generation of competent politicians, officials and even writers.[14] The towns thus became the mainstay of democracy and the wall that withstood the waves of reaction represented by the lords who tried to recompense themselves by turning on the peasantry.

Immediately in 1437, the land courts gave the lords the right to force their runaway subjects to return to the land.[15] As the verdict was not promptly implemented the peasants enjoyed freedom from oppression during the reign of King George (who depended on the towns) and for a short time at the beginning of the Jagiellon rule. The weak King Wladislaw, who had grown up in quite a different environment, gave free rein to the lords so that in 1487 serfdom was made law and the Czech peasant was left to the mercy of his landlord. Until 1781 he remained tied to the soil and his children were allocated to the estate as laborers as the lord thought fit.

This first blow to the foundations of the revolutionary achievements required many years to take effect. Respect for justice which the great Hussite preachers had instilled into the nation lived on in subsequent generations. During their frequent rebellions, the peasants got support from several sources: from the towns which granted asylum to fugitives, from eminent law experts like Victorin of Všehrdy who advocated their cause, and from peasant prophets such as Nicholas Vlásenický, the author of the legend of the Blaník Knights. In 1547, all this collapsed when the uprising against Ferdinand I failed.[16]

The revolt was led by Prague and other towns together with a handful of nobles. Some of these were Hussites, the rest were Bohemian Brethren who withdrew their support after the defeat of their evangelical allies in Germany. The king isolated Prague and tricked it into capitulation with the rest of the rebellious towns. Although the towns retained their representation at the diet, their democratic autonomy became paralyzed by the introduction of sheriffs, the king's own creatures. In spite of this defeat, the towns revolted again in 1609 led by Wenceslas Budovec. They tried to enforce the memorable Letter of Majesty and took up arms when the solemn pledge was demonstratively violated by Vienna. After two years of war, the revolution lost the fatal battle of the White Mountain (1620) which led to the utter destruction by the Habsburgs of political and religious freedom, and to the European-wide counter-reformation.

For more than a hundred years international conditions favored the Habsburgs to the extent that their triumph seemed final. During the Thirty Years' War, which had been sparked by the Czech revolt, the fortunes of war swayed to and fro, and almost at the last moment Prague very nearly fell to the Swedes but the recatholized population of Prague maintained the defense until the peace treaty was signed. The counter-reformation, which up to that time was ready to retreat, could now begin to wipe out systematically all that was left of Hussitism, with efficient support from the monarchy. It started with the Renewed Ordinances of 1627 whereby the towns as one estate were reduced to one single seat while each member of the new estate of prelates had one seat. Catholicism became law while the evangelical religion was declared a crime against the state. German was placed on an equal footing with Czech, thus opening the way for Germanization supported by a host of the new German and Romance lords who had very cheaply bought land in the enslaved country. The effort to eradicate everything reminiscent of the Hussite past concentrated on burning evangelical books which the Jesuit emissaries ferreted out up and down the country to deprive people of their last moral support, their last consolation.

A hundred years after White Mountain the work of the counter-reformation might have seemed completed. This was the period which Alois Jirásek portrayed in his tragical historical novel "The Darkness." In 1729, after about fifty years of propaganda at home and abroad, the counter-reformation invested a substitute saint, John of Nepomuk, the alleged martyr of confession, to erase the memory of Hus. "The swan (the new saint) will overcome the goose (hus in medieval Czech

means goose) and all the power of hell," said the inscription on the trium-
phal arch erected for his canonization in Prague. The much desired saint
failed to fulfill expectations;[17] within a decade the monarchy was reeling
under the threat of invasion by its various neighbors, especially the king
of Prussia. Wars filled almost all the forty years of the reign of Maria
Theresa, laid waste her lands, snatched the rich Silesia and forced her to
turn away from the powers of darkness and let in the light of enlighten-
ment. The ideals which had been trampled down in Hus' own country
survived in the countries which had reformed their churches, in Germany
and especially in England, and acquired a new meaning through the results
of modern research which ripened in the atmosphere of freedom. Then
they returned to the country of their origin to bring strength and comfort
to the tiny residue of fighters whom centuries of persecution could not
root out.

The Thirty Years' War deprived the nation of its urban and aristocratic
scholars and thinkers whom the Habsburgs, under pressure of public
opinion abroad, granted the paltry freedom of free exodus. Some of the
exiles bled to death on the innumerable battlefields of the Thirty Years'
War, others disappeared obscurely in foreign parts. The Czechs became
a nation of serfs toiling on the latifundia of new foreign lords and tied to
the soil more rigidly than ever before. Escape was punished by death
or a savage prison sentence, rebellions were brutally crushed and the
participants ended up on the gallows.

The beginning of the eighteenth century brought a slight improvement
to the old believers in remote parts of the country. In 1707, Charles XII
of Sweden obtained permission for the Silesian evangelicals to build six
churches of which the one at Těšín became a famous center for book
traffic and the organization of escapes. This brought back to life the
older and almost moribund confraternities which had been founded in
Lusatia after the battle of White Mountain. In Žitava, V. Klejch, a fugitive
from Litomyšl, set up a lively book business issuing small pocket books
which itinerant distributors peddled in the wide borderland of Bohemia
and Moravia while guiding whole families to evangelical settlements in
Saxony and Lusatia. In 1732, the first Czech congregation was founded
in Berlin and another one in the nearby Rixdorf in 1737. Henceforth,
the kings of Prussia and mainly Frederick II forcefully supported the
Czech evangelicals as part of their anti-Habsburg policy aiming at the

conquest of Bohemia. This plan never materialized but Frederick remained after 1740, an unintentional contributor to the Czech national revival. Hundreds of Czech families emigrated under escort of Prussian soldiers and founded several settlements in Silesia with assistance from Switzerland. In Berlin, J. B. Elsner, a senior member of the Unity and part of its Polish branch, published a large edition of almost all the Czech writings of J. A. Comenius and had many of them circulated in the Czech lands. The great peasant rebellions, first in Bohemia in 1775 and then in Moravian Wallachia, 1777, received moral support from Prussia. Both were ruthlessly suppressed but paved the way for the freeing of the peasants through the *"Robot-Patent"* and for the end of religious persecution. In 1781, when Joseph II issued his famous Toleration Edict and abolished serfdom, he was led, above all, by the endeavour to save the Czech lands from the king of Prussia whereby he incidentally laid the foundations for the Czech national rebirth.

The Toleration Edict stopped the pernicious process of sapping the nation's strength which was near exhaustion. It saved men like Palacký for the nation and made it possible for Šafařík to do his magnificent work in Prague. After the collapse of Metternich, the two men stood at the head of the famous Slav Congress of 1848, the greatest joint action of the Austro-Slavs. The abolition of serfdom restored to life the core of the nation and gave it access to the by now virtually Germanized cities and towns and to higher education. This yielded the first generation of intellectuals and national leaders, the generation of Joseph Dobrovský which grew up ceaselessly fighting against all aspects of darkness and became proudly aware of the culture of Hus, the Hussite revolution, the Czech Brethren and eminent émigrés like Comenius and Paul Stránský (the author of the enlightened book, "The Czech State") had created. Their writings and works written about them began to appear in their own country helping to fill the great gap which the battle of White Mountain had created.

The achievements of the Hussite revolution which had laid the foundation for national revival, have to this day remained a powerful force in our national life. The proud memory of the ethical ideas[18] of the revolution has become an inherent part of Czech national consciousness which guided the literary, and since 1848, the political phases of the revival. Spokesmen for enlightened circles in the whole world have been paying tribute to Hus and his followers to this day.[19] As Ernest Denis put it, the small nation has become a creditor to the world. This will remain so as long as anybody is willing to struggle for the ideals of the Hussite revolution, for truth and justice following the motto of John Hus: Truth prevails.

NOTES

* In the present (English) edition, Chapter One is the last chapter (9) of the first volume of the original Czech edition (1965). Accordingly, Chapters Two and following correspond to Chapters One and following in the second volume of the Czech edition (1966).

Notes to Chapter One

1. *SL*, 64. A later text adds "But later it (the body) was transferred to Čáslav and buried in the church." *SLŠ*, 48. The body was likely moved in 1436-1437 by his family.

2. For details, Pekař, 3, 207-208; Urbánek, 266-267.

3. Urbánek, 268-271; Tomek, 4, 308ff. For Nicholas Sokol see Dobiáš, 2, 51ff.

4. For the Konopiště negotiations see Biskupec, 574-89. For the German translations of some of the reports see Procházka, F. F., *Miscellaneen der Böhmischen und Mährischen Literatur* (Prague, 1785), 267ff. from the Prague University MS XVII A 16, preserved in part in Prague Cathedral Chapter MS D 741. 108-9. More recently, J. Sedlák described the negotiations in *Táborské traktáty eucharistické* (Brno, 1918), 39-41, and analyzed Nicholas' tract and printed Příbram's tracts, 56-106. For Pelhřimov's tract see, Sokol, V., "O zvelebení v pravdě svátostí těla a krve Pána našeho Jezukrista" *JSH*, 2 (1929-suppl) 1-4. The cited Cathedral Chapter MS names the participants. From Prague: Smil Holice of Šternberg

and Šimon of the White Lion; from Tabor: Chval of Machovice and Matěj Louda. For the more difficult questions they were joined by Peter Payne and the priest Jan Čapek. From the party of Prague were also present Jakoubek, John Kardinál, John Příbram, Peter English, John Rokycana, a certain Jaroslaus, George Albus and the priest Wacha. Master Jiřík, Havlík of Sušice, Markold, Nicholas of Pelhřimov, Čapek, Prokop, Chřenovský and Kvirin signed Příbram's formula. Sedlák in the above cited work printed and analyzed three other Taborite tracts although assigned authorship incorrectly to Peter Payne. See my *LČ Rok.*, 109-110. One of the authors may have been the Slovak Taborite priest of Lukáš of Nové Mesto on Váh who in 1424 was tortured to death in Rožmberk's Krumlov. See my article in *ČNM*, 96 (1922), 191.

5.   See Procházka, *Miscellaneen*, 272-279 and my article in *ČNM* 88 (1914), 314.

6.   These are published by me in *JSH*, 8 (1935), 6-7.

7.   ‚The minutes of the disputation record this date. See *JSH*, 8 (1935), 10. The arbitrators, chosen to conduct the disptue, and who had also presided at Konopiště, are named here. See *ČNM*, 88 (1914), 314. Cf. Biskupec, 589-593.

8.   See Novotný, V. (ed.), *Kronika velmi pěkná o Janovi Žižkovi*, (Prague, 1923), 20, (*Chronican Vet. Collegiati*, 31, cf. Palacký, III, 2, 230 and Pekař, 4, 157).

9.   In November 1423 Žižka received a letter from Ambrose and John Hvězda warning him of an attempt on his life. See my *Listy B. J. Žižky* (1949), 24-25, [Cf. F. G. Heymann's dating of 1424 in *John Žižka and the Hussite Revolution* (New York, 1969 repr.), 399.]

10.   *SL.* 64, Tomek, 4, 366-376 gave an overview of property held by both brotherhoods in 1427 based on data from two lists of that year now published by Bezold, 2, 163-167. The short list (167) is full of errors. Cf. Tomek, 4, 379 and *UB*, 1, 612.

11.   Jecht, 83.

12.   Dlugosz, 4, 329.

13.   *UB*, 1, 382 cf. Altmann, 6167.

14.   Dobiáš, J., "K dějinám českého jihovýchodu v 1425," *ČČH* 39 (1939), 345.

15.   Palacký, III, 2, 232 dated the outbreak of the fighting on 14 February. See Tomek, 4, 318; *SL*, 64; *UB*, 1, 386.

16. *UB*, 1, 381-82.

17. Tomek, 4, 319. I might also draw attention to the university addresses of the Prague preacher, apparently Peter Mladoňovice, from 9-15 April, sharply attacking Tabor whom he called Babylon compared to Prague as Jerusalem. See my article in *JSH*, 22 (1953), 30-31.

18. Tomek, 4, 319-324.

19. For the sources of the information on the brotherhoods' wars see my article in *JSH*, 17 (1948). For Poděbrady's change of camps see his letter to Korybut on 9 July 1425 apologizing for not being able to come to his aid. *AČ*, 3, 303.

20. Bartoš, *Manifesty*, 258.

21. Dobiáš, *ČČH*, 39 (1933), 341-356 drew attention to the importance of Sigismund's note from his residence on 16 September 1425 in *UB*, 1, 407. Dobiáš' penetrating revision of these events is well worth reading. Cf. Urbánek, *Morava*, 272ff described the conditions in Moravia and the difficulties they represented for purposes of study. He also shows that on 2 February Dobeslav Puchala conquered the fortified monastery in Dolany, and Peter Holý the castle Hluboký.

22. My conclusion is based on the reports of the Taborite raids of 1425 which I printed in *JHS*, 17 (1948), 80. Here is written: "Postea circa Wenceslai festum placitaverunt et concordaverunt cum Pragensibus et eis edherentibus." This is followed by reports of the conquest of Vožice. The date, 17 October is an estimate. It is however a fact that during the lengthy negotiations Hvězda and Heřman of Borotín died. I reject the assertion in *SL*, 66 that the Taborites and Orphans wanted to lay siege to Prague.

23. See *AČ*, 3, 252-254 for the names of the delegates and the hostages for the brotherhoods. Those for Prague are unknown.

24. Among the hostages from the brotherhoods are named the Moravian nobles, Hyncík of Holštejn, Beneš of Boskovice and Nicholas of Lamberk. *AČ*, 3, 253. Beneš signed the truce with Albrecht of Austria in 1433. Neumann, 115. Because of the inadequacy of sources we can only guess at who from Moravia signed the 1424 treaty.

25. The text of the truce, which is undated, was drawn up before 17 October 1425. *AČ*, 3, 253 and Tomek, 4, 328ff.

26. Tomek's opinion (4, 338) is based on Theobald, cap. 59, that Korybut took the initiative, cannot stand up to the clear statement in the Vršovice treaty.

27. For the synod see my "Sněm husitské revoluce v Betlémské kapli," *JSH* 18 (1949), 97-102.

28. According to Theobald, cap. 59, the burgrave of Karlštejn and representatives of the Plzeň *Landfrid* presented the assembly in Prague with four requirements, over which the deliberations of the assembly broke up on 21 January without agreement except on the issue of peace between archbishop Conrad and Prague. Tomek, 4, 339 and his, *Základy*, 1, 477.

29. *AČ*, 3, 256-259 and *UB*, 2, 509-511. Cf. Palacký, III, 2, 248 and Tomek, 4, 340-341. In addition to the Písek assembly, there was likely one for the Tabor region. See my "O čest táborského hejtmana," *JHS* 22 (1953), 78-80.

30. See Rieger, B., *Zřízení krajské v Čechách* 1 (Prague, 1894) 68ff. Support for my conjecture that a change in the brotherhoods' point of view on the question of the regions occurred at this time are the Písek and Tabor regional assemblies. [Cf. Klassen, J. *The Nobility and the Making of the Hussite Revolution* (New York, 1978), 50-53.]

31. Bartoš, *Husitská revoluce* I (Prague, 1965), 187, n. 15. Cf. *FRB*, 5, 434, *UB*, 1, 418. I assume the reference is to the election of a regional captain and most likely to John Královec. The first reference to his election to the leadership in Hradec, Čáslav and Kouřim regions is in 1 April 1428. *UB* 1, 606. He is mentioned among the participants at the battle of Ústí, 16 June 1426. The reason for the election of a captain was the visit from the Moravian Orphan leader, John Tovačovský, asking for military aid. Urbánek, *Morava*, 286.

32. I accept the observations of Toman, 133 and Urbánek, R., *Lipany a konec polních vojsk* (Prague, 1934), 198, n. 92 that the name Orphans occurs first on 20 May 1426, whereas in the text of the Vršovice peace and in the simultaneous truce between the Hussites and the Podbrský association (*AČ*, 3, 252) the reference is to the Orebite brotherhood.

33. Kejř, 56-58 and my article on Prokop in *SH*, 8 (1961), 194.

Notes to Chapter Two

1. 'König, E., *Kardinal G. Orsini* (Freiburg, 1908), esp. 48.

2. For Reinlein see Bartoš, *Husitika*, and Munich ms. 8365, 167-232. Reinlein had been in Regensburg in the summer of 1420 to preach a crusade. He undoubtedly was responsible for the arrest and burning, in

1421, of the priest Ulrich Grünsleder for translating Hus' works. See *Andreas von Regensburg*, 350-362. Peter the prince of Portugal stopped in Regensburg on 20 March 1426 on the way to the court of King Sigismund. *Andreas von Regensburg*, 332-333.

3. Sources and literature on the wars up to the battle of Ústí have been compiled by Ermisch, H., "Zur Geschichte der Schlacht bei Aussig" *NASG*, 47 (1926), 5-34. He included some of the less accessible reports of the battle. See also *CDS*, 1, B 4. Czech and German literature includes Palacký, Bezold, Tomek, Toman, 348-366, Kroker, E., "Sachsen und die Husitenkriege" in *NASG*, 21 (1900), 7-23 and Jecht, 100-112. For the military side see Frankenberger 2, 115-130, Durdík, 171-175 and Urbánek, R., *Z husitského věku* (Prague, 1915), 115-118 and Lužek, 37-44.

4. See my introductory essay in Molnár, A., *Boleslavští bratří* (Prague, 1953), 10-12 for Roháč at Mladá Boleslav, *UB*, 1, 454, names among the Orphan gentry: Viktorin of Kunštát, Smil of Holice, Diviš Bořek, J. Rušinovský, Jeník, captain of Litomyšl, Aleš Vřestovský, Jiřík of Vizenburk and Jiřík of Chvalkovice and a Rožmberk. Cf. Tomek, 4, 343.

5. Palacký, III, 2, 257; Tomek, 4, 347; Lužek, 42 and Toman, 353.

6. *SL*, 66-69 and *SLŠ*, 51; cf. Kroker, *Sachsen*, 21, and Toman, 356.

7. Ermisch, *Zur Geschichte*, 38-39, 41, 45. The elector, however, exonerated his general.

8. See *SL* and Lužek, 43.

9. *Hrady*, 14, 41 and 324 and Lužek, 44.

10. For Korybut's letter to Vitold on 26 March 1426, *CW*, 717 and for the address of a French poet and diplomat, Alain Chartier, see Bartoš, F. M. (ed.), "Persuasio Alani Aurige ad Pragenses," *Filologický sborník* 7 (1922), 172-178.

11. *CW*, 717. The imperial diet to which he was delegated was announced on 8 December 1425 for 9 February 1426. Sigismund reached Vienna after 3 March 1426 and already on 10 April he announced a new diet for Nürnberg. RA, 8, 430-431; Altmann, 6502.

12. Bartoš, *HR*, 1, 191, and *SL*, 71; Tomek, 4, 351 and Toman, 361.

13. Bartošek, 595 and *SL*, 69 and Urbánek, R., *Věk poděbradský*, 1, (Prague, 1915), 218.

14. Bezold, 2, 85-86 and *Andreas*, 355-356.

15. *RA*, 8, 491.

16. *Andreas*, 424.

17. Stöller, 39ff., *SL*, 70; Bartošek, 596.

18. See my *Korybut*, 29.

19. The resolutions are published by Tomek in *VKČSN* (1878), 253-257 and Nejedlý, 347-353.

20. For the circular of 1417 see Bartoš, *HR*, 1, 36 [and Kaminsky, Howard, *A History of the Hussite Revolution* (Berkeley, 1967), 240-46].

21. *UB*, 1, 474; *CE*, 2, 202 and my *Korybut*, 211.

22. *AČ*, 1, 206. I attribute the decree of 29 August 1421 and of 21 July to Jakoubek (*LČ Jak.*, 57 č. 85).

23. Tomek, 4, 9, 192ff and 5, 233.

24. For Christian see Gellner, G. "Jan Černý a jiní lékaři češti do konce doby jagellovské." *VKČSN* (1934), 148-153. For his relationship to Čeněk of Vartemberk, *Documenta*, 635 and to Ulrich of Rožmberk, *AČ*, 3, 4. For Mladoňovice see my article in *KR*, 30 (1963), 79-85. For Příbram and Payne, see *LČ Rok.*

25. *LČ Jak.*, 58, č. 88 and *LČ Rok*, 10, č. 11.

26. Sedlák, *Studie*, 2, 161-164. See also my article in *JSH* 9 (1936), 29-34. Cf. Pekař, 1, 108-110 and my "Vrcholná bitva M. J. Jakoubka," *KR*, 28 (1961), 245-248.

27. Grünhagen, 107ff and 113ff. His book is based on documents in *UB* which even Palacký and Tomek did not fully utilize.

28. *UB*, 1, 497—the report of Rodenberg and his letter in *UB*, 1, 523-24.

29. Theobald, 1, 241.

30. See "Píseň o pražské příhodě," *Výbor z české literatury husitské doby* 1 (Prague, 1963), 327-331; *SL*, 70-71 and Prokeš, 204.

31. It is possible that his sister Helena, who since the death of John of Regensburg, headed the government of the duchy of Silesia gave him the signal to attack. *SSRSiL*, 6.

32. Svojše of gentry stock, resided in Prague, where he was a magistrate of the Old Town council 1424-1425 as well as a military captain of the city. Tomek 4, 333, 363. In 1429, he had made his peace with the city after a quarrel. *AČ*, 4, 383; Urbánek, *Věk*, 2, 27. For Rozvoda, see Tomek, 4, 410.

33. Tomek, 4, 410.

34. One of the reasons for Hussite opposition to Korybut was their suspicion that he allowed the Polish army to bring with it prostitutes and that he himself had committed adultery. *KR*, 26 (1959), 43.

Notes to Chapter Three

1. Hirsch, in *ADB*, 7, 464-75, Lindner, T., *Geschichte des deutschen Reiches unter König Wenzel* 2 (Braunschweig, 1880), 404-408; Hintze, O., *Hohenzollern und ihres Werk* (8th ed., Berlin, 1916), 80-82, and Bezold, passim.

2. *UB*, 1, 478-84; *RA*, 9, 11-14; Andreas, 433-35.

3. *RA*, 9, 30ff for the diet. See also Toman, 369-401; Bezold, 2, 97ff and Juritsch, G., *Der dritte Kreuzzug gegen die Hussiten* (Leipzig-Prag, 1900), 16.

4. Frederick sent one of his confidents a letter (Bezold, 2, 161-163) addressed "zu dem B," interpreted by Tomek, 4, 379, to mean Diviš Bořek. I agree with Bezold (2, 107) that Heník of Kolštejn was meant, especially since in July 1427 he sought a meeting with a major Lusatian noble. (*UB*, 1, 524) Heník's attack on Slaný also suggests involvement with Frederick.

5. *AČ*, 3, 261-264 and my *LČ Jak.*, 59, č. 89.

6. Tomek, 4, 363.

7. Stöller, 44-47; Andreas, 339; Antoch, 104.

8. Jecht, 127-138; *SL*, 71-72.

9. For Prague's and Žatec's *UB*, 1, 519, 522. It appears a defense of the Four Articles was also sent. An unknown Catholic theologian responded. See Prague Chapter, ms N50f, 26-32.

10. Radford, L. B., *Henry Beaufort* (London, 1908); Emden, A., *Biographical Register of the University of Oxford*, 1 (1957), 139. [See also Holmes, G., "Cardinal Beaufort and the Crusade against the Hussites" in *EHR* 88 (1973) and Schrith, K., "Kardinal Heinrich Beaufort und der Hussitenkrieg" in Bäumer, R. (ed.) *Von Konstanz nach Trient* (Munich, 1972), 119-138.]

11. Printed by me in *Communio Viatorum* 6 (1963), 52-54. He knew about Prague's answer to the elector as is indicated by his use of the word 'communitas', clearly of Czech origin, and especially by his expectation for a response from the community of the Prague allies which Prague had promised the elector but which had not materialized because of the outbreak of war. Cf. *UB*, 1, 542 and Twemlow, J., *Calendar of Entries in the Papal Registers, Papal Letters*, 7 (1906), 35.

12. *RA*, 9, 52-53.

13. Bartošek, 596 and the Nürnberg poet, Hans Rosenblüt in his

"Spruch von Beheim" in Liliencron, R., *Die historische Volkslieder der Deutschen von 13. bis 16. Jahrhundert* (Leipzig, 1865-69), I, 61-67, and Kraus, A., *Husitství v literatuře* 1 (Prague, 1917), 61-63. Cf. Juritsch, 43 and Bezold, 2, 117 who relies on Andreas' (450) account.

14. Antoch, 105 and Jecht, 147.

15. Theobald, I, 2, 245.

16. Theobald and Pešina of Čechorod, *Mars Moravicus* 1 (Prague, 1677), 521 gives additional names: Zajimač of Kunštát, John of Pernštejn, Smil of Holice. By Peter Jr. of Strážnice was likely meant Wenceslas. [See Klassen, J., *The Nobility and the Making of the Hussite Revolution* (New York, 1978), 123, 134-139 for Menhart of Hradec.]

17. Truhlář, J., *Catalogus codicum manu scriptorum latinorum,* 1 (Prague, 1905), 231.

18. See my *HR,* 1, 118; Bartošek, 597 and *SL,* 72.

19. Bartošek, 597 mentions an M. Albertus who is surely Albert of Metelsko, brother of the Týn Horšův military captain, Henry. *Hrady,* 9, 119.

20. Bezold, 2, 120. The Podbrský association had been in continuously extended truces with the Prague allies since 1422. See *AČ,* 3, 264-267; Tomek, 4, 389 and Bartošek, 598.

21. Pope Martin V on 11/12 November 1427 forbade the disputation at the request of Bishop John Železný (*UB,* 1, 555) who sent notes also to Plzeň and Karlštejn. Prague Univ. MS VI c 22. The participants nevertheless met at Žebrák with John of Valdek presiding for the Catholics and Smil of Holice for the Hussites. Cardinal Beaufort sent Dr. Simon of Tišnov on 21 September; the Hussites sent Peter Payne. The Catholics charged the Hussites with breaking up the disputations from the very beginning. *UB,* 1, 555-557. See also Odložlík, O., "Z počátků husitství na Moravě," *ČMM,* 49 (1925), 161-164. [See also Cook, W., "Negotiations Between the Hussites, the Holy Roman Emperor, and the Roman Church, 1427-1436." *East Central Europe* 4 (1977).]

22. Bezold 2, 167 shows Kolín as belonging to the royalist noble Hašek of Valdštejn. His list of royalists is however unreliable. It seems likely that Kolín was handed to the royalists by inside conspirators. Troops of the lords Krušina of Lichtenburg and Otto of Bergov aided in the attack on Prague. Antoch, 106.

23. Tomek, 4, 389-92.

24. Antoch, 206; Bartošek, 597; *SL*, 74.

25. For Náchod see *UB*, 1, 527; for Čapek, *SL*, 72-73. Cf. Antoch 109.

26. See *UB*, 1, 602; Urbánek, *Lipany*, 193-194 and my article in *JSH*, 34 (1965).

27. Phillip, A. *Quellen aus deutschem historischen Seminar der Universität*, 1 (Innsbruch, 1910), 134-36.

28. For the expedition, the author of *Chronicon vet. collegiati*, who participated in the campaign, as well as *SL*, Bartošek and numerous Silesian documents and chronicles are our major source. Grünhagen collected the Silesian material, some of which has been printed by Palacký in *UB*. Tomek, 4, 395-403, adds useful information, as does Heck, R., "Śląsk w czasie powstania husyckiego," in *Szkice z dziejow Śląska* 1 (Warsaw, 1955, 2nd ed.), 192-193. For Luzice see Jecht, 166ff.

29. See Beck and Loserth in *ZVGMSch* II (1897), 64-67; Stöller, 50-51 and Varsík, 23-27.

30. Bartošek, 598; Windecke, 236-37; Andreas, 467; *UB*, 1, 625-27 and Bezold, 2, 135-36.

31. Stöller, 51.

32. Werminghoff, A., *Die deutschen Reichskriegsteuergesetze von 1422 und 1427 und die deutsche Kirche* (Stuttgart, 1916).

33. *UB*, 1, 589.

34. Tomek, 4, 442.

35. *CIM*, 3, 65 and Kejř 55, 161.

36. For the siege of Bechyně and Lichnice see Bartošek, 598-99; *SL*, 75 and Theobald, 1, 297.

37. His tract "De existencia vera corporis Christi" was published by Hardt, 3, 884-932. See my *LČ Jak.*, 59-60 for dating.

38. *SL*, 75; *AČ*, 1, 220-222; Tomek, 4, 409.

39. See *UB*, 1, 638 and 614; *RA*, 9, 204, 202.

40. Bartošek, 509.

41. Bezold, 2, 3 and 5 n. 4 and Macek, J., *Prokop Veliký* (Prague, 1953), 207.

42. *CW*, 813 and Chroust, A., in *Deutsche Zeitschrift für Geschichtswissenschaft* 5 (1891), 369.

43. Tomek, 4, 415-416.

44. For the Lutsk meeting see Goll, 197.

45. *CW*, 813.

Notes to Chapter Four

1.   *UB*, 2, 22-25; Bartošek, 599; Andreas, 675-77; Aeneas Sylvius, ch. 47. From the Hussite side: Payne's speech in my *Petri Payne Anglici Positio* (Tabor, 1949), 81-90. See also Tomek, 4, 424-426; Herre, H., *Die Hussitenverhandlungen auf dem Pressburger Reichstage vom April 1429* (Rome, 1899), 2, 307-316; Neubauer, in *ČČH* 16 (1910), 171-175; Bartoš, *ČMM* 49 (1925), 171-195; Macek, *Prokop Veliky*, 74 and Varsik, 40.

2.   .She died in sorrowful exile. See my article in *JSH*, 10 (1937), 15-30 and Riezler, S., *Geschichte Bayerns*, 3 (Gotha, 1889), 270-277.

3.   The invitation to the doctors of the University of Paris is in Vienna ms 4576 f. 331-2. See also Valois, N., *Le Pape et le Concil*, 1 (Paris, 1910), 87-88. [See also Black, A., "The Universities and the Council of Basle: Ecclesiology and Tactics" *Annuarum Historiae Conciliorum* 6 (1974).]

4.   At the meeting in Lutsk (Dlugosz 4, 368) he had stated that if the pope did not call a council, he would himself. I'published Payne's speech in *ČMM* 49 (1925).

5.   .See documents nos. 1-6 in my "Z bratislavské," *ČMM* 49 (1925).

6.   It was likely drafted by Prokop Holy but signed by the Taborite captain, Jacob Kroměšín, the Orphan Koudelník of Březnice and František of Kotvice. Jacob and Koudelník were the guardians of the seals belonging to the field armies.

7.   Ebendorf, doc. no. 6 in my "Z bratislavské" and *UB*, 2, 24.

8.   It was likely he who brought Orsini's letter to the king. Orsini forbade negotiations with the Hussites. Ebendorf, doc. no. 1 in "Z bratislavské". The cardinal's death on 9 October 1430 certainly aided the cause of peace.

9.   Altmann, 7194ff and 7263, Bezold, 3, 8; *RA*, 9 has a large number of pertinent documents.

10.   Herre, H., *Die Hussiten Verhandlungen*, 315-316.

11.   The official records of the diet are both in Czech and Latin. See *AČ*, 6, 421-22 and *UB*, 2, 514-516. Cf. Hlaváček, 92. A private German record is in Siegel, K., *ZVGMS* 22 (1918), 180-182. Cf. *Oesterreichische Zeitschrift für Geschichte* 2 (1836), 328.

12.   Peter Turnov, of Prussian origin, in 1423 introduced the Hussites to them with the article "Ritus et mores Grecorum" which I published in 1915 in *VKČSN*.

13.   *AČ*, 6, 421; *RA*, 9, 304; Bartošek, 600 and *UB*, 2, 42.

14.   As was customary he provided the delegation generously with meat and wine and tried to reduce the possibilities of friction between the Magyar burghers and Moravian lords who just last year had been up to the Bratislava walls on a military expedition. On the composition of the council see the letter of J. Glockner of 12 August in *CDLS*, 2, 2, 101-102. For the Hussite requirement of a council see *UB*, 2, 50-51.

15.   See Glockner cited in n. 14 above. Cf. Sigismund's letter to the Polish king in *CW*, 860 and Bezold, 3, 11-13. See also *UB*, 2, 50-51, *CW*, 870-71 for a German translation of a letter from Prokop to Sigismund.

16.   *CW*, 862.

17.   *SL*, 76, Bartoš, *ČSPS*, 30 (1922), 103.

18.   Laurence, 329.

19.   *UB*, 2, 64-66 and Prokeš, 206, n 206 and Tomek, 4, 455+ 470. Mladoňovice and Příbram did not return.

20.   For the negotiations see *AČ*, 1, 222-25; Tomek, 4, 414-416, 434-35; *SLŠ*, 56 and Čelakovský, J., in *Sborník příspěvků k dějinám města Prahy*, I, 2 (1928), 88-89.

21.   Zimmerman, J. V., *Pokračovani kroniky Beneše z Hořovic* (Prague, 1819), 151ff.; cf. Tomek, 4, 441-43.

22.   *ČKD*, (1863), 570. For the tracts that resulted from these disputations see my *LČ Rok.*, 22, nos. 76-79 and 103 nos. 13-14. See also Biskupec, 593-96.

23.   *LČ Rok.*, 1; Tomek, 4, 440-41; Prokeš, n. 199. The synod hoped that peace between the two churches would come through a new translation of the Bible directed jointly by Prague and Orphan theologians. See Kyas, V., *Česká předloha staropolského žaltáře* (Prague, 1962), 19 and my article in, *Strahovská knihovna* 3 (1968) and Souček, B., *Česká apokalypsa v husitství* (Prague, 1967).

24.   *LČ Rok.*, 22 no. 17.

25.   *LČ Rok.*, 22 no. 19 and Macek, *Ktož jsú Boži bojovníci* (Prague, 1951), 262-309 who unfortunately omitted the biblical references.

26.   *UB*, 2, 87-89.

27.   Bartošek, 599.

28. Jecht, 190-195; Anděl, 68-69; Antoch, 107.

29. Grünhagen, 161-168; Tomek, 4, 412-414.

30. Antoch, 105-106 and for the Orphans' raid on Plané, UB, 2, 59.

31. Hrady, 11, 30-31, 144.

32. Jecht, 222-25; Grünhagen, 180-182; Tomek, 4, 427-28.

33. Bartošek, 600; Antoch, 106. For Šarovec, see Hrady, 2, 102. See also AČ, 1, 255.

34. RA, 9, 305.

35. Jacob, E. F., The Fifteenth Century (Oxford History of England), (Oxford, 1961), 238.

36. Jecht, 266.

37. Jecht, 235-236 gives the names of the Hussite leaders who signed the truce.

38. Jecht, 230-33; Mětšk, F., "Peter z Přiseč" KJ, (1955), no. 36.

39. Bartošek, 599; Hrady, 12, 37.

40. These hardly warrant the term diet as given by Hlaváček, 92-93. For the sources see Siegel, ZVGM, 22 (1918), 180 and UB, 2, 77-78; Tomek, 4, 444-48. For the Glorious campaign see Bezold, 3, 28-51. He used unpublished sources such as the valuable description of the German commander, Ludwig of Oetingen; see also Zapletal, F., Přerov za válek husitských (Prague, 1965), 38.

41. UB, 2, 85; Bezold, 3, 29 n. 1.

42. See my Husitství a cizina, 226. For Lubich, who participated in Hus' execution see my Čechy, 415. See also Kraus, Husitství v literatuře, 2, 208-24.

43. Palacký, III, 2, 330.

44. Palacký, III, 2, 332 and Gritzner, E., in NASG 33 (1912), 142-144.

45. Bezold, 3, 39, n. 1.

46. See JSH, 7 (1934), 10.

47. Bezold, 3, 59, n. 2.

48. Bezold, 3, 110-11; Tomek, 4, 458; UB, 2, 116, 128-29, Rynešová, 117; CW, 895 and Andreas, 473. For the protocol of the Hussites, sent to Frederick, upon which the following is based, see JSH, 5 (1932), 90-91. Cf. Bezold, 3, 44-45.

49. UB, 2, 109.

50. UB, 2, 135.

51. Teig, *Dodatky*, 40-41; Tomek, 4, 455; *MUP*, I, 2, 6. For the purpose of the negotiations, my *Manifesty*, 304; for Sigismund's delegation, Rynešová, 117.

52. Bezold, 3, 171-75 and *RA*, 9, 402-450. [Bartoš lists the names of the representatives in *HR*, II, 68.]

53. Andreas doubted the elector's goodwill. See my *Husitika*, 85-88, my *Husitství a cizina* and *RA*, 9, 426.

54. *SL*, 79.

55. See my *Manifesty*, 302-305 and my article in *JSH*, 13 (1940), 128-129.

56. My *Husitství a cizina*, 222ff, my article in *ČNM*, 10 2 (1928), 73-77. Prokeš, J. in *ČNM*, 102 (1928), 1-38 and Pekař, J., in *ČČH*, 34 (1928), 370-82. For the response of a Spanish theologian, perhaps J. Palomar, to the manifesto, see *JSH*, 7 (1934), 56-59. Bantle, F. X., in *Scholastik* 38 (1963), 537-53 analyzed the newly discovered response to the former Prague professor Nicholas of Javor, an opponent of Hus and the Hussites at Constance and Basel.

57. Bartošek, 602; Grünhagen, 182-190; Tomek, 4, 487-91.

58. *CW*, 895; Bartošek, 602; Toman, 367.

59. Windecke, 279-80; *UB*, 2, 144; Antoch, 107; my article in *KJ*, (1962) no. 1 and Varsik, 47ff.

60. Bartošek, 602; *CW*, 899; Antoch, 104 and Varsik, 75-76.

61. Grünhagen, 103-107; Tomek, 4, 461-63.

62. Bartošek, 602-603; Tomek, 4, 464-5.

63. *UB*, 2, 132. For Nürnberg's letter, *UB*, 2, 120-121; cf. Bezold, 3, 66ff. [See Spunar, P., "Antihussitische Verse aus Schlesien," *Basler Zeitschrift für Geschichte und Altertumskunde* 74 (1974), 189-200.]

64. *UB*, 2, 161.

65. *RA*, 9, 452-53, 459-60; *UB*, 2, 164.

66. *UB*, 2, 170-172; Bezold, 3, 74-79.

67. Grünhagen, 198-203; Jecht, 255-70.

68. '*UB*, 2, 175.

Notes to Chapter Five

1. *UB*, 2, 332; Tomek, 4, 473; Kejř, 57.

2. For the Kutná Hora diet, Bartošek, 603 and the Taborite Confession of 1431 in Lydius, B. (ed.), *Waldensia id est Conservatio verae Ecclesiae*,

Demonstrata ex confessionibus, 2, (Dortrecht, 1617) 1. Biskupec (597) wrote that at the diet 12 persons were elected ". . . ex statu baronum, militum, clientum, civitatum et communitatum de regno Bohemiae, legi Die adherentium, quibus ab omnibus commissum erat de providendo bono ordine inter se et sacerdotes partium utrarumque." See Palacký, III; 2, 362 and Pekař, 4, 212.

3. We can surmise its membership as follows: for Prague, William Kostka, Simon of the White Lion, John of Smiřice and John Reček; for Tabor, Matthew Louda and Nicholas of Padařov; for the Orphans, William Temlík of Žatec and Křišt'an of Louny. The lords were perhaps represented by Smil Holice of Šternberk and possibly Menhart of Hradec. It is not known whether Prokop Holý was on the committee.

4. In 1430 Jeník of Mečkov was still captain in Litomyšl but by 21 May 1433 Kostka was. Hoffmann, F., "Litomyšl v husitském revolučním hnutí," *Sbornik k 700. výročí Litomyšle* (Litomyšl, 1959), 61; *UB,* 2, 144. See also my article in *KJ,* (1960), no. 7 and (1963) no. 5.

5. Goll, 196ff.

6. Both a certain Puchala and Paul of Sovinec hosted Korybut after his release from confinement. Prokop Holý visited him there. Goll, 204.

7. *UB,* 2, 205; Dlogosz, 4, 437-41 and Morawski, K., *Historya universytetu Jagellonskiego,* 1, 272 and Goll, 219.

8. See the "Confessio Taboritarum" in Lydius, *Waldensia,* 1-303. Parts of the confession are in Biskupec's *Chronicon.* See Höfler, 597-700. From the point of view of Prague we have two of Rokycana's writings. See my *LČ Rok.,* 22-23.

9. Truhlář, J., in *VČA,* 9 (1900), 293-94.

10. Biskupec may even have lived in the same college as Hus and Jakoubek and have grown up near Bethlehem chapel. Hus bestowed his degree on him. Schmidtová, A., *ThPf KR* 27 (1959), 151-52. Biskupec illustrated his indebtedness to Jakoubek in that he relied on his Commentary of John's Revelation in his own translation of the Revelation. See *ČSPS* 67 (1959), 13. See also Confessio Taboritarum in Lydius, *Waldensia,* 267.

11. *RA,* 9, 493ff and 10, 126ff and Bezold 3, 89ff and my article "Manifesty nuncia Cesariniho husitům z roku 1431" in Jenšovský, B., and Mendl, B., eds., *K dějinám československým v období humanismu* (Prague, 1932), 178-79.

12. "Manifesty nuncia Cesariniho," 180.

13. Siegel, in *MVGDB*, 54 (1915), 13-20; Bezold, 3, 112-113 and Werminghoff, *Reichkriegsteuergesetze*, 87ff.

14. It is likely that the Hussites had in their hands the military plans which accompanied the declaration of the crusade. *RA*, 9, 544-45 and Bezold, 3, 113-114.

15. See Prague chapter ms. 03 1.106. For Kuneš of Zvole see Jireček, H., *Život právnický v Čechách a na Moravě* (Prague, 1903), 226 and Sedláček in *OSN*, 27, 722-23.

16. *Hrady*, 12, 131; Pekař, 3, 225. See also *UB*, 2, 235 where one of the Orphan captains complained that Beneš had not participated with them in battle.

17. *UB*, 2, 210-214 and Stojkovic, in *MC*, 182.

18. *SL*, 81.

19. Jecht, 282ff.

20. Jecht, 286; *Hrady*, 10, 283; Grünhagen, 210.

21. 'Jecht, 288-300; *CDLS*, 2, 274-78 and 230, 12 and 32 and *UB*, 2, 190-97.

22. *UB*, 2, 215; Urbánek, R., *Z husitského věku*, 156-57. See my articles in *JSH*, 6 (1933), 46 and "Manifesty nuncia Cesariniho," and Macek, *Prokop Veliký*, 113-122. For a poem describing the campaign by a Nürnberg poet see Liliencron, R., *Historische Volkslieder*, 1, 332ff. The beginning of an elegy by a contemporary poet, Osvald of Wolkenstein, is printed in *Verhandlungen des historischen Vereins für Oberpfalz* 51, 89. A song on the victory of Domažlice by Laurence of Březová is in Čapek, J. B. et al. (eds.), *Píseň o vítězství u Domažlic* (Prague, 1951).

23. As M. John Borotín wrote on 24 July, "exercitus Boemorum i-acebat inter Planam et circa silvam magnam hwozd" in Podlaha, A., *Soupis rokopisů kapituly pražské* 2 vols. (Prague, 1910-1922), 2, 453.

24. Fechner, H. G., "Cesarini bis zu seiner Ankunft in Basel" (diss. University of Marburg, 1907), 79ff. See n. 34 for the warning Poggio Braciolini sent the nuncio against the crusade against the Hussites.

25. For the participants see *RTA*, 9, 560.

26. *UB*, 2, 228-231. For Cesarini's manifesto see my "Manifesty nuncia Cesariniho," 188-91.

27. Bartošek, 604.

28. He was to be captain there to 1430, although his replacement,

John Královec, is not mentioned there until 1432. Toman, 233 and *Hrady,* 13, 102. Buzek was the son of the Prague master builder Pilík. He changed careers, becoming a successful soldier for the Prague and Orphan camps. See my article in *JSH,* 33 (1964), 85-88.

29. *UB,* 237, Segovia, 27.
30. Hanušek of Louny wrote about this on 7 August 1431, *UB,* 2, 23.
31. Rynešová, 126. See the report of 14 August 1431, *UB,* 2, 238.
32. Frankenberger, 3, 94, *AČ,* 6, 424.
33. Segovia, 27; Urbánek, *Z husitského věku,* 151 and Theobald, 1, 289.
34. See the report of its commander in Neumann, A. (ed.) *Studie a texty k náboženským dějinám českým* (Olomouc, 1923-1925), III, 2, 122.
35. Segovia, 28. Some of the details have been preserved in "Bratrské rozmlouvaní mladého rytíře," *Hlasy ze Sionu* (1867), 92.
36. Theobald, 1, 290.
37. *UB,* 2, 243, Rynešová, 127 and Hofman, L., *ČČH,* 7 (1901), 143f.
38. The cardinal paid his soldiers generously. *UB,* 2, 239.
39. Wackernagel, R., *Geschichte der Stadt Basel,* 1 (Basel, 1907), 474-75, 635; *CB,* 2, 35 and Hofman, *ČČH,* 7 (1901), 185, n. 21. Most likely Frederick, who was connected with the circles pressing for a council, sent the manifesto. Cf. Valois, 1, 89.
40. Hefele, C., and Leclercq, H., *Histoire des Conciles,* VII, (Paris, 1916), 2, 682; *MC,* 1, 101; *VČA,* 53, (1944), 98 and Valois, 1, 118.
41. *MC,* 1, 135 and Stojkovic, 113.

Notes to Chapter Six

1. Bezold, 3, 148; Jecht, 300-302.
2. Urbánek, 295-300 for the sources and for a mysterious group, the "Prostředci" who are mentioned only by Bartošek, 604. They took weapons, hoping to remove all unlawful taxes and to assure themselves the freedom of the chalice. They were said to number 14,000 but were defeated by Duke Albrecht. Vok of Sovince conquered Přerov in 1427 but it was most likely bought back in 1436. Zapletal, 29.
3. Pešina of Čechorod, 563, *Chronicon Treb.,* and *SL* describe the celebrations. See also Nejedlý, 38 and my article in *KJ* (1962), no. 4.
4. See chapter five, note 22. It was likely sung by the students of

Nazareth and Queen's Colleges affiliated with Bethlehem chapel and Charles University who probably harmonized the whole composition.

5. The Basel ambassador from Feldkirch reported the king to say that the Hussites intended to elect themselves a head and twelve priests for administering the church. See Krofta, *ČČH*, 17 (1911), 36. For the accident see *SL*, 83, Bartošek, 605 and Tomek, 4, 496.

6. For Přemek's agreement, *AČ*, 6, 125. Cf. Grunhagen, 216-217. For the expeditions, Jarník, H., *ČMM* 93 (1919), 350, Varsik, 1, 76.

7. *SL*, Frankenberger, 3, 99.

8. A description of these events probably appeared immediately after the retreat but is unfortunately lost. Prokop Lukáč, *Rerum boemicarum Ephemeris, sive Kalendarium historicum*, November 9 (Prague, 1584) had it at his disposal as most likely did Veleslavín, Daniel, Adam, in *Kalendář hystorický*, November 9 (Prague, 1578) and Pešina (see n. 3 above). See also Dudík, B.D., *Forschungen in Schweden für Mährens Geschichte* (Brünn, 1852), 401-402. Cf. Palacký, III, 5 and 20 and *Chronicon Treb.*, 62. The original author was most likely an experienced soldier who had participated in Žižka's expedition. He suppressed less glorious aspects and played up the illustrious parts.

9. My main source in Pešina, 567-69. See my article in *JSH*, 31 (1962), 83-87.

10. 'The Council's delegates, sent to Nürnberg to deter the lords near Bohemia from signing a truce, spread reports that Prokop lived in Kutná Hora having lost the respect of the Hussites. According to rumor he had betrayed his brothers, and that when he sent to Prague for a physician, people said he should be sent a hangman instead. *MC*, 1, 140. In reality Prokop lived most likely at Vlašim and the Taborite brothers remained loyal to him as is shown by the fact that they did not send a representative to the diet in the new year. See also Toman, 369-370; Dobiáš, 2, 59-63.

11. *UB*, 2, 228-230.

12. Hofman, "Husité a concilium," 294-295; *MC*, 1, 145-46, 193 and my *Husitika*, 29.

13. *Chronicon Treb.*, 62.

14. We have no record of the development of the Orphans' ideas on worship as we do in the decrees of the Prague and Tabor synods. Undoubtedly the Orphans had similar sessions. The rapprochment between Prague and the Orphans and their efforts to include Tabor can be seen in the

manifesto from the pen of Peter Payne (English), sent abroad in November (*MC*, 1, 153-70). It is moderate, and indirectly and favorably responded to the invitation to Basel. It was published in German and immediately nailed to the gates of the city hall, where it caused considerable excitement. The Council issued a warning against it and hastily prepared an answer (ibid., 170-74). A former student in Prague, the Ulm pastor, Henry Neithart, was given the task of translating it into Latin. The only known answer to the manifesto is that of the French abbot, Geoffrey of Lerin. Neumann, *Studie a texty*, IV, 3-4, 61-69. For the manifesto see Pekař in *ČČH*, 34 (1928), 370-82, and my *Husitství a cizina*, 228-31. For Rokycana's part see my *LČ Rok.*, 24, no. 5 and Prokeš, J., *VKČSN*, (1929). The agreement is in *MC*, 1, 182-184; *AČ*, 3, 268-70; Windecke, 335ff.

15. *MC*, 1, 184, Rieger, *Zřízení krajské*, 1, 73 and Hlaváček, 93-94.

16. For example, John Královec ceased being captain of the domestic armies of the four eastern regions and became instead the captain of the region of Tachov. *Hrady*, 13, 102.

17. Lydius, 2, 316-32 and *MC*, 1, 140.

18. *Chronicon Treb.*, 62-63; Bartošek, 606; *MC*, 190-92. The Diet had both lower and upper estates represented.

19. Jecht, 322-44.

20. Ibid., 343-44.

21. My *Čechy*, 399.

22. *CDLS*, II, 2, 383.

23. Jecht, 335-37, 350 and 530.

24. Hofman, "Husité a concilium," 148ff.

25. Valois, *Le Pape*, 1, 142, n. 2. Both apologies in Segovia, 95-108, 109-117 and in Neumann, *Studie a texty*, 4, 49-60, cf. Bezold, 3, 184.

26. For Prague's complaint and the answer of the delegates see *MC*, 1, 204 and 212. For the Cheb meeting, *MC*, 1, 217-27; *UB*, 2, 281-4.

27. For Nider see Klapper, J., in Stammler, W., and Langosch, K., *Die Deutsche Literatur des Mittelalters, Verfasserlexikon*, 3 (Berlin, 1943), 560-65, and my *Husitika*, 60-63.

28. Fleischmann met Hus in 1414. Novotný, V., *M. Jana Husi korespondence a dokumenty* (Prague, 1920), 213; see also Bezold, 3, 165-168. For Toke see my articles in *JSH*, 14 (1941), 1-8 and *JSH*, 15 (1942), 29. For Parsperger see Leidinger, G. (ed.), *Chronicon Hussitarum* (Munich, 1903), 278-79, 293. The Council sent him to Prague in 1433. He died in

1449 at the age of 64 years. See also Janner, F., *Geschichte der Bischöfe von Regensburg*, 3 (1886), 454-86.

29. *MC*, 1, 211-12.

30. See my *Husitika*, 2, 6 and Weigel, M., in *Mitteilungen des Vereins für Geschichte Nürnbergs* 29 (1928), 174-225. He died in 1454.

31. *MC*, 1, 211-24.

32. Slawik, J., *Husité na Chebsku* (Cheb, 1955), 6 located the house in the former Dominican monastery. For part of the speech see Prokeš, 58. Cf. my article on Tokes cited above n. 28.

33. *MC*, 1, 212.

34. "In causa quatuor articulorum, quam prosequuntur, lex divina, praxis Christi, apostolica et ecclesiae primitivae, una cum conciliis doctoribusque fundantibus se veraciter in eadem, pro veracissimo et evidenti iudice in hoc Basiliensi concilio admittentur." This is the celebrated "iudex in Egra (Cheb) compactatus," or the Cheb arbiter or judge.

35. Palacký, III, 3, 41 and Urbánek, *Věk Poděbradský*, 4, 559.

36. *MC*, 1, 211-4.

37. Hofman, *Husité a concilium*, 302 with reference to Denis, *Huss et la guerre des Hussites* (Paris, 1878), 411.

38. For the report and the king's answer see above n. 26. Prokop's delegation arrived there at that time most likely with the safe conduct of some influential person of the king's party. The king sent his answer with John of Maulbronn, who had been sent to him by the Council in order that he might report on the Cheb meeting. John was to send the response to Prokop after consultation with the Council. See Stojković's item in *MC*, 1, 212.

39. Urbánek, 301-302; Grünhagen, 220, 227-29.

40. Goll, 223-24; Macek, J., *Husité na Baltu a ve Velkopolsku* (Prague, 1952), 34-35; Tomek, 4, 527.

41. Varsik, 2, 5. Blažek of Borotín ruled there until he gave it up to Sigismund in 1435. According to Varsik, 2, 37, John Vrbenský conquered Skalice at that time.

42. *MC*, 1, 227-29, 240-41.

43. *MC*, 1, 246-48. According to Rokycana all fourteen who had been at Cheb were chosen, plus Kostka, Menhart of Hradec, Wenceslas of Strážnice, Přibík of Klenovy and Beneš of Mokrovous.

44. Valois, *Le pape*, 1, 175ff and Goll, 224-25 for Eugene's attempt to get Polish mediation.

45. *SSR Pruss.*, 3, 499-504. Sigismund sent the letter to the Council on 16 January 1433 accompanied by complaints against the Poles and the Czech heretics. *MC*, 1, 275-77.

46. The administrators of the truce for the Hussite party were Roháč and Beneš of Kolovraty. On 7 September Jacob of Vřesovice was added. The field armies got the Silesian princes' agreement to buy the castles which they had in their power. The agreement was never carried out. *UB*, 2, 304-06, 313-17.

47. For the fall of Fridštejn, Jecht, 347. Its lord was Bohuš of Kováně who entered the service of Görlitz. For Pecky and Potštejn, two other castles laid siege to by the Hussites, see Bartošek, 608. For Lichnice, *Hrady*, 13, 73 and for other battles, Tomek, 4, 532-33.

48. 'Stöller, 76-77. For Albrecht's military order see Toman, 416-20.

Notes to Chapter Seven

1. See Bartoš, *HR*, 1, 151 and Janner, F., *Geschichte der Bischöfe von Regensburg*, 3 (1886), 414-50. He died in 1437.

2. As for the motives, the nobles may have resented the fact that the spokesmen for the Hussites included the priest Prokop and Kostka. It is also true that neither noble knew Latin. Wenceslas' thinking is reflected in the inscription he had engraved in the castle in Velké Meziříčí in 1435 where he expresses satisfaction with the conquest of Prague and undoubtedly also with the defeat of the field armies at Lipany. See Hejnic, J., in *Listy filologické*, 86 (1965), 134-39.

3. *MC*, 1, 263.

4. Namely the Prague burghers, John of Krajnice, the Prague scribe, Nicholas of Humpolec, a member of the delegation just returned from Basel, and Jacob of Vřesovice.

5. Laurence was undoubtedly German and his original name was likely Laurence Roesen as he signed it on a copy of a Bible ordinance of 1423. In my article in *SH*, 2 (1954), 97-103 I showed that he was the writer of the invaluable journal published by Palacký in 1857 in *MC*, 1 under the name of Peter of Žatec.

6. Palacký, 3, 72. For the arrival of the delegation with wagons loaded with books, see *CB*, 2, 250. Cf. Segovia, 316 and for Louda's reports, see Chelčický, "Replika Rokycanovi" in *Listy filologické*, 25

(1898), 272. They stayed three months, longer than expected. *PŽ*, 80.

7. See *RA*, 10, 602 and 585 where there is valuable data augmenting what is known about the work "Quomodo Bohemi vocati productique sint ad Basiliensem synodum," which Palacký attributed to Aeneas Sylvius but which likely was written by Jacob Sobius, the editor of a collection of well-known sources entitled, *Fasciculus rerum expetendarum et fugiendarum* published by Gratius, Orthvinus (Cologne, 1535) and reprinted in 1690 by Brown, Edward, in London, 313. See my article in *JSH*, 13 (1940), 129.

8. The slogan most likely originated with Nicholas Biskupec who likely thought of emblazoning it on the Taborite banner carried to Basel. See my articles in *JSH*, 17 (1948), 10 and *JSH*, 18 (1949), 118.

9. *Čechy*, 388.

10. For William see Kluckholn, A., in *Forschungen zur deutschen Geschichte*, 2 (1862), 519-615.

11. Mansi, J., *Sacrorum conciliorum nova amplissima collectio*, 30 (Paris, 1901), 260 and my *Husitika*, 67 and *PŽ*, 201; *MC*, 1, 258 and *CB*, 2, 300ff.

12. *PŽ*, 17; Mansi, 30, 260; *CB*, 5, 3 and Aeneas Sylvius, c. 49.

13. Wackernagel, R., *Geschichte der Stadt Basel* 1 (Basel 1907), 480. For the imperial diet *RA*, 10. For the book trade, Lehmen, P., *Erforschung des Mittelalters* (1941), 70-80. For literature on the Council see *Histoire de l'Eglise* 14 (1962), 227-28 and 237-38 and Theodora von der Mühl, *Vorspiel zur Zeitwende. Das Basler Konzil* (1959), 228-231. [Cf. Krchňák, A. *Čechové na basilejském sněmu* (Rome, 1967).]

14. For Landriani see Hofman, "Husité a concilium," 152-54 and Schofield, A., "The First English Delegation to the Council of Basel" in *Journal of Ecclesiastical History* 12 (1961), 166-196. He tried to get Oxford to send six doctors well acquainted with Hussite ideas. *CB*, 2, 235. See *PŽ*, 220 and my article in *SH*, 99 regarding Hussite lodgings.

15. *PŽ*, 23; *PŽP*, 291.

16. Hofman, Husité a concilium, 306; my *Husitika*, 58-59, 70.

17. Mansi, 29, 382-85 and 30, 251-54; *CB*, 2, 236-41.

18. *CB*, 2, 303, 13, 21. See my *Čechy*, passim for Capra and Mauroux. Both interferred rudely during Hus' trial.

19. *LČ Rok.*, 28 č. 10. See Jacob, E. F. "The Bohemians at the Council of Basel 1433," *Prague Essays*, Seton-Watson, R. W. (ed.) (Oxford, 1949), 94-97.

20.   See my edition, *Orationes, quibus Nicolaus de Pelhřimov. . .*
(Tabor, 1935)–henceforth *Orationes*, 3-32. Cf. Jacob, 97-99.

21.   *Orationes*, 86-113, Jacob, "The Bohemians," 103-105. Ulrich
died in 1448 as dean in Čáslav. Hrdina, K., M. J., *Kampanus, Mecenáši
Karlovy university* (Prague, 1949), 15. Cf. Jacob, "The Bohemians," 89.
CB, 2, 325 for the Council's resolutions of 26 January.

22.   I published his speech in *Petri Payne Anglici positio* (Tabor,
1949), 1-40; *CB*, 2, 326 and 5, 40. Cf. Jacob, "The Bohemians," 111-15.
For Maulbronn's reaction see *RA*, 10, 587. Cf. *LČ Rok.*, 105 č 17.

23.   Mansi, 29, 699-868, 1271-80.

24.   *LČ Rok.*, 29, č 12. The speech is unpublished. Cf. *DPŽ*, 102.

25.   For Charlier see my introduction in *Orationes*. See also *Anton-
ianum* 5 (1930), 406-412 and my *Husitika*, 30, 44-45 and 58.

26.   See my edition of *Replika proti Mikuláši*, 38-82.

27.   See my article in *JSH*, 7 (1934), 5-8.

28.   *Orationes*, 114. See his "Tractatus quos collegit ann. 1430 Nuren-
berge et in consilio Basiliensi contra hereticos" in *Romanische Forschung-
en*, 6, 436 no. 6. He crossed Bohemia in 1421 with the army of the archbishop of Trier.

29.   Mansi, 30, 475-85 and 29, 1105-53. See also my *Husitika*, 64.

30.   *Husitika*, 41-80; Jacob, "The Bohemians," 111-115 and Mansi,
29, 1105-53 for Palomar's speech.

31.   Jacob, "The Bohemians," 110-11. For the English delegation see
Emden, A., *A Bibliographical Register of the University of Oxford to AD.
1500*, 1-3 (1957-59). Beaufort, although invited, did not attend. This was
a loss for the Hussites who expected him to be an ally. Deprived of Payne,
protected by Hussite power, the English opponents found another to
sacrifice. Paul of Kravař, of Silesian origin, a graduate of Montpellier, of
the University of Paris, and of the University of Prague, was Vladislav's
physician until Polish politics changed in 1433. After that he went to Scot-
land where he fell into the hands of the inquisitor who had him burned on
23 July. See Bednář, F., in *ČMM*, 39 (1915), 67-76 and my article in
Věstník Matice Opavské (1933). [See Spinka, M., "Paul Kravar and Lol-
lard-Hussite Relations" in *Church History*, 25 (1956) and Moonan, Law-
rence, "Pavel Kravar, and Some Writings once Attributed to Him," *The
Innes Review* (Glasgow) 27 (1976): 3-23.]

32.   *CB*, 2, 369; *PŽ*.

33.   Valois, *Le Pape*, 1, 215ff.

34.   *RA*, 10, 567, 593-94.

35.   Vansteenberghe, E., *Le Cardinal Nicholas de Cues* (Paris, 1920) 213ff and my article in *Communio Viatorum* 5, 1962, 44.

36.   *PŽ*, 119; Segovia, 324; *MC*, 1, 441. Further details are in Munich library MS 19.524 f. 1. entitled "De tractatu Bohemorum" and in *CB*, 1, 308. Of the eight members of the commission whom we know by name, Branda and Cervantes, Archbishop Talaru and Dr. Toke favored agreement with the Czechs. Palomar, the Meissen bishop Hoffmann and Konrad the bishop of Regensburg opposed it.

37.   The other three were Kostka, Louda and Mokrovous. All fought against the brotherhoods the following year. *PŽ* is silent on the negotiations mentioning only where they took place. *CB*, 2, 375 mentions the resolution to send a delegation to Prague. Cf. *MC*, 1, 441 where the writer states that the solution was suggested secretly by some Czechs. The official letter of the leaders of the delegation, Prokop and Kostka, expressly states that the proposal came from the Council and that their delegation approves. *AČ*, 3, 396 and *PŽ*, 243.

38.   The proceedings are in *CB*, 2 and 5, 50-51; *MC*, 2, 346-47 and in *PŽ*, 178-85.

39.   *UB*, 2, 371-73.

40.   The Franciscan letter in *PŽ*, 186. See my article in *SH*, 3, (1955), 139-42. I printed the letter to Rokycana in *ČČM* 101 (1927), 125-126. Cf. *PŽ*, 216 and Bianco, F. J., *Die alte Universität Köln*, 1 (Köln, 1855), 171.

Notes to Chapter Eight

1.   As they left they sang Latin and Czech Easter hymns. *CB*, 5, 51-52; *PŽ*, 247-48; *RA*, 10, 585.

2.   For the Franciscan Matthew Döring, see my *Lipany*, 87 and my article in *JSH*, 13 (1941), 8-11. See the journals of Charlier and Ebendorfer in *MC*, 1 and the committee's instructions there, 378-80. Bishop Philibert died in Prague when on a trip there in 1439. See Pekař, 2, 246 and Lhotsky, A., "T. Ebendorfer," *Schriften der MGH* 15 (1957) and Emden's above cited dictionary, 3, 1719 for Sparrow.

3.   By 24 May when joined by the Cheb delegates, the total number was ninety horsemen. *MC*, 1, 365.

4.   Toke gained the sympathy of many Hussites with his heartfelt speech to Prague on 20 May. *MC,* 1, 390-95, 371. He formulated the position eventually accepted by the Council. Before he left Prague he wrote his tract on the Church, under instructions from the Council. *MC,* 1, 479.

5.   *LČ Rok.,* 30, no. 14; *MC,* 1, 399-401, 414.

6.   *MC,* 1, 414-430. See Třeboň ms. A/19f 151b-2 for a Hussite response to Palomar.

7.   *MC,* 1, 370.

8.   *MC,* 1, 371, 709.

9.   *MC,* 1, 374, 713.

10.   Prokeš, 63ff.

11.   *SLŠ,* 67.

12.   Stöller, 77 and Varsik, 106ff.

13.   *SLŠ, Chronicon vet. Coll.;* Bartošek, 611.

14.   It is unclear why the Taborites did not participate. See Goll, 229 and Macek, J., *Husité na Baltu,* 59-77 who used the Danzig archives.

15.   Odložilík, O., "Husyci na brzegu Baltyku w 1433 roku," *Rocznik Gdański* 7 (1933), 44; Goll, 234-235; Bartošek, 611. The Orphan expedition prompted Conrad Bitschin, the town scribe, to write the extensive *Epistola Ecclesiae deplanctoria,* parts of which M. Toeppen printed in *SSR Pruss.,* 3, 512-518. Cf. Hledíková, Z., in *ČsČH,* 13 (1965), 419-27.

16.   They are listed in *MC,* 1, 407.

17.   Prokop was given an unknown estate most likely by the Taborite captains meeting at Nymburk on 12 May 1430. See my article in *KJ,* 1963 no. 5.

18.   Tomek, 5, 594; Segovia, 438; Bartošek, 613.

19.   For the extent of the *Landfrid* at this time see the atlas by Čepelák, V., in *Sborník pedagogického institutu v Plzni, Dějepis a zeměpis,* 3 (Plzeň, 1962), 67-69.

20.   *CB,* 2, 309 and 3, 63. See also Stammler-Langosch, *Deutsche Literatur des Mittelalters,* 3 (1943), 618-619.

21.   Toman, 371-72; Urbánek, *Lipany,* 126, 233; *UB,* 2, 379; *SLŠ,* 66 mistakenly names Prokop and Frederick of Strážnice as leaders of the raid.

22.   Bartošek, 611; *SLŠ,* 66. Cf. Toman, 124-26. The cause of the uprising was the truce Prokop and Pardus signed with the lord of Rožmberk on 28 September. See *SH,* 8 (1961), 193. Tvaroh died in battle at the

beginning of February. He had been an official of Hlouška, a suburb of Kutná Hora. Kejř, 120.

23. My *HR,* 1, 204 and Siegel, in *ZGMSch,* 22 (1918), 180.

24. Prokeš, 63-66.

25. One bishop apparently said, "even if Paul himself should come down from heaven, he would not teach us." Dudík, *Forschungen,* 462; Segovia, 600. See also Aschhach, I., *Geschichte der Wiener Universität* (Wien, 1865), 265.

26. *MC,* 1, 444-45. He was a priest in Chrudim which belonged to the Prague association but after the uniting of the Prague and Orphan churches it likely became part of Orphan territory.

27. *CB,* 2, 463; Segovia, 431.

28. A fragment of Kalteisen's tract is in Palacký, III, 3, 118. Cf. my *Husitika,* 70-72. See also *MC,* 1, 723-31 for Ebendorfer's tract. A second tract, a year later, "Professio me incitat," written against all Four Articles is in Vienna ms. 4074, ff. 20-147. For the University of Vienna's attack, see Palacký, III, 3, 118 and Prokeš, J., *Husitika vatikánské knihovny v Římě* (Prague, 1928), 31-32 and Jenšovský, B., *Zprávy zemského archivu* Vol. 6, 16. It seems Tokes also wrote an opininon on the chalice. Vienna ms. 4790, f. 13. If I am not mistaken two paragraphs of Palomar's confidential speech are in Třeboň ms. A/11. f. 131b-2.

29. For Cusa's verdict on the Council, see my article in *Reformační sborník* 7 (1939), 122.

30. Charlier's mission was assumed by John Turonis, Philibert's scribe, who also is responsible for the journal found among Charlier's writings and hitherto mistakenly ascribed to him. *MC,* 1, 446-71.

31. *CB,* 1, 74.

32. Urbánek, *Lipany,* 232. One of the victims of the plague was Rokycana's loyal follower, Simon of the White Lion. Erben, J. (ed.) *Výbor z literatury české* 2, (Prague, 1868), 361. See Peter Chelčický's comments on requisitions and raids in Müller, J. Th., in *ČČH,* 13 (1907), 167.

33. It is possible that the Bohemian nobles were aided at the diet by the Moravians. That the nobility formed separate curia is in *MC,* 1, 741. For the death of Vřešt'ovský in 1442 see *Hrady,* 2, 230. As the regent he became lord of Kutná Hora which was thereby taken from the brotherhoods. In January he named his council. Kejř, 233. Cf. *MC,* 1, 456 and Hlaváček, 95.

34. These were the first so-called Compactata which became the final Jihlava agreement printed in *MC*, 1, 495-501 and *AČ*, 3, 398-412. Their basis was the commentary on the three articles which the delegates brought from Basel. The second two documents are a response to the questions and objections raised by the Hussite theologians. The course of the rest of the negotiations are only partially recorded in the journal of the Council's scribe in Segovia, 581-84. See also 592-98. The Czech arbiters elected to supervise the observance of the Compactata were Prokop, Rokycana, Ambrose and Payne. *MC*, 1, 845.

35. *MC*, 1, 467.

36. Mansi, 30, 821. Martin Lupáč was sent to Basel where he was harshly treated. Segovia, 596-98, 601-2; *MC*, 1, 735 and *CB*, 3, 27-31, 33-34.

Notes to Chapter Nine

1. Segovia, 584-86, 592.

2. The Council and Sigismund (who did not want to leave Basel) each gave 4,000. I printed Palomar's letter, exhorting the people of Plzeň in *JSH*, 8 (1935), 15. He sent 3500 gold pieces and paid six weeks' wages for the soldiers. Segovia, 673f.

3. Přibík was most likely among the seven barons whose letter was read to the Council on 8 February in which they complained that the army promised for 17 January had not materialized. Segovia, 592. He had enough helpers among the captains of the royal party with whom he repeated that brave action at the beginning of May. Bartošek, 612. He approached the Basel delegation in January in Cheb and was accepted into the Church with one other person. Cf. Tomek, 4, 632.

4. Urbánek, *Lipany*, 135.

5. For the meeting of the lords see Segovia, 673 and Schofield, A., in *Slavonic and East European Review* 42 (1964), 316, 328. Part of the nobility refused fealty to Albrecht because they feared that the rural and townspeople would lose faith in them and thus the cause of peace would be set back. This information is based on a letter of the English abbot, Nicholas Frome who mistakenly included the Bohemian nobility. The letter is valuable in that it gives us the date (after March 28) of the meeting, which was not a meeting of the Brno diet. *JSH*, 18 (1949), 91-92.

6. As early as 1431 part of the Hussite nobility offered the royal party an alliance against the brotherhoods but nothing came of it. *MC*, 1, 189.

7. *Chronicon vet. coll.*, 93.

8. *Reg.* 200. He also became the chief notary for the land court.

9. For the complaint of the Taborites against Čapek see Urbánek, 255-256.

10. ꞏChaloupecký, V., *Jiráskovo Bratrstvo v dokumentech* (Bratislava, 1937), 234; Urbánek, R., in *VKČSN* (1939), 11 and Urbánek, *Lipany*, 138.

11. Urbánek, *Lipany*, 138; Rynešová, 1, 170. Cf. *SH*, 8 (1961), 193, no. 28ꞏ

12. Urbánek, *Lipany*, 139ff, 241, n. 33.

13. ꞏIbid., 261ꞏ

14. ꞏ[See Bartoš' Czech edition for a lengthy analysis of the modern Czech historiography of the battle. *HR*, 2, 171-173, n. 17.]

15. For Prokop's fate see Oliva, O., in the journal *Historie a vojenství* 4 (1954). Reports from the seventeenth century stated that Prokop was starved to death in the Vartemberk castle. If there is any substance to the report, the reference is likely to Prokůpek (little Prokop) and the castle in question was perhaps Veliš, belonging to Henry of Vartemberk, who was mortally wounded at Lipany. See my article in *JSH*, 19 (1950), 25-26.

16. See my article in *JSH*, 7 (1934), 42-44.

Notes to Chapter Ten

1. ꞏSegovia, 674; *CB*, 3, 116-17; *RA*, 11, 377.

2. Theobald, 1^2, 308; *SLŠ*, 67ꞏ

3. Palacký, III, 3, 160; Bartošek, 613, 623.

4. Toman, 13.

5. For the semi-official diet see the German report perhaps translated from the Czech in *UB*, 2, 419-22.

6. Toman, 126. It seems Keřský fled despite his word of honor which, if I am not mistaken, explains his behavior at the diet in Čáslav in 1441 and his end at the hands of a hangman in 1446. Urbánek, *Věk poděbradský*, 1, 765, 2, 89.

7.   *UB*, 2, 421; *MC*, 1, 741.

8.   Henry of Vartemberk, the son of Čeněk, and lord of Veliš, is also mentioned among the lords by our two main sources for the meeting. *MC*, 1, 506, 736. Sedláček, *Hrady*, 5, 256 states, however, that he died on 28 October 1434 from wounds suffered at Lipany. Cf. Tomek, 4, 651.

9.   According to Ebendorfer, 737, Lupáč was sent instead of Mark of Hradec. This is the last we hear of the conservative Mark. Menhart of Hradec took along Prokop of Plzeň and perhaps other conservative masters. Prokeš, 214, 329. See Prokeš, 78 for the peace between Menhart and Rožmberk.

10.   *UB*, 2, 425-29; *MC*, 1, 741-45; Lydius, 342-53 and Prokeš, 214, n. 326.

11.   *MC*, 1, 505-523, 736-41.

12.   All nine members of the 1433 delegation were present again except for the deceased, Dr. Sparrow and John of Maulbronn, now an abbot. In addition John Nieder and two new men, Tileman, the provost from Coblenz and Thomas of Courcelles, a cannon from Arras. The bishop of Lübeck was there but as the confident of Sigismund.

13.   Menhart of Hradec, Wenceslas of Kravař and Hynek Ptáček of Pirkštejn. For the *Landfríd*, see *AČ*, 10, 250-54 where the date is wrong. See my article in *JSH*, 18 (1949), 91-92. For the diet see *CB*, 5, 109. According to the report here Albrecht called the diet on the advice of Palomar and several barons. It demanded the recognition of the Four Articles which Albrecht refused saying it was a matter for the Council. Many lords promised fealty to Albrecht, others left indignantly and many were absent. He named as captains, John of Lomnice who, after Prince Wenceslas of Opava, was the first to sign the *Landfríd*. Albrecht wanted above all financial aid which was promised to him. Lomnice soon had to yield his office to the Hussite, Vaněk of Boskovice. See Zapletal, 50.

14.   Grünhagen, 260.

15.   *MC*, 1, 632-34.

16.   In 1433 Blažek of Borotín began to negotiate in Budín, the return of Trnava which he had captured in 1433. By January 1435 agreement had been reached and by March the town was in Sigismund's hands. About the same time the king had redeemed Skalice from John of Vrbno, although by March 1435 it was back in Hussite hands. The second major Hussite fortification, Topolčany, which dominated the "Czech highway,"

and which had been captured by the Hussite lord John Šmikovský of Žd'ár in the fall of 1431, also went to Sigismund. Šmikovský received his first payment in November 1434 and by the beginning of 1435 he had left. Čapek of Sány also laid claim to it on the basis of Sigismund's promise in August 1434. *MC*, 1, 741. It is not known when the Hussites lost Lednice and Žilina. They lost Likava in December 1434. See Varsik, 2, 3-55 and my report in *KJ*, 1966, no. 27.

17.   Printed by me in *JSH*, 4 (1931), 55-57 from the Stuttgart codex. The text was sent to Žatec and differed only slightly from the Latin translation of Rožmberk origin, reprinted in *MC*, 1, 536-37. A letter of a Hussite is joined to the Stuttgart text, which invited the nobility only to accept the Four Articles for thus they can turn the tables on the towns and compel the townspeople and sausage makers to return the property which they have taken, to repair the castles of the lords, to return the monasteries and the tithes which they have usurped. All of this the reactionaries expected from Sigismund's return. [The diet resolution's are in Bartoš' original *HR*, II, 183-184.]

18.   *MC*, 1, 539-43. Koranda is not mentioned by name, but as 'plebanus Taboritarum.' Simon Kovářů is unknown in the sources unless he is the Simon of Strážnice, brother of the priest, Frederick, whose policies he defended. He appears in 1439-61 in Kolín. Vávra, J., *Dějiny Kolína* (1878) 66.

19.   With the possible exception of the burning of Rožmberk's town, Soběslav, although this was likely a response to an attack from that noble. Ryněšová, 181.

20.   The demands were collected in two sets: one of the nobility upper and lower, and one of the towns and then likely edited into one draft and thus sent to Sigismund. *MC*, 1, 658. See Theobald, 1, 312 for those of the barons, *AČ*, 3, 419-20 for those of the gentry, *MC*, 1, 537-38 and *UB*, 2, 440 for the towns' (Latin) and *AČ*, 3, 420-21 for the Czech version. Cf. Hlaváček, 98ff.

21.   See my *Čechy*, 459. [Klassen, J., *The Nobility and the Making of the Hussite Revolution* (New York, 1978), 48-51, 58.]

22.   *AČ*, 3, 437 and Prokeš, 79-82, 146-47.

23.   This beautiful Bible, copied by John called Aliapars, was described by Matějček, A., in *Sborník Žižkův 1424-1924* (Prague, 1924), 149-56.

24. Theobald, 1, 311; Tomek, 4, 672, ns. 6. 9.

25. The sources for the Brno diet are the journals of Charlier, Eben-dorfer and Jean de Turonis in *MC*, 1, 524-673, 745-57, 791-810.

26. Two of them mentioned in n. 25 plus Bishop Philibert, Palomar, Berruer and Tileman.

27. Valois, *Le Pape*, 1, 362-98.

28. *MC*, 1, 661-63.

29. *CJM*, 1, 216-19; *AČ*, 3, 427-31; *MC*, 1, 662-64; *UB*, 2, 445-48.

30. *MC*, 1, 614 and my article in *SH*, 6 (1959), 218.

31. He got 600 gold ducats as did Menhart, whereas Ptáček received 400 and his helper, Aleš of Šternberk, 300. *MC*, 1, 615. Cf. *ČČM* (1828), IV, 57; *AČ*, 1, 41; *CB*, 3, 543. For modern literature, Salaba, J., in *ČNM* (1934), 23-25 and Cikhart, R., in *JSH*, 8 (1935), 64-66 and 21 (1952), 116.

32. *SL*, 92; Windecke, 394-96; Cochlaeus, 394-96 and *AČ*, 3, 436-37.

33. Yet it was not entirely unique. Martin V had been elected in 1417 by a conclave which was then described as the representative of the Council of Constance. See my *Husitství a cizina*, 166, 172.

34. Höfler, 2, 832-35 and *JSH*, 19 (1950), 14.

35. Tomek, 4, 693, n. 13, 711, n. 26; *MC*, 1, 673.

36. Rokycana was absent. *MC*, 1, 692. The barons were represented by Menhart and Ptáček, the gentry by Diviš Bořek and John of Smiřice. Each Prague town sent two and Louda and two rural burghers were present. Charlier's and Ebendorfer's journals are the main source. *MC*, 1, 674-700 and 757-65.

37. *MC*, 1, 681.

38. Palacký, III, 3, 194.

39. *SL*, 93.

40. *MC*, 1, 765-83, 811-67; *SL*, 93-96; Bartošek, 618. Cf. Hoffmann, F., in *Vlastivědný sborník Vysočiny, oddíl vědy společenské*, 1 (1956), 55-66 and my *Jihlavská kompaktáta*.

41. See my article in *JSH*, 8 (1935), 78-86.

42. A collection of these documents were published in Czech in 1513 and in Latin in 1518. See *LF*, 9 (1961), 261-62. See also *AČ*, 3, 398-444 and Urbánek, *Věk*, 1, 101-14.

43. *UB*, 2, 457-58. A similar letter by the bishop of Olomouc is in Dobrovský, J., *Beiträge zur Geschichte des Kelches in Böhmen* (Prague, 1817), 15-20 and Bretholz, B., in *MIOeG* (1900), 676-78.

44. See my article in *ThPĭ (KR)* (1963), 79-85.

45. *AČ*, 3, 445-46; *MC*, 1, 834. For Laurence of Březová's allegorical warning against the deceit of the emperor see *SH*, 5 (1957), 60-63.

Notes to Chapter Eleven

1. *AČ*, 3, 446-49.
2. *MC*, 1, 872, 825-28.
3. *MC*, 1, 831.
4. *UB*, 2, 468.
5. Sigismund, on 12 July, praised Louda and five other nobles who yielded towns to him. They were Kostka, Diviš Bořek, Smiřický of the Prague alliance and Sokol and Vřesovice of the Taborites. For Louda and Pelhřimov's denunciations of him see my article in *JSH*, 1 (1928), 53. For John Kunvald, Tomek, 6, 1-5. For the public scandal, *MC*, 1, 832.

6. The information is scarce on this subject. It is quite certain, however, that the nobility dominated the government at the expense of the towns who were represented by Paul Dětrichovice, *SLŠ*, 77 and perhaps by John Kunvald, Tomek, 6, 7. [Heymann, F., "The Role of Bohemian Cities during and after the Hussite Revolution" in *Tolerance and Movements of Religious Dissent in Eastern Europe*, Király, B., ed., (New York, 1975), 27-41.]

7. *Reg.*, 183-87; *SLŠ*, 70-71; *Chronicon vet. Coll.*

8. For Rožmberk's mediation, *CJM*, 3, 155-56, 171-72. For Nicholas' response, Biskupec, 707-711 and 728-730 and Rokycana's response, *MC*, 1, 837.

9. *CJM*, 3, 167-73, 177-79, 200-202.

10. *MC*, 1, 850; *AČ*, 3, 451-52; *SL*, 98.

11. *AČ*, 3, 452-53; Palacký, 3, 236.

12. *AČ*, 1, 46, 51 the case of Ulrich of Rožmberk.

13. *MC*, 852; *CJM*, 3, 194-97; Kejř, 154.

14. Biskupec, 729; Tomek, 6, 18; *SLŠ*, 71, 73; *MC*, 1, 855, 857. See my article in *JSH*, 34 (1965).

15. *MC*, 1, 841. Vřesovice gave up the towns of the Žatec association in July at the latest but only now, 19 November, was he compensated for Chomutov and several estates. *Reg.*, 193-94 and Müller, A., *Quellen und Urkundenbuch des Bezirks Teplitz-Schönau* (1929), 133.

16. *MC*, 1, 852.

17. *MC*, 1, 845.

18. *SLŠ*, 88.

19. *MC*, 1, 857; *CDLS*, II, 2, 668-70. Cf. Urbánek, *Věk*, 1, 125.

20. *MC*, 1, 858.

21. Hejnic, J., in *Sborník národního musea*, Series A, 15, no. 4 (1961), 238-55 and Boháček, M., in *ČSPS* (Prague, 1955), 38-39.

22. *UB*, 2, 476-80 and Brno ms. Cerr. II, 361, 98-99.

23. Palacký, IV, 1, 140; Šafařík, P., in *ČČM*, 48 (1874), 107 and *MC*, 1, 861-62.

24. *AČ*, 3, 455-56; *MC*, 1, 864; Tomek, 6, 31 and Klier, Č., in *ČČM*, 79 (1905), 4.

25. *MC*, 1, 865. For Christian's election see Krofta, K., in *ČČH*, 17 (1911), 42-43.

26. For the impact of Rokycana's departure, *RA*, 12, 131-33, 137. For his activity in Hradec Králové, *SL*, 100.

27. *RA*, 12, 124ff.

28. Tomek, 6, 31, n. 9 and 33. See also 8, 154 and 9, 348 for the church of Mary of the Snows, i.e. Želivský's church. Paul Dětřichov entered the council of state. *SLŠ*, 77.

29. Kalich was held by John Řitka of Bezdědice, against whom Sigismund tried to gain Heník of Valdštejn by giving him the Byčkovice estate. *Reg.*, 200; *Hrady*, 14, 372; Toman, 295-97; my article in *JSH*, 32 (1963) and Rynešová, 226.

30. See Sylvius's song in *VKČSN* (1897); Palacký, 3, 254-7; *SL*, 103-4; *SLŠ*, 78; Bartošek, 620-21; Windecke, 434-35; Lupínek, F., *J. Roháč z Dubé* (Kutná Hora), 1937; Urbánek, R., *Z husitského věk*, 178-80.

31. *AČ*, 3, 465-68. Most likely John of Kunvald, no longer considered a Hussite, was meant. It is possible that several foreigners were placed in German towns. See Rynešová, 227-28.

32. It is unlikely that a similar attempt was made at this time although see *Reg.*, 206 where Sigismund complains that he was wrongfully judged by the land court.

33. *RA*, 12, 259; Urbánek, *Věk*, 1, 252. Frederick likely acquired Kolín through his second wife of the Polek family. See Hejnic in *Sborník Národního musea*, 238-55, and my article in *KJ*, (1962), no. 19. For the letter of challenge, *SL*, 104. For Sigismund's illness, Ebstein, W., in *MIÖG*,

27 (1906), 678. For Queen Barbara and her Czech friends, Urbánek, *Věk*, 1, 252ff. Among these was Ptáček who likely warned against executing Roháč, not only as a relative but also as a member of the nobility, and also perhaps because he had parted company with the king. A noble was not supposed to be tortured and could be judged only by the land court.

34. Windecke, 448. See Linder, 2, 417 and my article in *JSH*, 10 (1937), 36-41; Pekař, 4, 284-86; Palacký, III, 3, 265.

35. Svejkovský, 11. For history's judgement see Lea, H.C. *Geschichte der Inquisition im Mittelalter* 2 (1909), 531.

36. Prokeš, 86-97.

37. For Palomar see my *Husitika*, 22, 57. For Příbram, my *LČ Rok.*, 62-63, nos. 1-2 and n. 61 to which should be added the ms. which Prokop Lupáč had in his *Rerum boemicarum Ephemeris* (Prague, 1584), 24, XII.

38. Prokeš, 220, n. 410. He was the victim of a double-cross from the conservatives who had drawn up instructions according to Palomar's wishes. See *ČČM*, (1920), 193-195. See also Prokeš, 219, nos. 401 and 408, and 91-92, 177-78.

39. Brown, E., *Fasciculus rerum expetendarium et fugiendarum* (London, 1690), 319-21. The requests represented the diet's resolutions.

40. Re the south Slavs, the Hussites refer to Gregory VII's letter of 1080 to Vratislav.

41. Příbram at one point, not satisfied with Procop's defense of children's right to the chalice, seized the podium from him. Prokeš, 222, n. 416. Lord Přibík of Klenové, according to the testimony of Sylvius, was equally resolute in his defense of the chalice. For Peter, see Šimák, J. V., *Dějinné paměti okresu mnichovohradišťského*, 1 (1917), 42-43, 135, 142 and 7, and my article in *Acta Universitatis Carolinae* 2 (Prague, 1958), 20-23.

42. *MC*, 1, 1082; Prokeš, 97.

43. Prokeš, 100, 111; Urbánek, *Věk*, 1, 392. The Council cancelled Rokycana's election by electing its own Prague archbishop who failed ignominiously in Bohemia. Prokeš, 120.

44. *SLŠ*, 96. He likely died in Austria where on 5 October 1439 Albrecht named him legate for Bohemia. Urbánek, *Věk*, 1, 451. See also Döllinger, J. J., *Beiträge zur politischen, kirchlichen und Kulturgeschichte*, 3 vols. (Regensburg-Vienna, 1862-82), 2, 414-41.

45. See my article in *Reformační sborník*, 7 (1939), 137.

46. See my article in *SH*, 3 (1955), 116ff. For a discussion of these reforms and the Hussite contribution to them see Beer, K., (ed.), *Die Reformation Kaiser Sigismunds* (Stuttgart, 1933); Dohna, L., *Reformatio Sigismundi* (Göttingen, 1960), and my defense of my position in *Communio viatorum* 8 (1965), 123-124. [Cf. de Vooght, P., "Les Hussites et la Reformatio Sigismundi," in Bäumer, R., (ed.), *Von Konstanz nach Trient* (Munich, 1972), 199-214. De Vooght disagrees with Bartoš' argument that the Hussites contributed substantially to the *reformatio*.]

47. For example, Toke's defense of the Council was printed in 1470 as well as by Hutten and in the Chronicle of Sebastian Franck. See my article in *JSH*, 15 (1946), 29. The '*reformatio*' was published five times between 1476 and 1500 and thereafter many times. See Haupt, H., in *Westdeutsche Zeitschrift, Ergänzungsheft*, 8 (1893). See also my article in *Naše věda*, 23 (1944), 126-30.

48. [Two accounts of his reign exist in English. Odložilík, O., *The Hussite King* (New Brunswick, 1965) and Heymann, F. G., *George of Bohemia* (Princeton, 1965).]

Notes to Chapter Twelve

1. See my *Manifesty* and my two articles in *JSH*, 7 (1934), 56-59 and 13 (1940), 128-29.

2. My *Čechy*, 248.

3. A Taborite manifesto of 1430 added fourteen requirements to the Four Articles. See Pekař, 4, 277-79 and Lancinger, L., in *Acta Universitatis Carolinae* 3 (Prague, 1962) [For Tabor's earlier development see Kaminsky, H., *A History of the Hussite Revolution* (Berkeley, 1967), 310-481.]

4. See my article in *ČNM*, (1921), 36 and my *Husitství a cizina*, 166-68; Krofta, K., *Listy z náboženských dějin českých* (Prague, 1936), 240-287; my *Světci a kacíři* (Prague, 1949), 222-223 and Heymann, F., in *Archiv für Reformationsgeschichte* 52 (1961), 1-16.

5. Hansen, J., *Zauberwahr, Inquisition und Hexenprocess im Mittelalter* (München und Leipzig, 1900), and Lea, H. C. *A History of the Inquisition in the Middle Ages*, 3 vols. (New York, 1888).

6. For Galka see my study in *Slavia*, (1965); for Heimburg, see Joachimsohn, P., *Gregor von Heimburg* (Bamberg, 1891) and my article

in *Vlastivědný sborník východočeský* 2 (1924), 20-24. For Lübeck, my article in *SH,* 4 (1956), 66-70 and for the Brandenburg Waldensians, Müller, J. T., *Dějiny Jednoty bratrské,* 1 (Prague, 1923) also in German as *Geschichte der Böhmischen Brüder* (Herrnhut, 1922) but without Bartoš' editorial comments. [For more bibliography on the Waldensians see Zeman, J. K. (ed.), *The Hussite Movement: A Bibliographical Study Guide* (Ann Arbor, 1977), 43-48.]

7. Molnár, A., in *Náboženská revue* 34 (1963), 154-63 and my article in *JSH,* 21 (1952), 41-48.

8. See my article in *ThPř* 21 (1954), 134-41. For Chelčický, see my article in *KJ,* (1963), no. 11 and my *Petr Chelčický* (Prague, 1958). [See also Zeman, *The Hussite Movement,* 152-157, and Wagner, Murray L., *Petr Chelčický: A Radical Separatist in Hussite Bohemia* (Scottdale, Pa., 1983).]

9. My article in *Archiv für Reformationsgeschichte* 31 (1934), and Thomson, S. H., in *Archive for Reformation History* 44 (1953) and Haller, J., *Die Ursachen der Reformation* (1917) [Zeman, *The Hussite Movement,* 225-258.]

10. See the article "Žižkův a husitský demokratismus" in *Z Husových a Žižkových časů* (1925) and Vaněček, V., *Dějiny státu a práva v československu do roku 1945* (Prague, 1970, 2nd ed.)

11. *AČ,* 22, 7-8; Graus, F., *Dějiny venkovského lidu,* 2 (Prague, 1957), 233. [Klassen, J., *The Nobility and the Making of the Hussite Revolution* (New York, 1978), 47-60.]

12. Hlaváček, J., *AČ,* 3, 249; and Bezold, F., *Zur Geschichte des Hussitenthums* (Munich, 1874).

13. See *SH,* 10 (1962), 71-92. [Eberhard, W., *Konfessionsbildung und Stände in Böhmen 1478-1530* (München, 1981), 78-119.]

14. Klik, J., *Národnostní poměry v Čechách od válek husitských* (Prague, 1922), offprint from *ČČH,* 17 and 18); Krofta, *Listy,* 136-45, and his article in *Le Monde Slave* 5 (1928), 321-51 and *Das Deutschtum in der tschechoslovakischen Geschichte* (Prague, 1934); Macek, J., in *ČsČh* 3 (1955), 4-29. The most promising document for an analysis of the towns' confiscation of church property is in *AČ,* 14, 369-79. For education see Winter, Z., *Život a učení na partikulárních školách v Čechách v XV a XVI stol.* (Prague, 1901). He concentrated on the 16th century.

15. *AČ,* 22, 11ff.; Krofta, K., *Dějiny selského stavu v Čechách* (Prague, 1949, 2nd ed.).

16.   See my articles in *KJ,* (1961), no. 40 and (1958) no. 7 and in *Reformační Sborník* 7 (1939), 163-67 and Krofta, *Dějiny selského stavu,* 125, 162.

17.   See my *Světec temna* in *Světci a kracíři* (Prague, 1949).

18.   See Pekař's and Urbánek's article in Odložilík, et al., eds., *Českou minulostí* (Prague, 1929), and Krofta, *Listy,* 141.

19.   See Kraus, A., *Husitství v literatuře, zejména německé* (3 vols., Prague, 1917-24). My own additions to this basic work can be found in *Světci a kacíři.* For a discussion of how Palacký was led to a study of Hussitism by the German historian, K. L. Waltmann, see my booklet, *František Palacký* (Prague, 1948).

INDEX

201